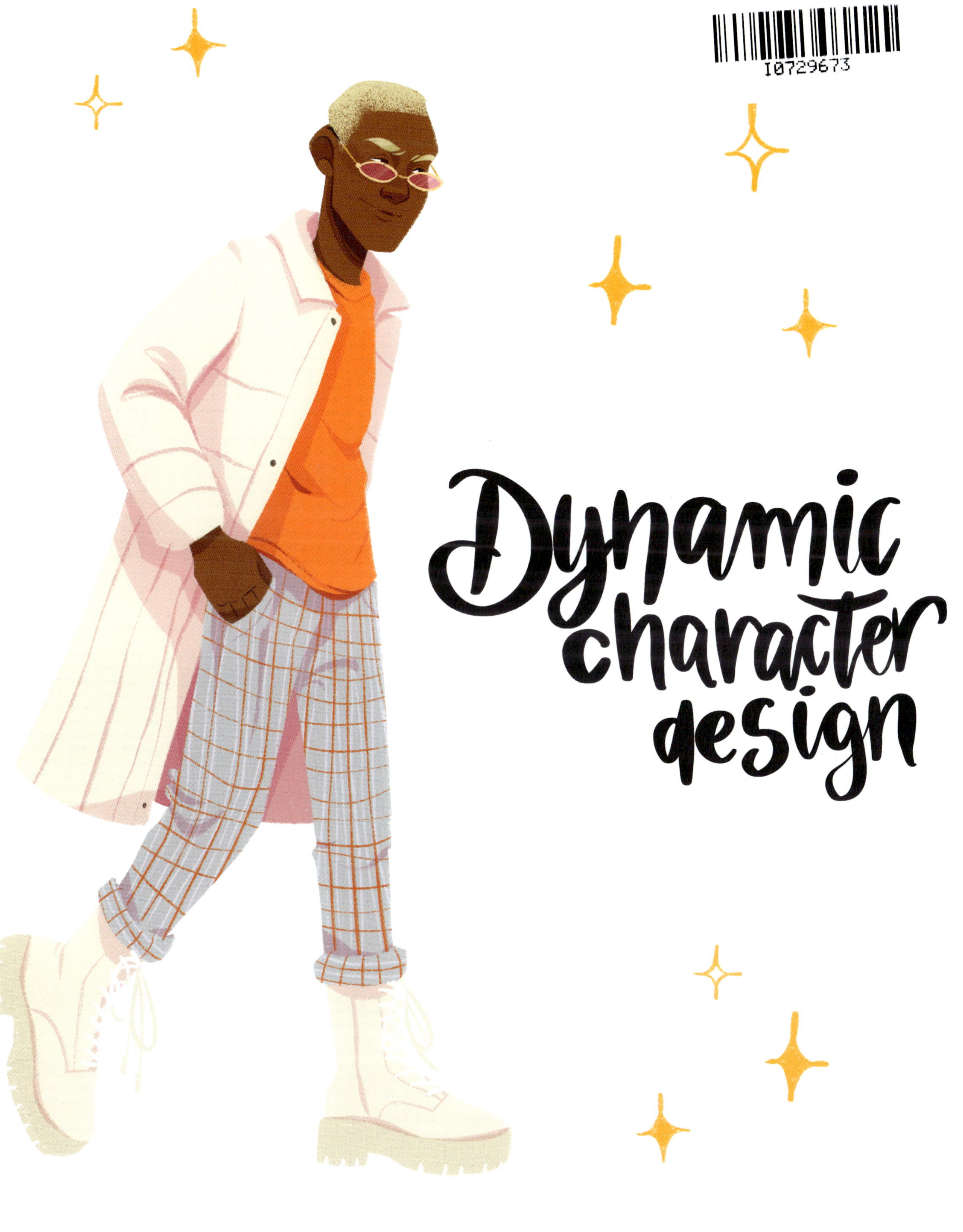

I0729673
Dynamic
character
design

MIX
Paper | Supporting
responsible forestry
FSC® C016973
www.fsc.org

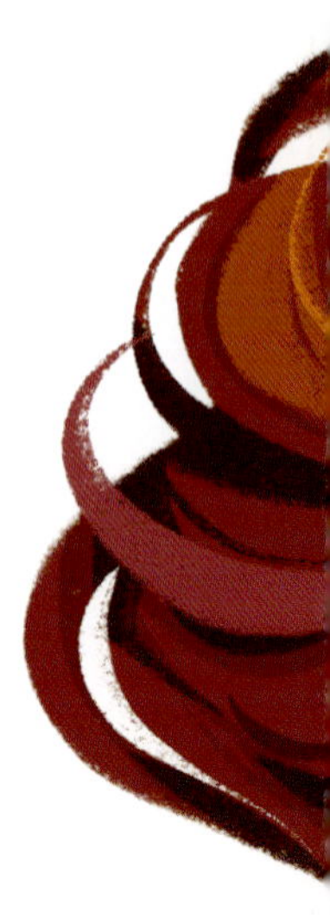

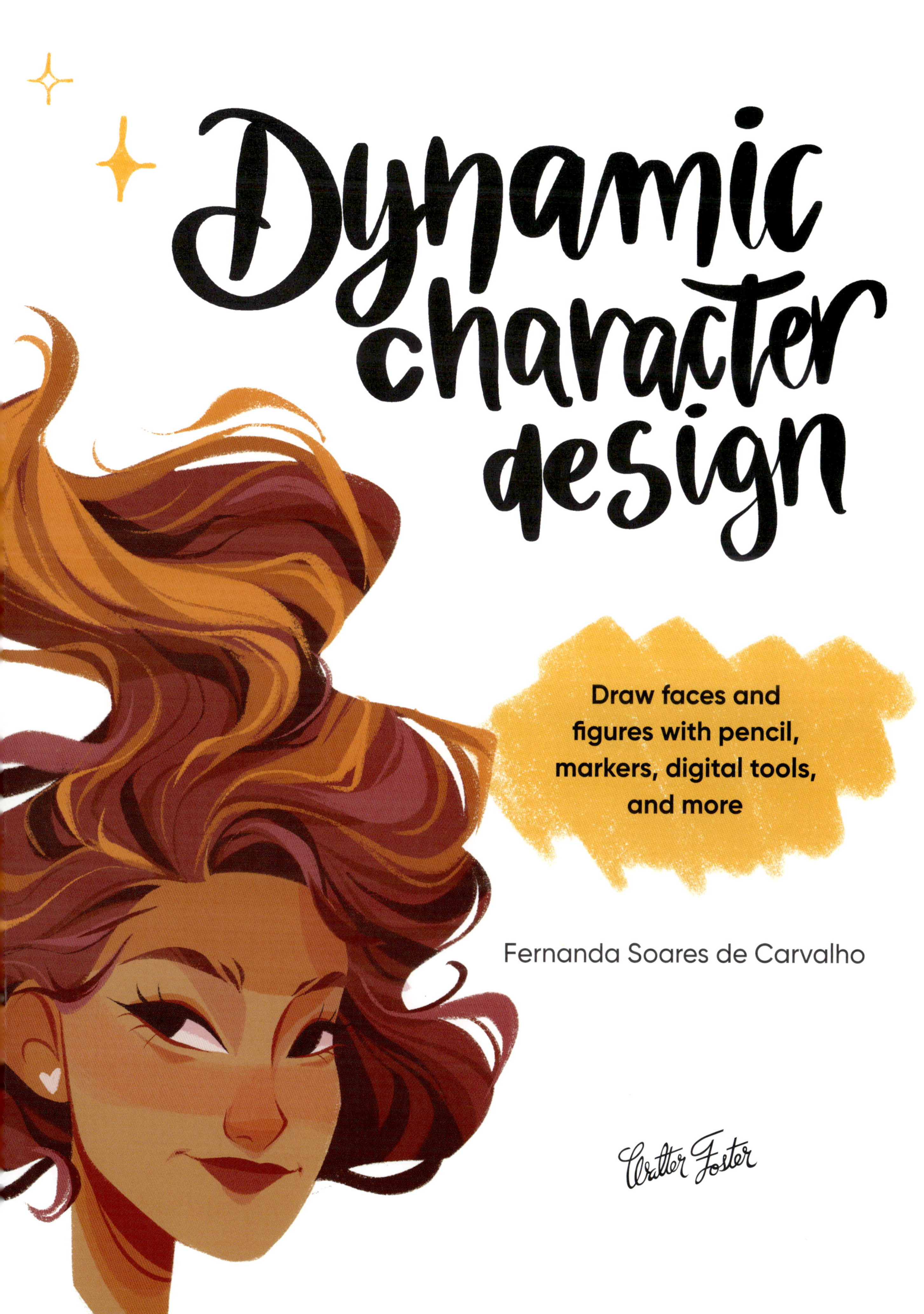

Dynamic character design

Draw faces and figures with pencil, markers, digital tools, and more

Fernanda Soares de Carvalho

Walter Foster

Contents

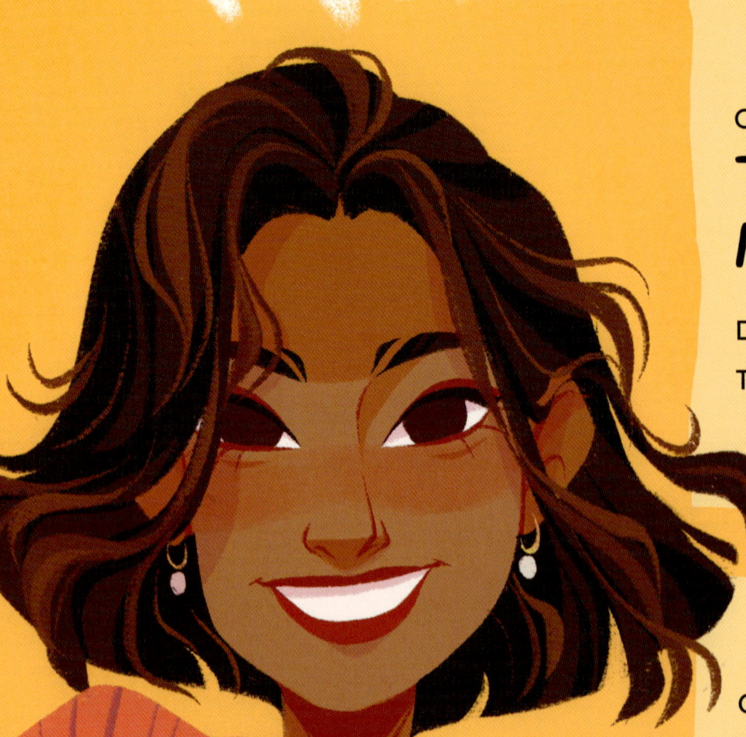

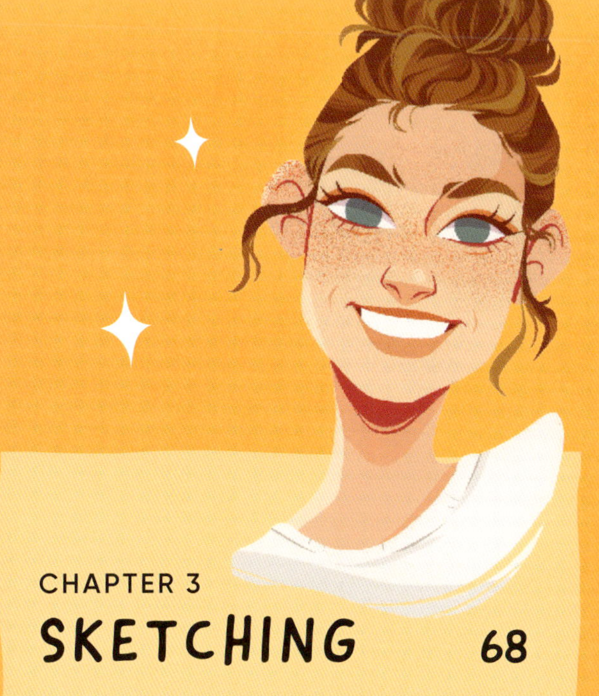

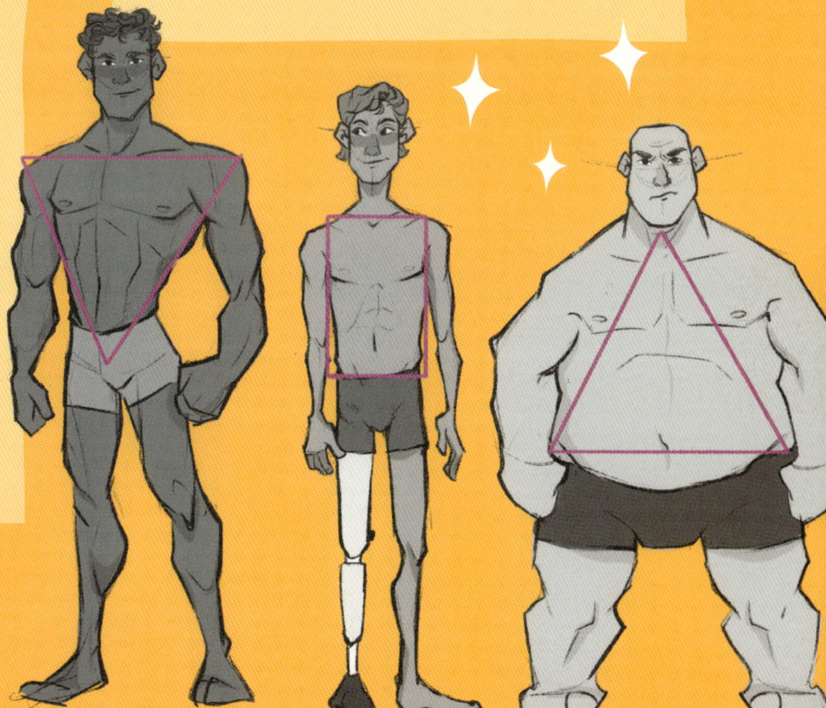

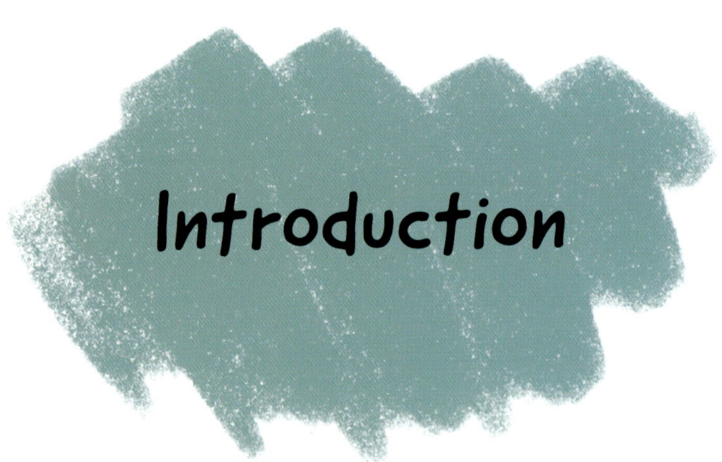

Introduction

Drawing has always been a big part of my life. Since I was a kid, I've always found joy in grabbing a piece of paper and some colored pencils and drawing my family, friends, stuffed animals, or dog. Then, after drawing things and people around me, my next step was starting to create my own characters.

I remember my family asking me, "Who is this?" while looking at a character I created out of my imagination, and my answer was, "No one! I've just got it out of my head."

I started to realize that I didn't want to draw just people I knew or things I could see in front of my eyes. I also wanted to let my creativity flow and create different characters with unique combinations of facial features, hair, body types, and other characteristics. I gave them names and even imagined a history for them and learned how to express their characteristics and personality through my drawings.

So that was when my love for drawing characters grew strong and became my favorite thing to do. For me, creating characters is much more than just a combination of different features. It is the ability to transmit personality, feelings, emotions, movement, and essence.

With some practice, trial and error, and lots of imagination, I developed the style that I currently have, which I will be always improving because there is always something to learn.

In this book, I'll go from the basics and first steps of drawing a face on to drawing different body types. From there, I discuss drawing with digital and traditional media, adding movement and dimension to your drawings, and how to interpret an image and turn it into a character. Plus I give many other tips and tricks to help you in your artistic journey.

I really hope that this book makes you enjoy drawing and creating characters as much as I do, and that, after reading and practicing, you develop the ability to add liveliness to your own characters.

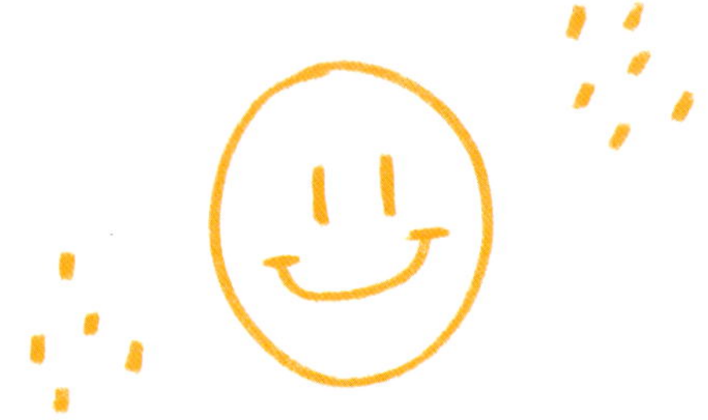

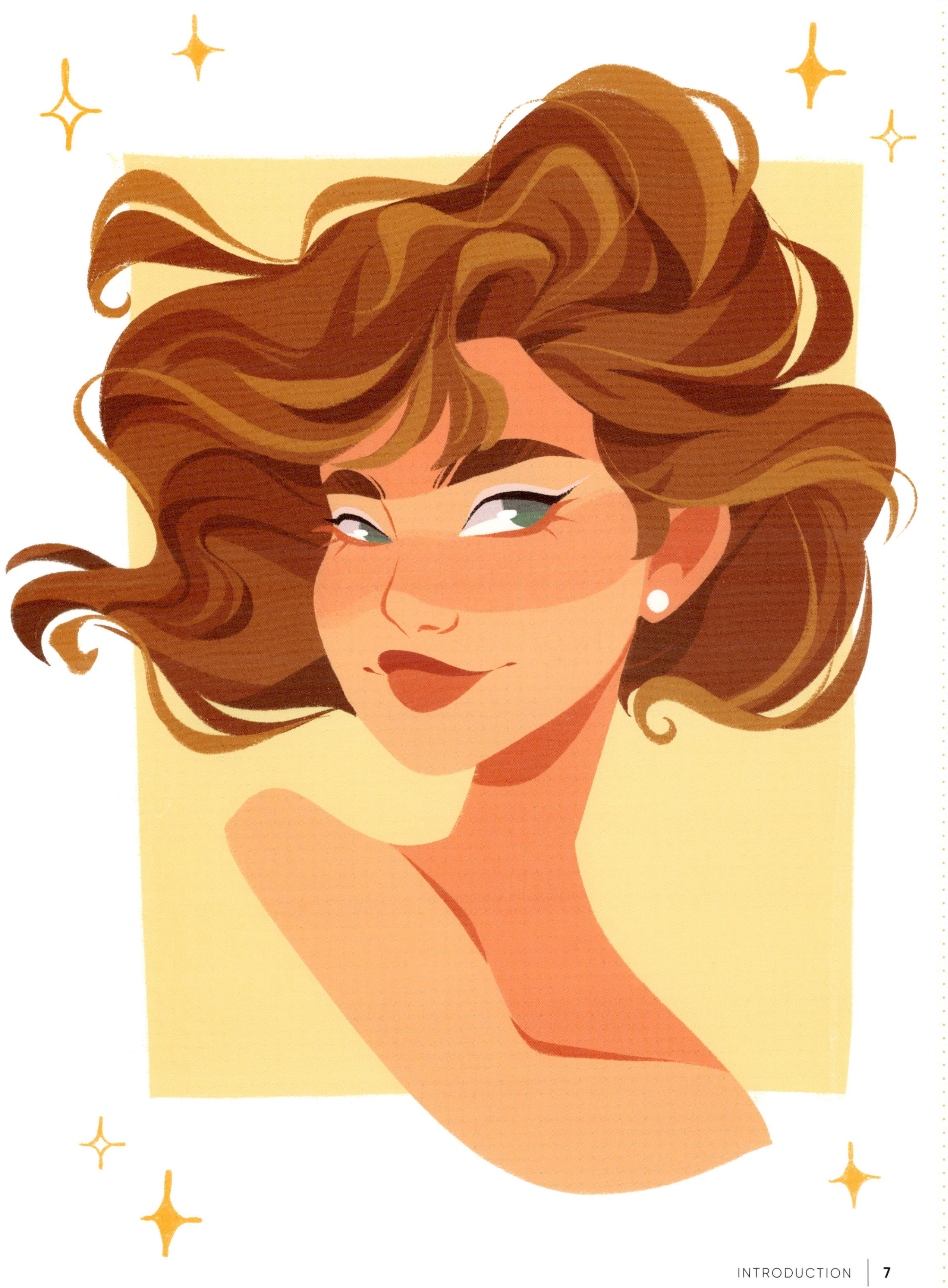

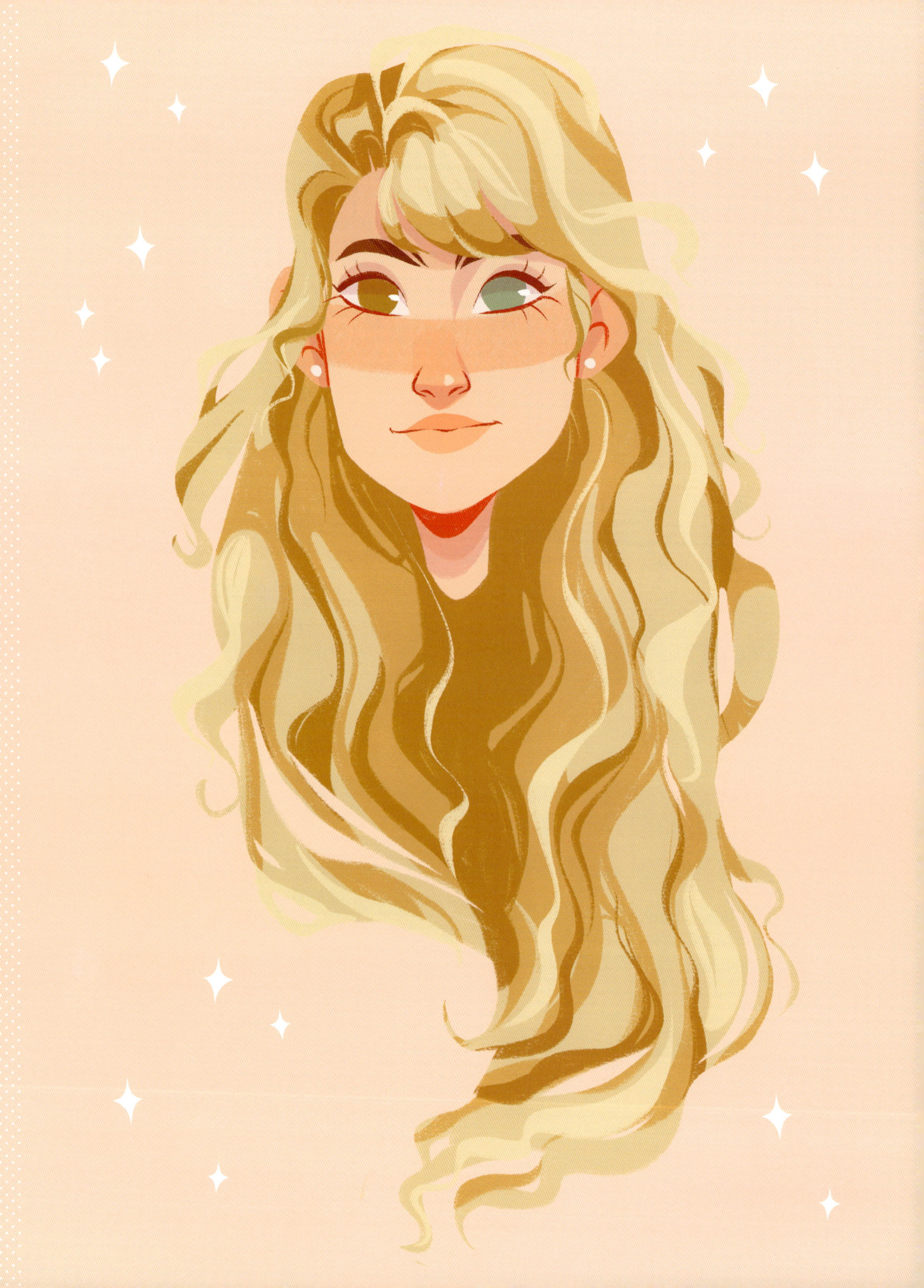

CHAPTER 1

Tools & Materials

The materials that you choose make a huge difference in the results of your drawing. You can have two completely different drawings if you just change one single pen, for example. Knowing which materials you are going to choose for each drawing and how to be creative with materials is an ability that every artist should cultivate.

In this chapter, I'm going to go through my favorite materials for traditional and digital art, and I will explain a little bit of how I use each material or tool for the results I want. However, don't forget to always be creative, experimenting with materials you already have and exploring textures and pencils to create many different art pieces.

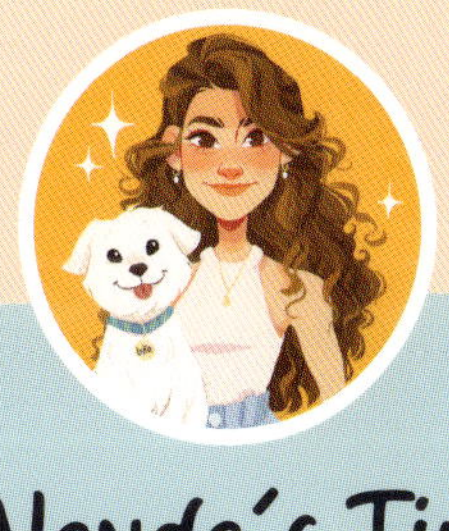

Nanda's Tip

As an artist, you are not defined by the tool you use but by how you use that tool.

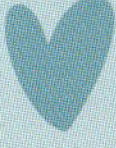

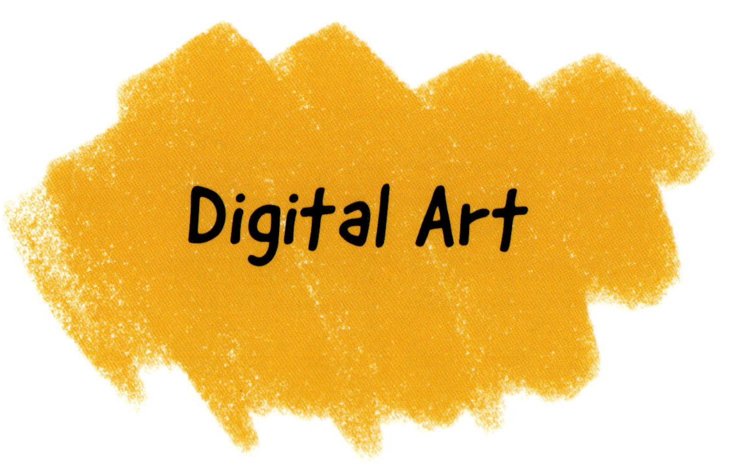

Digital Art

There are innumerous digital brushes and digital media out there, which can help you create many digital drawing styles. They can go from digital art that looks like an oil painting to a drawing that looks like it was made by a computer.

I use Procreate for my digital drawings, but these fundamentals apply to every digital media. In this chapter, I'll show you the brushes I use the most as well as in which stage of the drawing I use them. But remember, there are tons of other brushes that you can explore, so be creative with them! Don't limit yourself to the ones here.

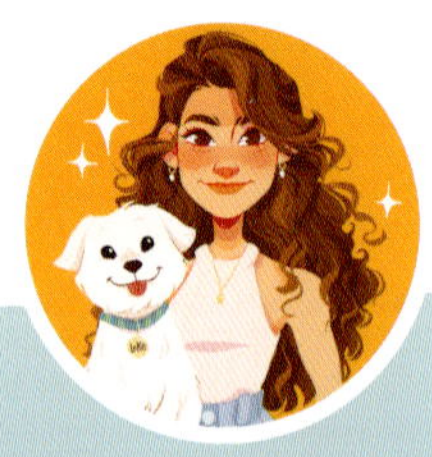

Nanda's Tip

If you don't use the same art software I have, try to select equivalent brushes from the options that you have available, considering textures, characteristics, and density compared to the ones I suggest.

On digital drawings, I usually use three to four different brushes. The quantity and type of brushes can vary a lot depending on what style of drawing you are aiming for, and it can also vary depending on what technique you use.

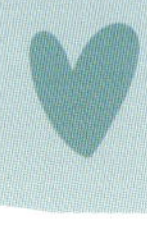

SKETCHING

For sketching, I like to use a simple pencil brush. It really doesn't make a lot of difference since I normally hide the layer that I used to do the sketch. These pencil brushes are usually thin and not so dense, so they're good for sketching.

ADDING TEXTURE

Finally, I add brushstrokes that have different textures. This is also a good time to try out new-to-you brushes to see what they can add to your drawing.

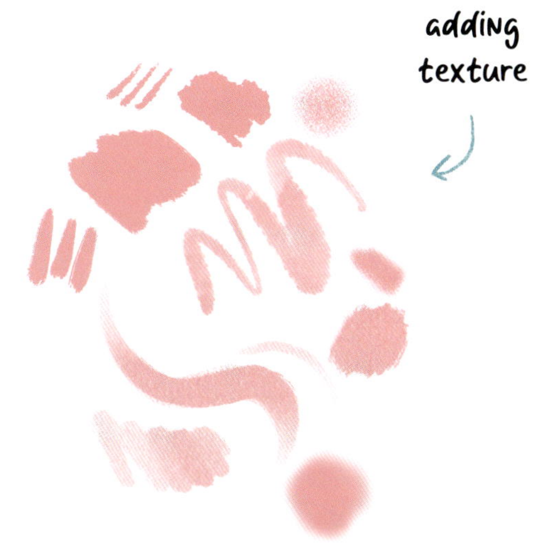

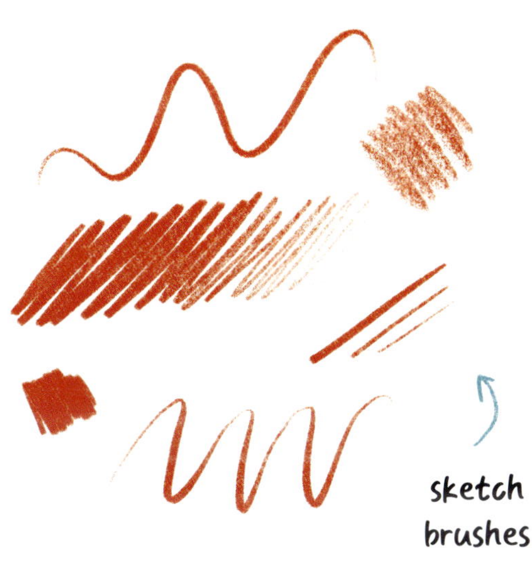

PAINTING

For painting and constructing the base of my drawing, I like to go for a brush with a bit of texture and high opacity to create a "chalky" effect.

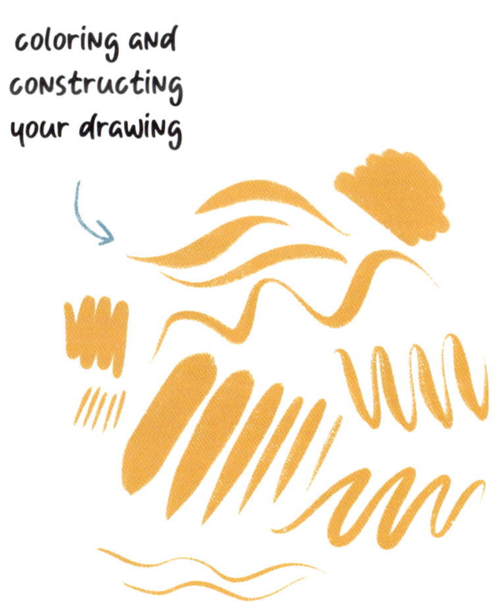

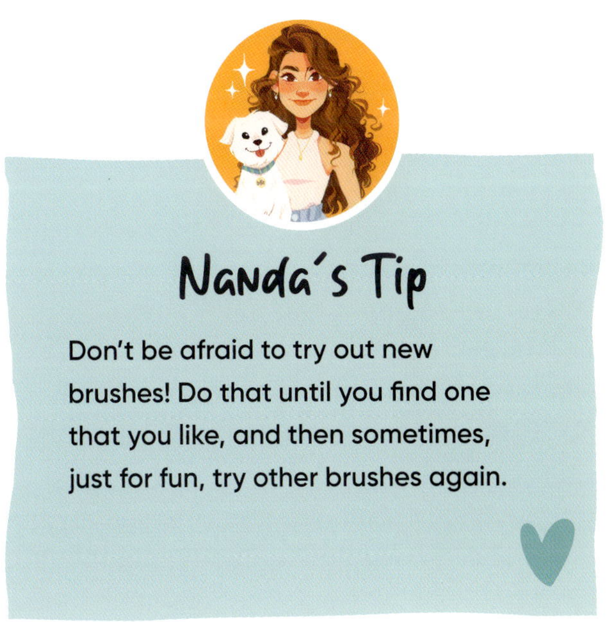

Nanda's Tip

Don't be afraid to try out new brushes! Do that until you find one that you like, and then sometimes, just for fun, try other brushes again.

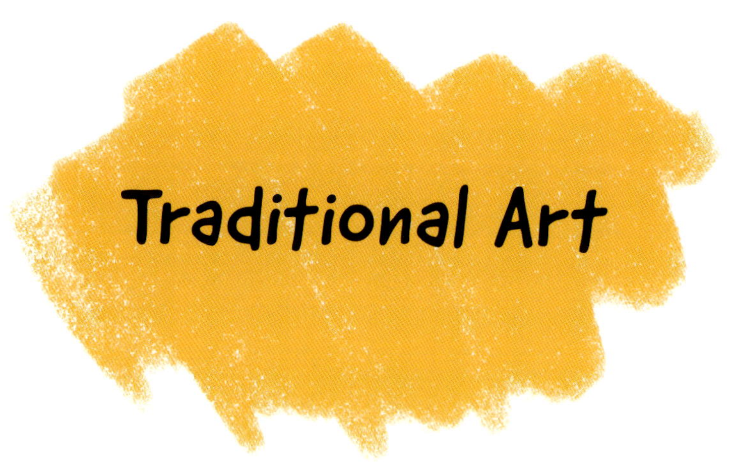

There are innumerable types of traditional art and just as many media used to create it. My personal favorites are graphite and colored pencils for sketching and alcohol- and water-based markers for a more elaborate drawing.

SKETCHING

When I'm sketching, I like to use graphite or colored pencils.

When choosing the graphite, I normally go for a normal HB pencil (top right), and then I add details and define some lines with a 5B pencil (middle right).

For sketching with colored pencils, I normally go with blue or red pencils, shown at right, because I think it gives a beautiful look to a sketch. You can choose whatever color you have available.

COLORING

For coloring, I like to use colored pencils, water-based markers, or alcohol-based markers, or a mix.

I like to make the base of the drawing with the alcohol-based markers because they don't smear as much as water-based, giving a beautiful and uniform look to your drawing.

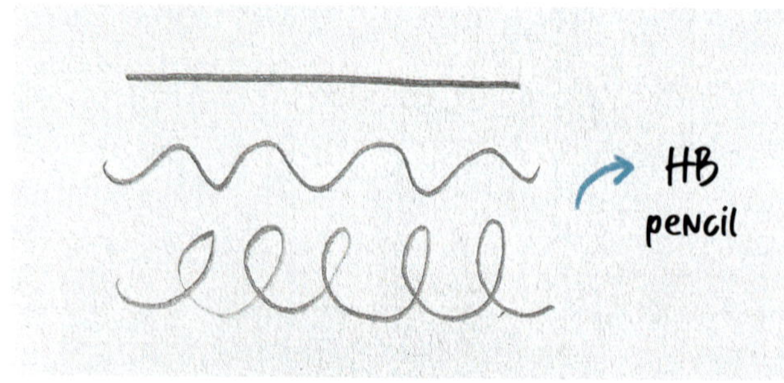

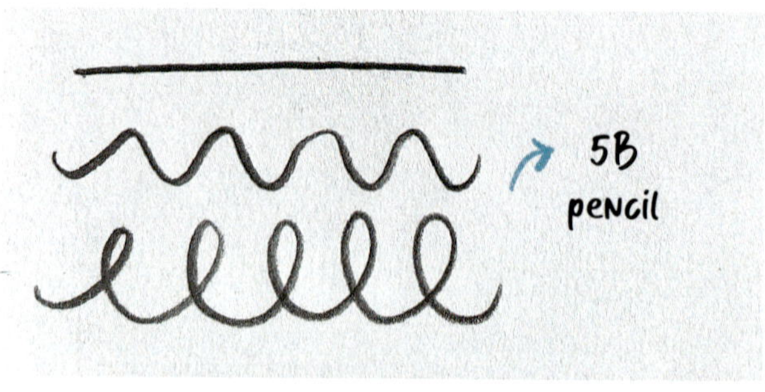

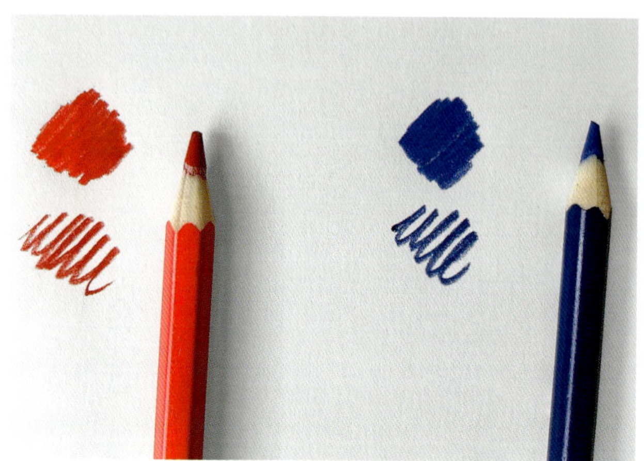

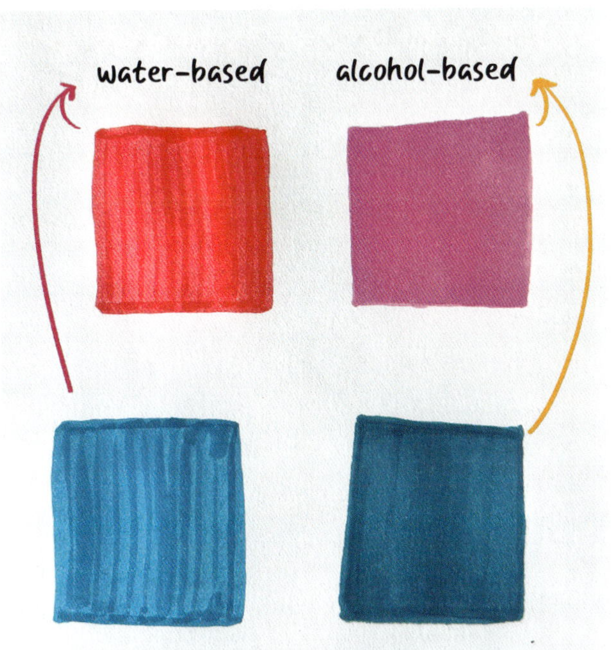

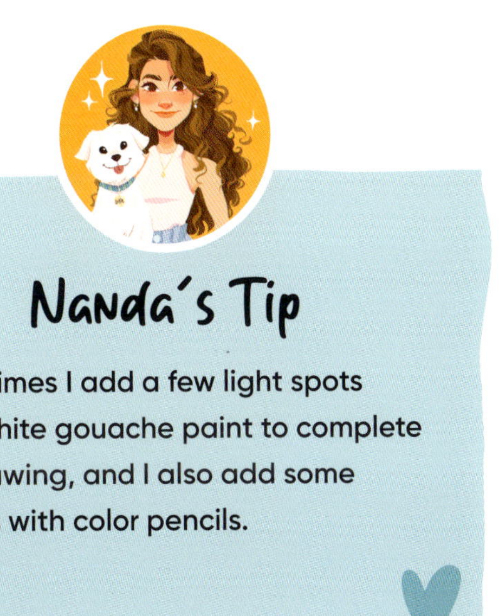

Nanda's Tip

Sometimes I add a few light spots with white gouache paint to complete my drawing, and I also add some details with color pencils.

I chose two different colors, shown above, to show you the difference between the water-based marker and the alcohol-based marker.

As you can see, the water-based ones smear much more than the alcohol-based ones, so I use alcohol-based for the base elements of my drawing, like the hair, skin, and facial features.

Then I add the details and shades and correct some mistakes with the water-based marker.

Here is a quick step-by-step to show you where and when I use each marker:

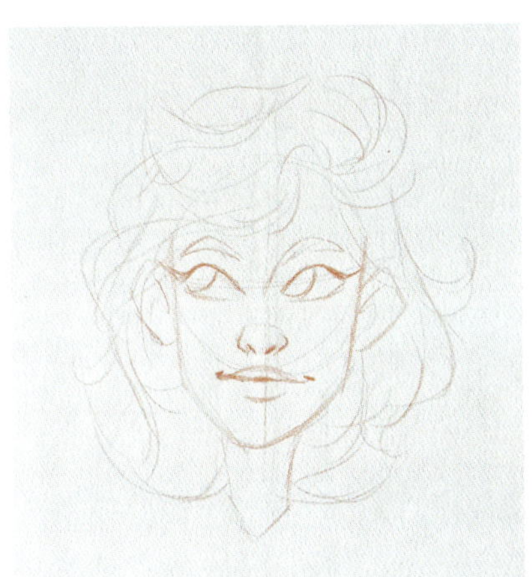

1. Make a simple sketch.

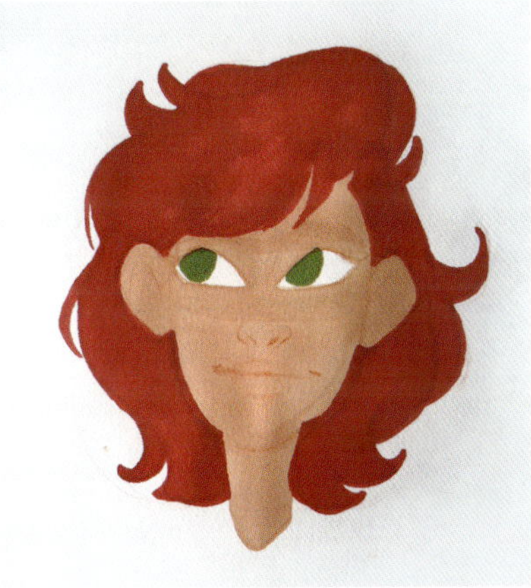

2. Add the base colors with alcohol-based markers.

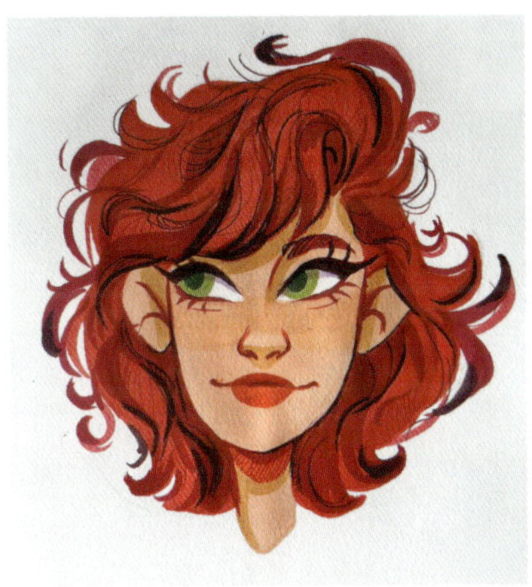

3. Add the shadows and details with water-based markers.

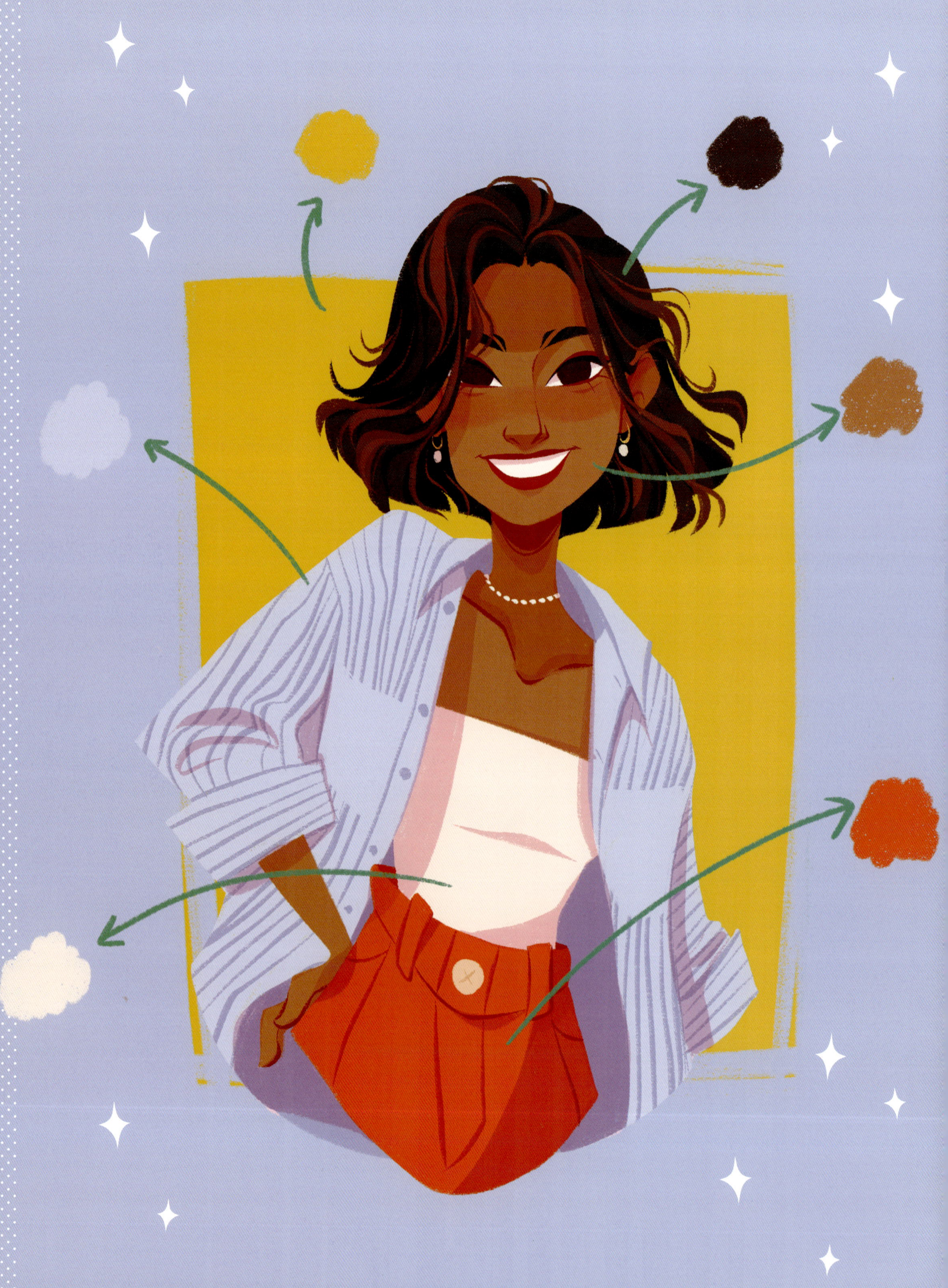

CHAPTER 2

Tutorials

In this chapter, we are going to go through tutorials on how to create characters with unique personalities and characteristics. You are going to learn the necessary techniques to draw a face and explore the shapes that are used to compose a range of facial expressions.

You will also gain an understanding of how to draw the hair and give it texture and explore the anatomy and body types of your characters. After practicing everything here, you'll be equipped with many tools that will allow you to express your unique art design in the characters you create.

Let's have some fun!

First Steps

CIRCLE

Okay, let's start with the basics. When drawing a face, a circle is the first thing you must do to guide you through the process. This will be your reference, your central point for every other component you will add to the face.

JAWLINE

After that first step, you will draw the jawline.

This point is when you can start creating different characters just by introducing small changes to the shape and size of the jaw you just added. (We will cover how to draw different characters a little later.)

GUIDELINES AND NECK

Next, you're going to define the lines that will guide where you're going to place the facial features (eyes, nose, eyebrows, ears, and mouth) and also draw the neck, making choices about its thickness and length, which will help define another characteristic of your character.

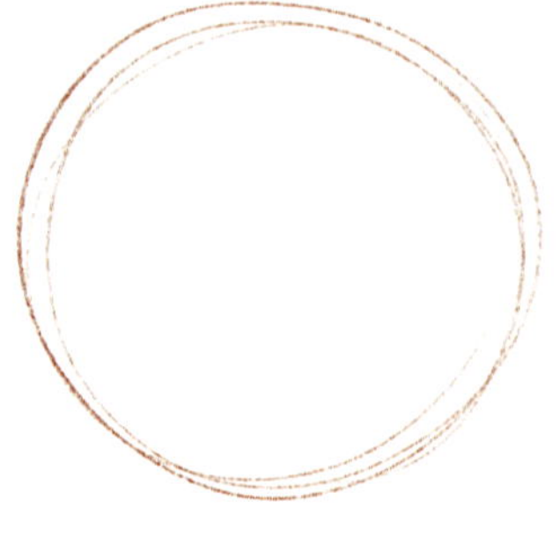
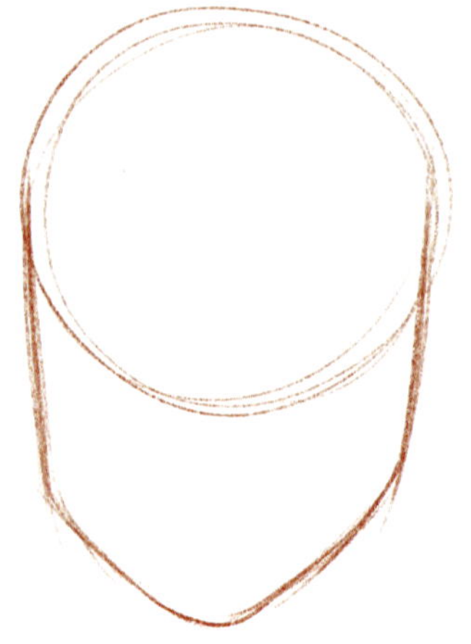
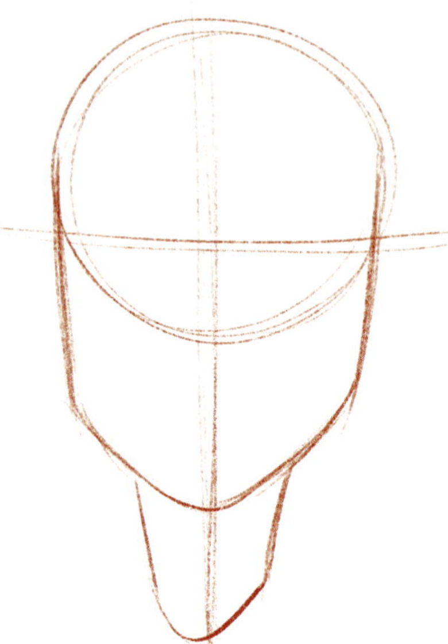

POSITION MARKS FOR THE FACIAL FEATURES

Now you're going to place a position reference for all the facial features (eyes, nose, eyebrows, ears, and mouth) so you have an idea of where you're going to draw them later.

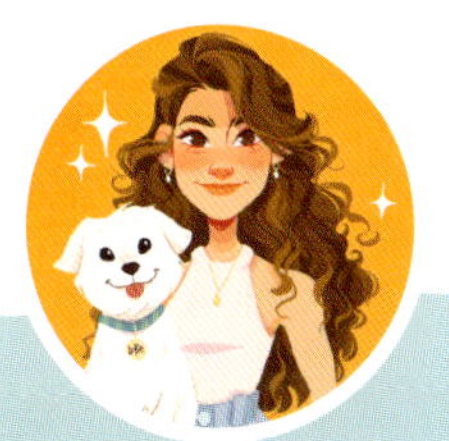

Nanda's Tip

Another important tip you will use through the entire drawing process is to draw loosely, which is to not make great effort trying to perfect your trace. Don't make shy and fearful strokes, but rather try to draw freely, without worrying about making mistakes, even if you need to erase and do it again.

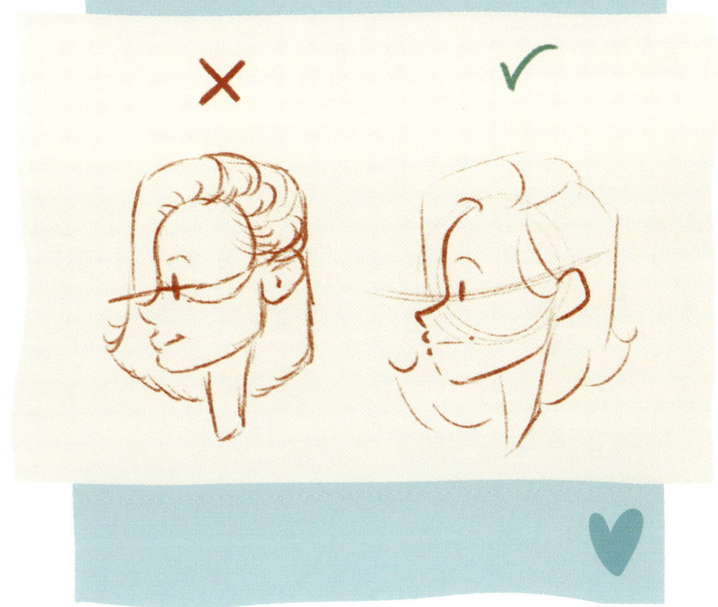

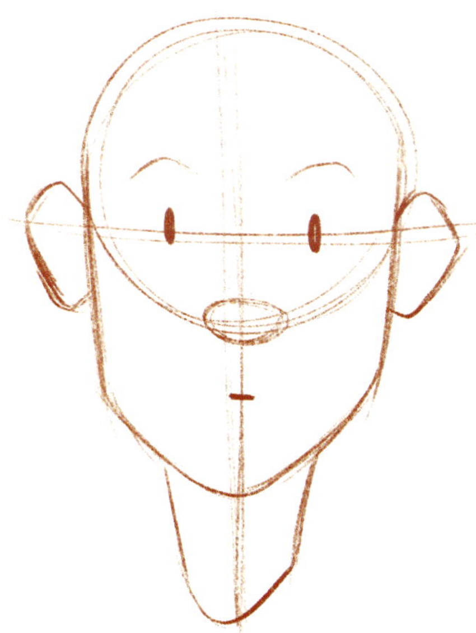

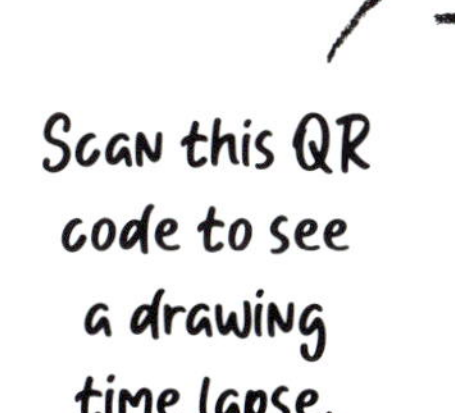

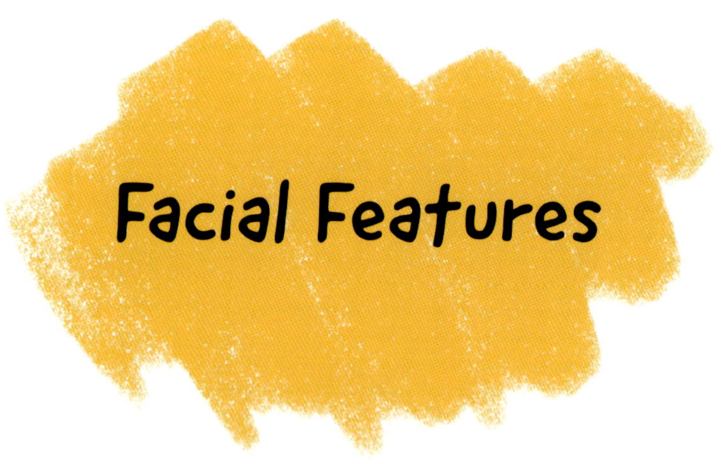

EYES

When I'm drawing a face, the most important and expressive part is the eyes. I always start with them, and they guide me through the whole character construction process.

Just by changing the eye shape and size, I can change the character's personality or expressions, making them go from happy to sad, angry to scared, and so on.

Your goal while drawing the eyes is to express emotion and the character's feelings, and it's an opportunity to show their unique personality traits. If you're just starting out, doing this through a drawing can be a little challenging, but I'm going to help you develop this ability.

Here you can start building the traits you want your character to have. Making the eyeline more arched or straight, or making the eye shape bigger or smaller, for example, can emphasize the personality of the character you're building.

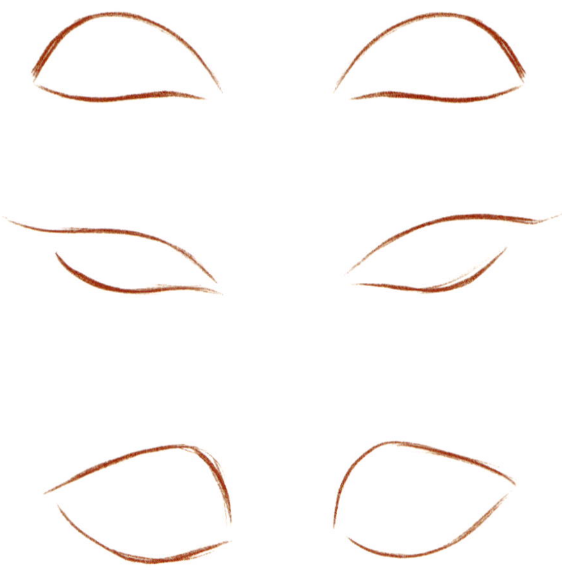

1. UPPER EYELINE AND WATERLINE

When drawing the eyes, the first step is to draw the upper eyeline and the waterline. They will guide you when drawing the irises, eyelids, and eyebrows and delimit the space your eyes are going to occupy. Remember to keep some size and format similarities between the two eyes. Because they are close to each other, small differences will be very visible.

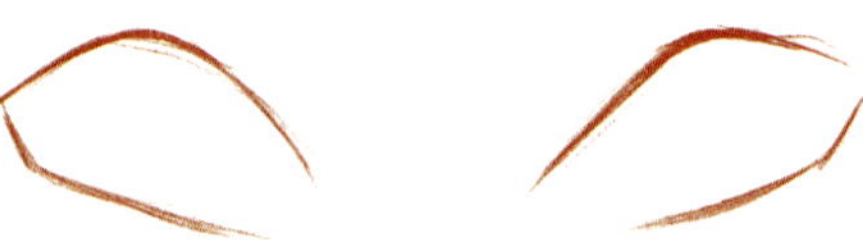

2. IRISES

The second step is drawing the irises. You're going to draw two circles looking in the same direction. Remember to keep the two irises a similar size and shape like you did with the eyes.

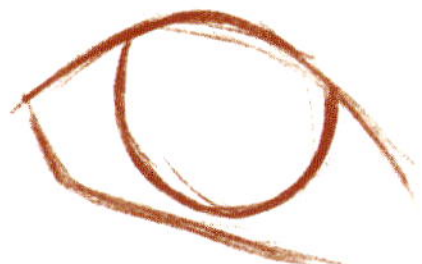 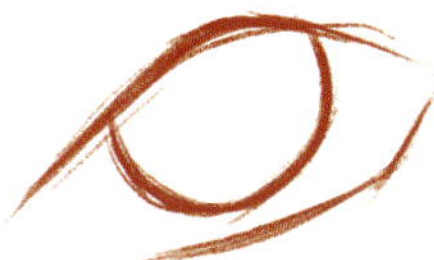

EYEBROWS

Next are the eyebrows. Keep in mind that this facial feature is really important to convey your character's emotion and personality. The eyebrows are as important as the eyes in these matters. I always draw them right after the eyes to try to make the set of eyes and eyebrows express the same characteristics together as one harmonic piece.

    I start by drawing the shape of the eyebrows, delineating their space and always trying to draw flowing and curvy lines to make them more natural.

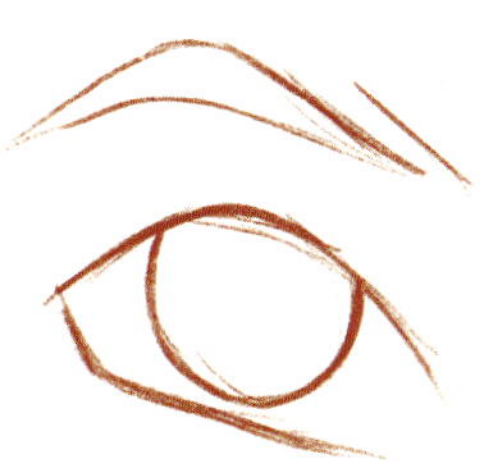 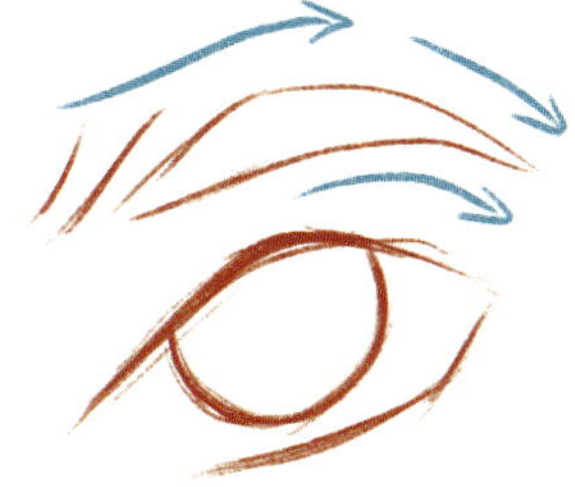

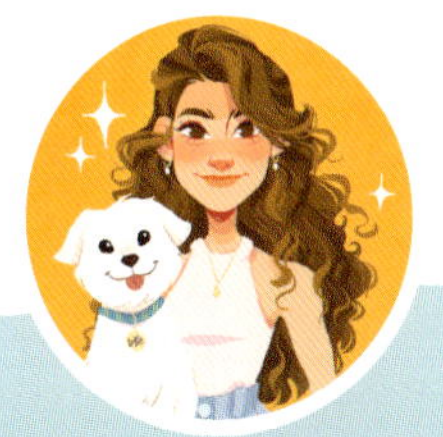

Nanda's Tips

- If you're having trouble drawing the irises looking in the same direction, you can draw two guidelines to make sure you're putting them in the correct place.

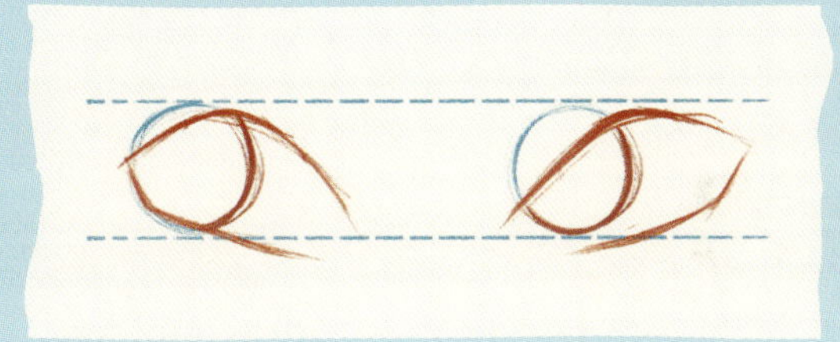

- To give your character a more realistic look and make the iris a perfectly circular shape and not an oval one, imagine you're drawing a circle that goes beyond the upper eyeline (if it helps, you can actually draw the entire circle).

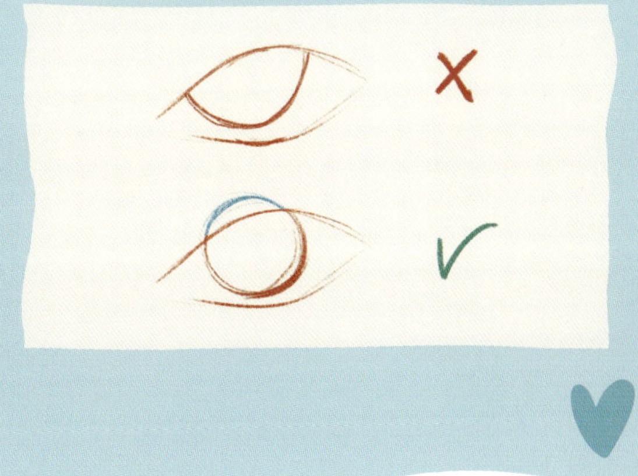

Eyebrows can be thick, thin, arched, straight, low, and more—there are several variations that can be used to add expression to the characters. Playing with the shapes will help you create more diverse characters.

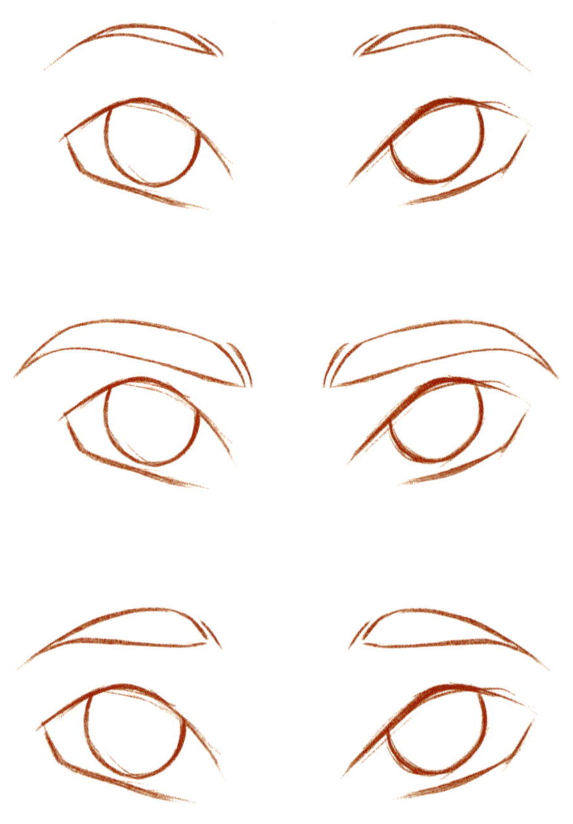

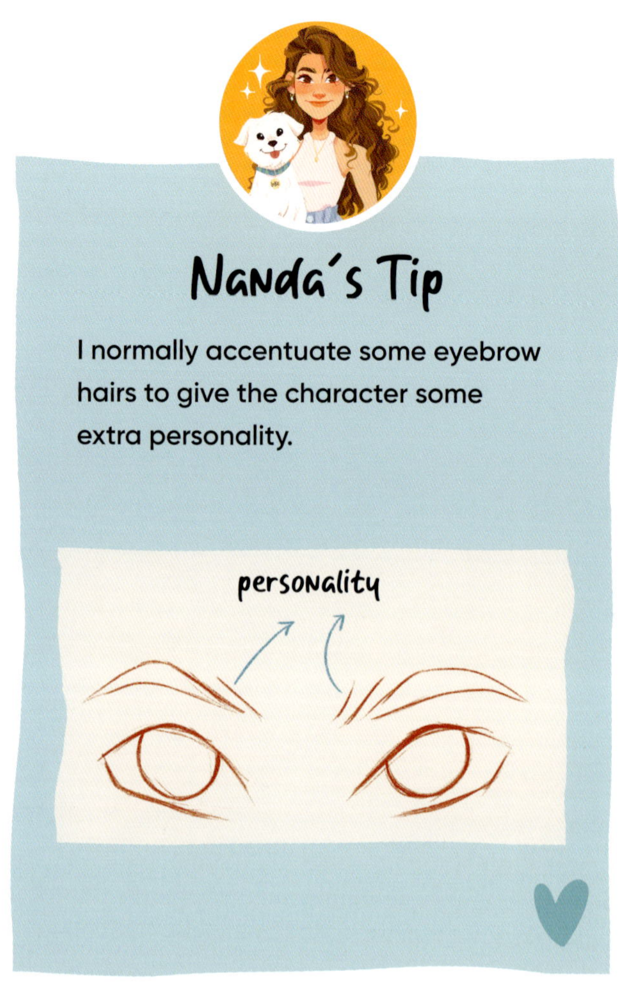

I normally accentuate some eyebrow hairs to give the character some extra personality.

ADDING DETAILS TO YOUR EYES AND EYEBROWS

Now that you have the basic shapes of your eyes and eyebrows, add the lashes, eyelids, and details to them. Details make your drawing more stylized and less artificial.

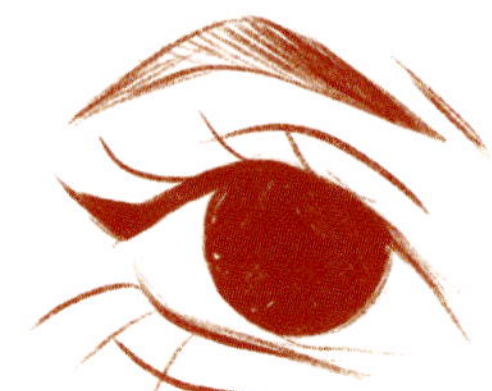

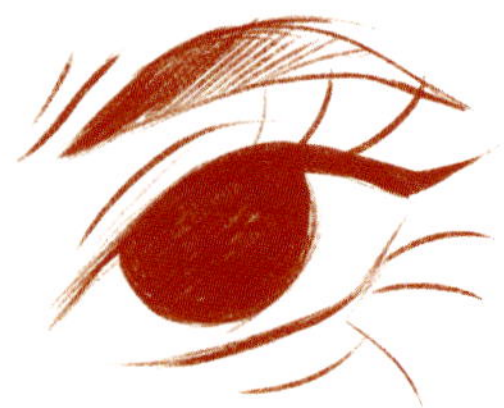

NOSE

Drawing the nose in three separate steps will give you a clearer idea of where to start and where to go from there.

1. CIRCLE

Start by drawing a circle that represents the base shape of the nose. It can be bigger or smaller depending on what size or type of nose you want your character to have. If the circle that you made is bigger, the other shapes that you are going to draw are going to lead to a bigger nose, for example.

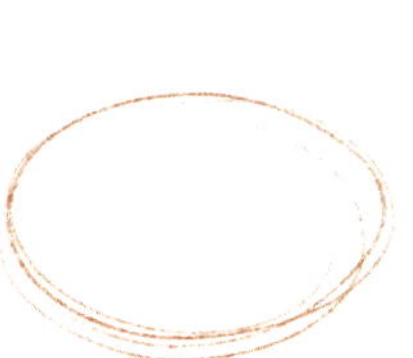

To create different types of noses, start with the base circle that you made in the first step. Just by slightly changing the lines of the nostrils and the edges of the nose, you can create innumerous nose variations.

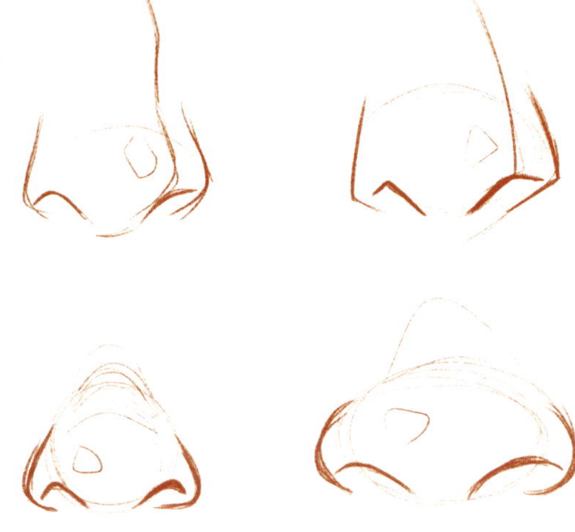

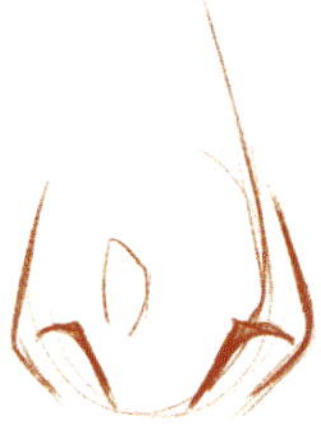

2. NOSTRILS AND EDGES

Next draw the nostrils. For this part I like to imagine them as two letter *L*s upside down. After that step, draw two other lines to construct the edge of the nose.

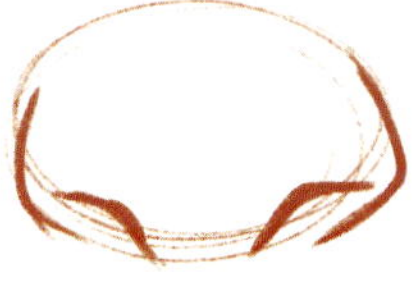

3. FINAL DETAILS

Finally, draw the shadows, shine, and last details of your nose to add some personality.

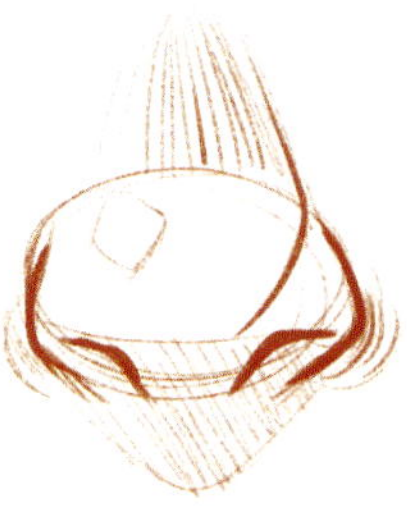

MOUTH

1. MOUTH SHAPE

When drawing a mouth, I like to start with the line between the upper and the lower lips.

Everyone has a different mouth shape. For some people, it can be an upside-down *U* shape. For others, the mouth could have a *V* shape. Variations are welcome, and playing with them will give you the skill to develop many different characters.

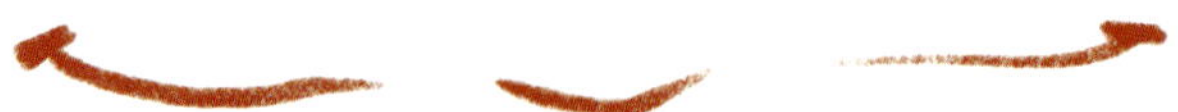

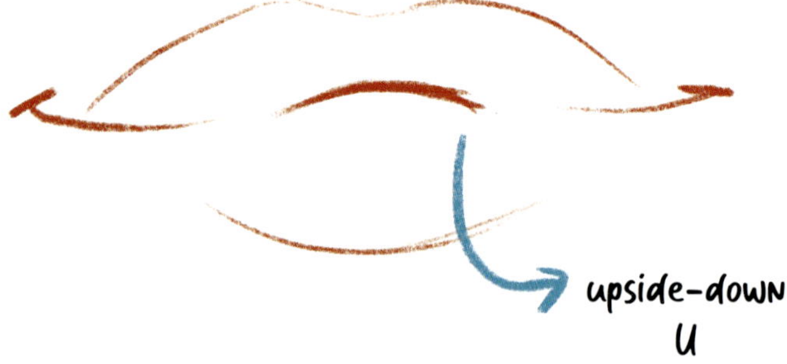

Here is where you can define some additional features of your character, like if they are going to be happy or sad.

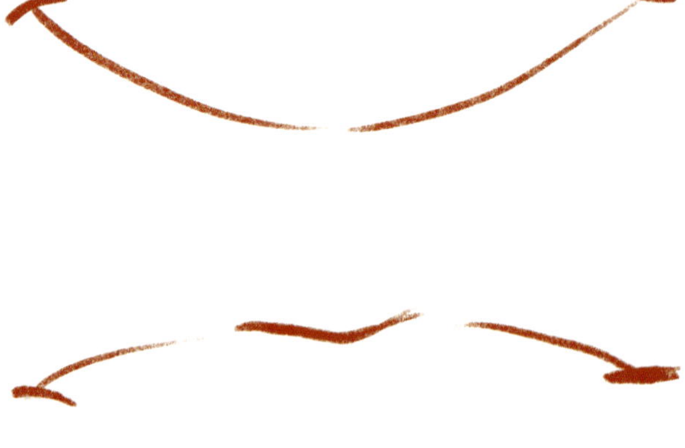

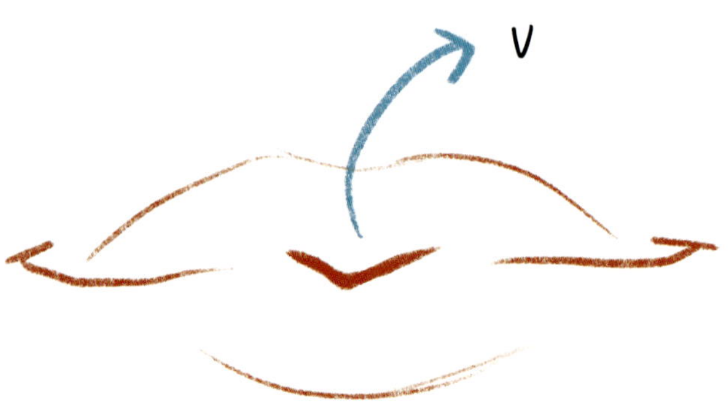

2. LIPS

After defining the shape of the mouth, draw the lips, which you can make in many distinct shapes. They could be bigger or thinner, a bit longer or shorter, and so on.

3. FINAL DETAILS

Finally, I add the shadows, following the shape of the mouth, to give the drawing some depth.

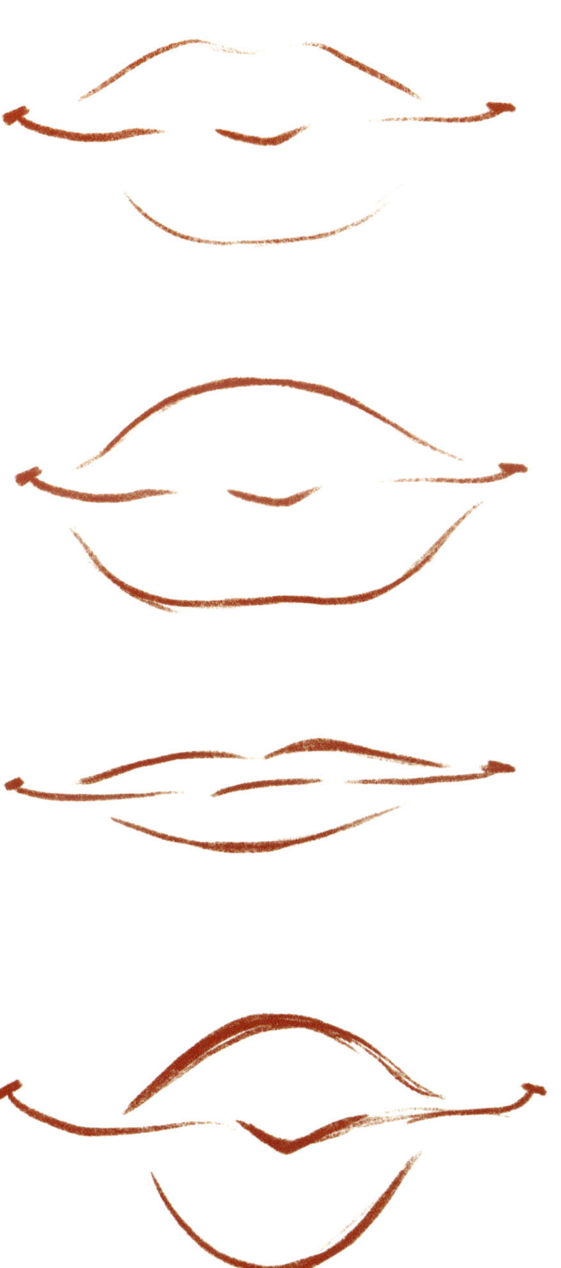

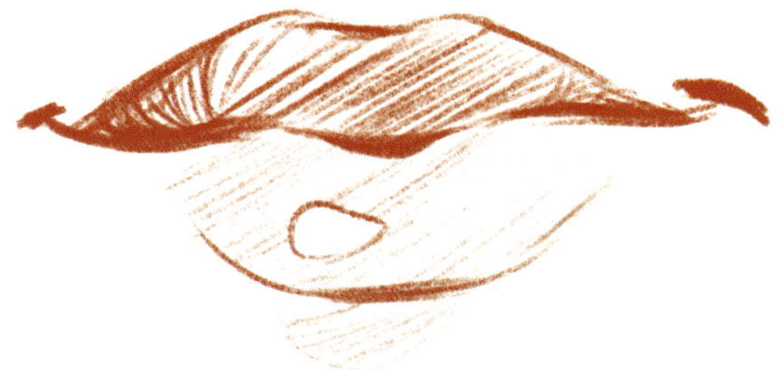

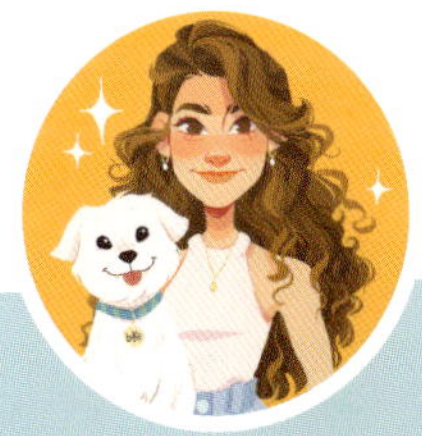

Nanda's Tip

Shadows are very important to your drawing. Under natural light or even during the night, shadowing should always have a presence on a character's face. Identifying and drawing these shadows give you the ability to express characters in a more stylized and realistic way.

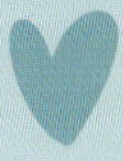

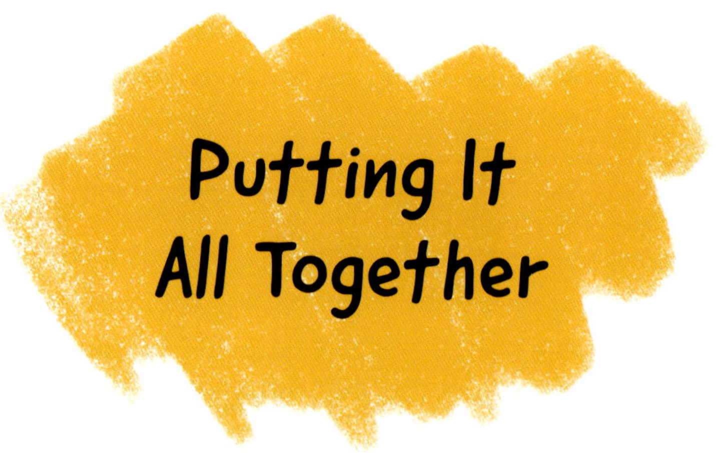

Putting It All Together

Now that you've learned how to draw each facial feature, you're going to put all of them together to create a character's face. Here you can experiment, trying different variations of the eyes, lips, nose, and mouth to create endless characters of different ages, ethnicities, backgrounds, and personalities. This is the time when all your drawing results in something unique and special, something that just you will be able to create.

At this stage, try not to worry about being perfect. Keep practicing—it's time to play with the facial features you've just learned how to do.

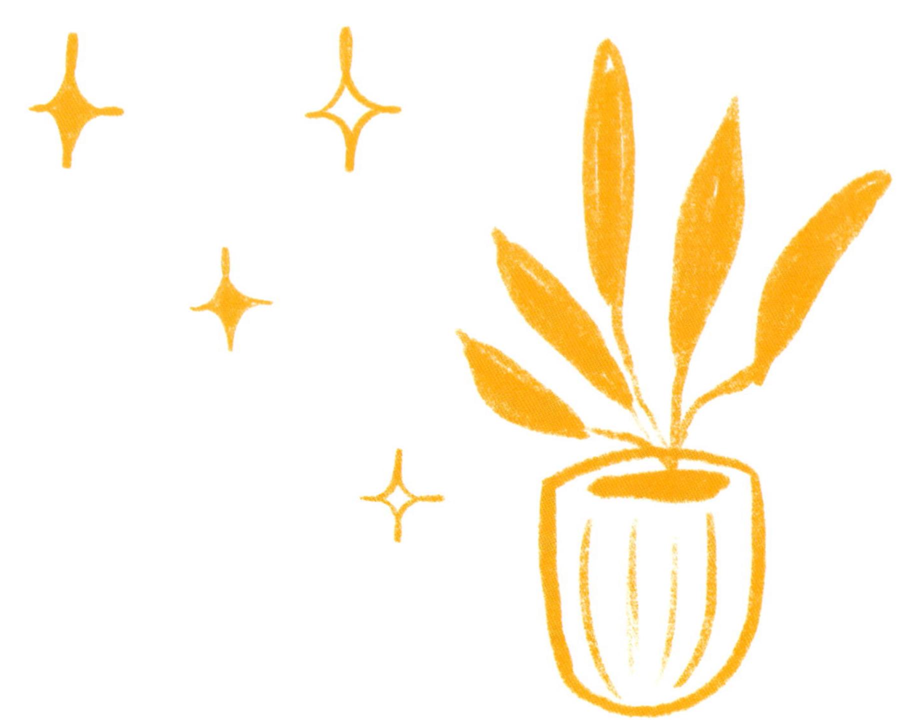

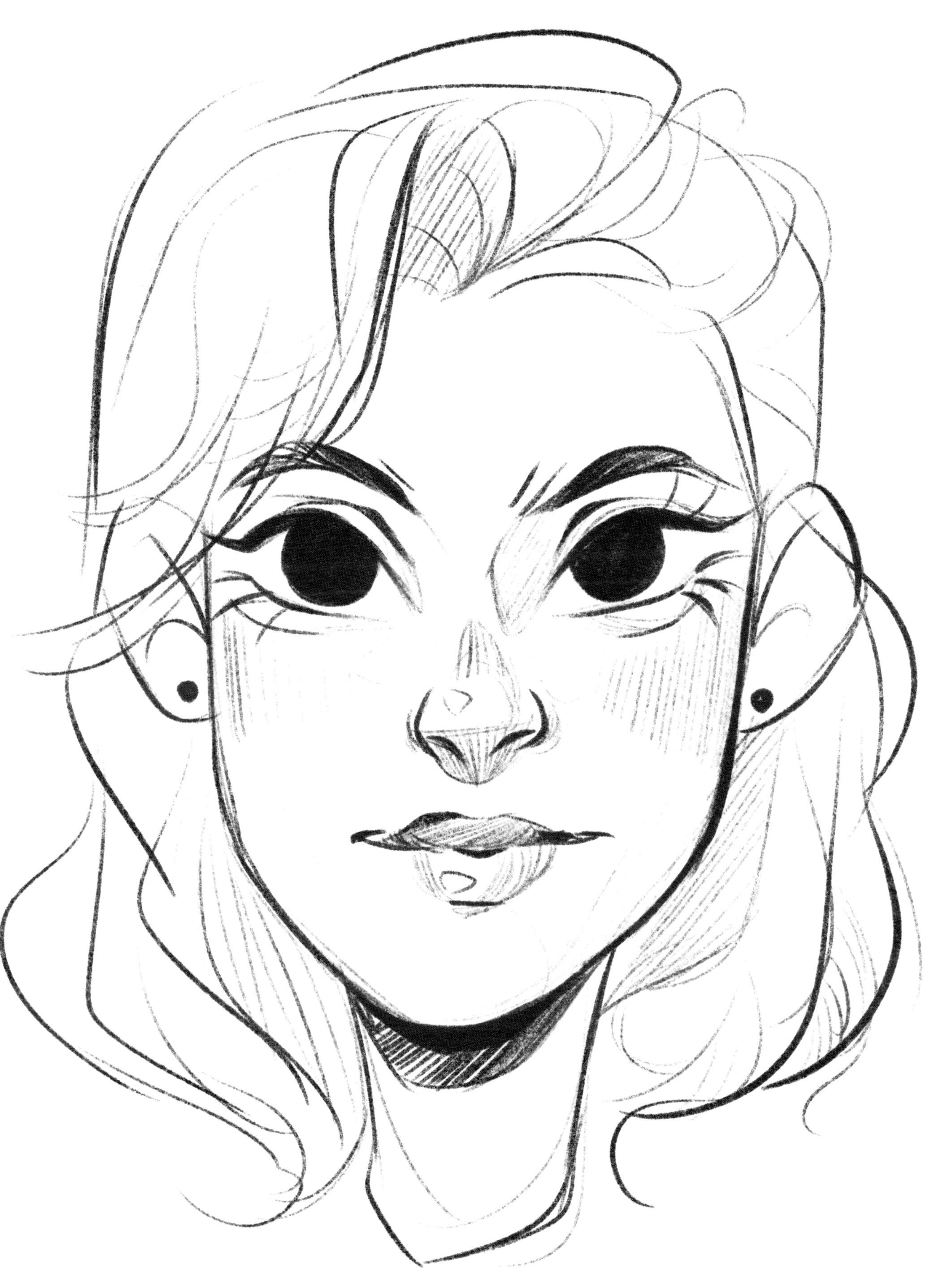

Front, Three-Quarters & Side Head

Now that you've learned how to draw the simple basic shapes of a face and also the facial features, you are going to learn how to draw the character you created from three different angles: front, three-quarters, and side. It's important when drawing the same character in different perspectives to keep their basic shapes the same size and proportions so they don't look like someone else from another angle.

The key is to simplify their head into two simple reference shapes so you can draw them from different perspectives.

After you have the basic reference shapes settled, you can begin adding the details and defining the lines that will build the face, then start on the facial features. After you have developed the ability to draw characters from different angles, you can change the reference shapes that build their faces to create a bunch of variations.

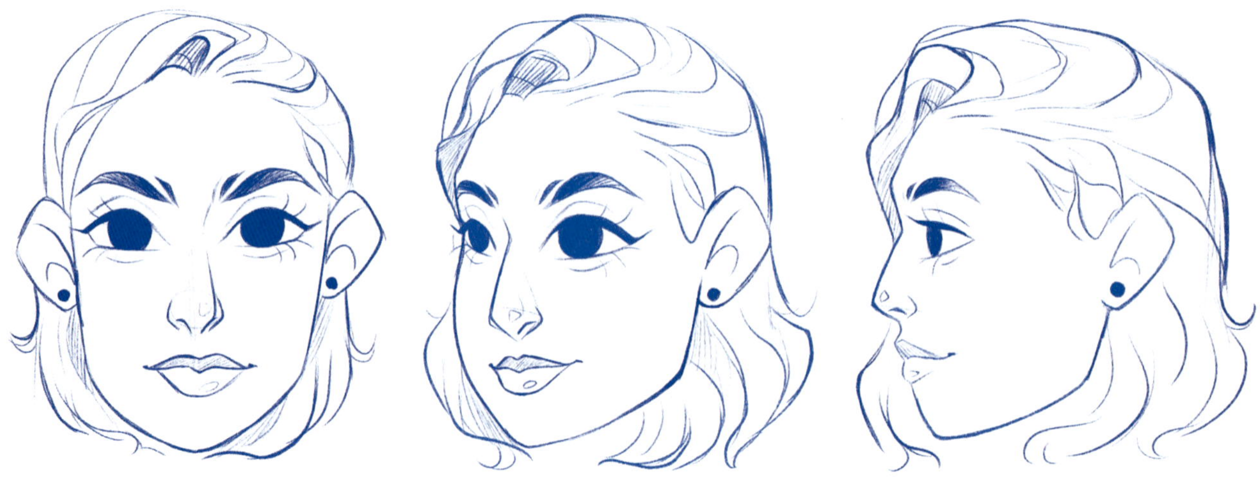

First you must have an idea of how the skull looks from those perspectives. This will be the base for building your character and will help you keep the proportions correct.

As you can see in these examples, the skull is divided into two big pieces (the cranium and the jaw), and keeping the ratio of those pieces is essential to making your character recognizable and proportional. Remember that each shape changes a little bit in every person. For example, one character may have a larger jaw than another, so you may want to draw the jaw shape larger too to help you later on.

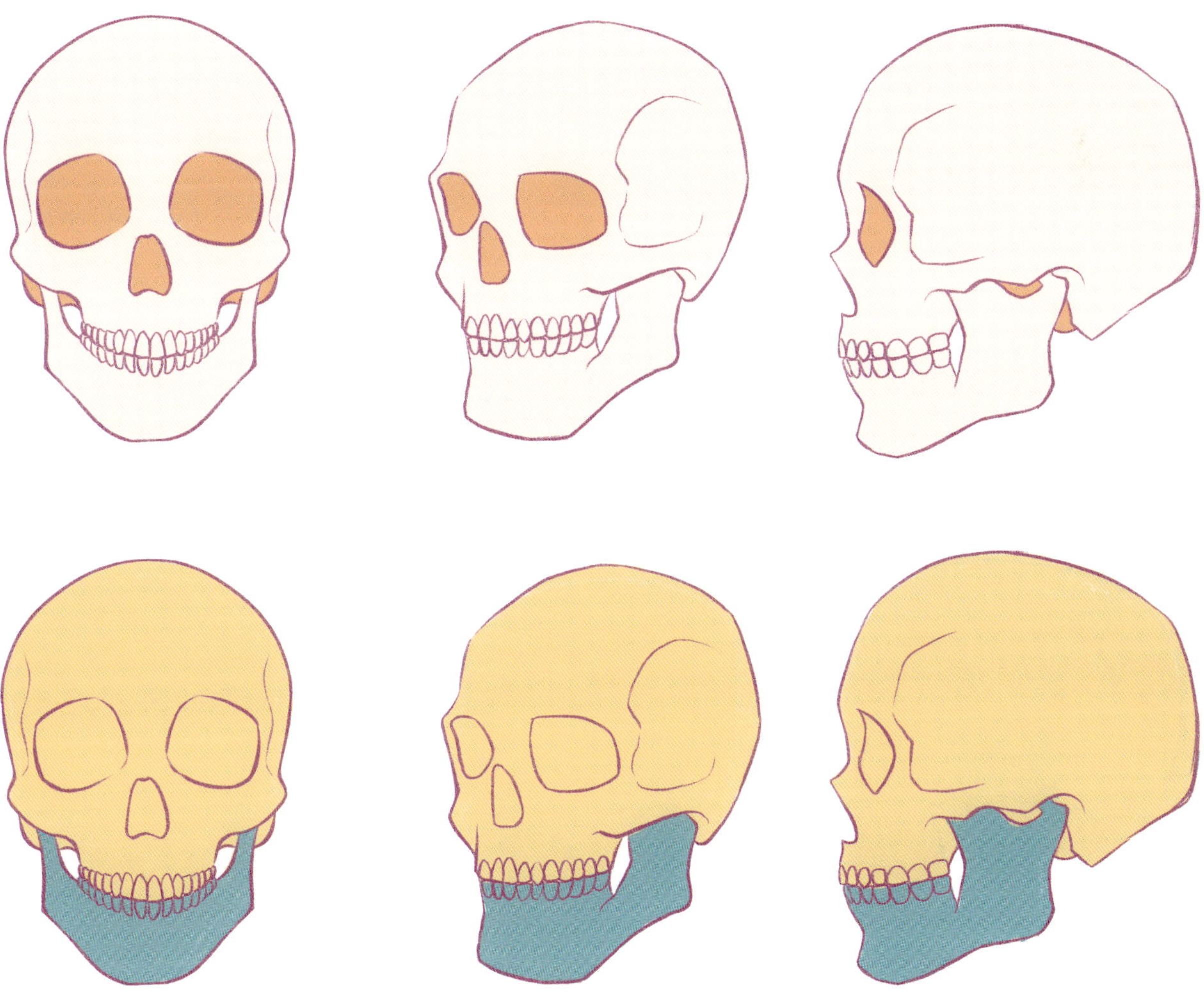

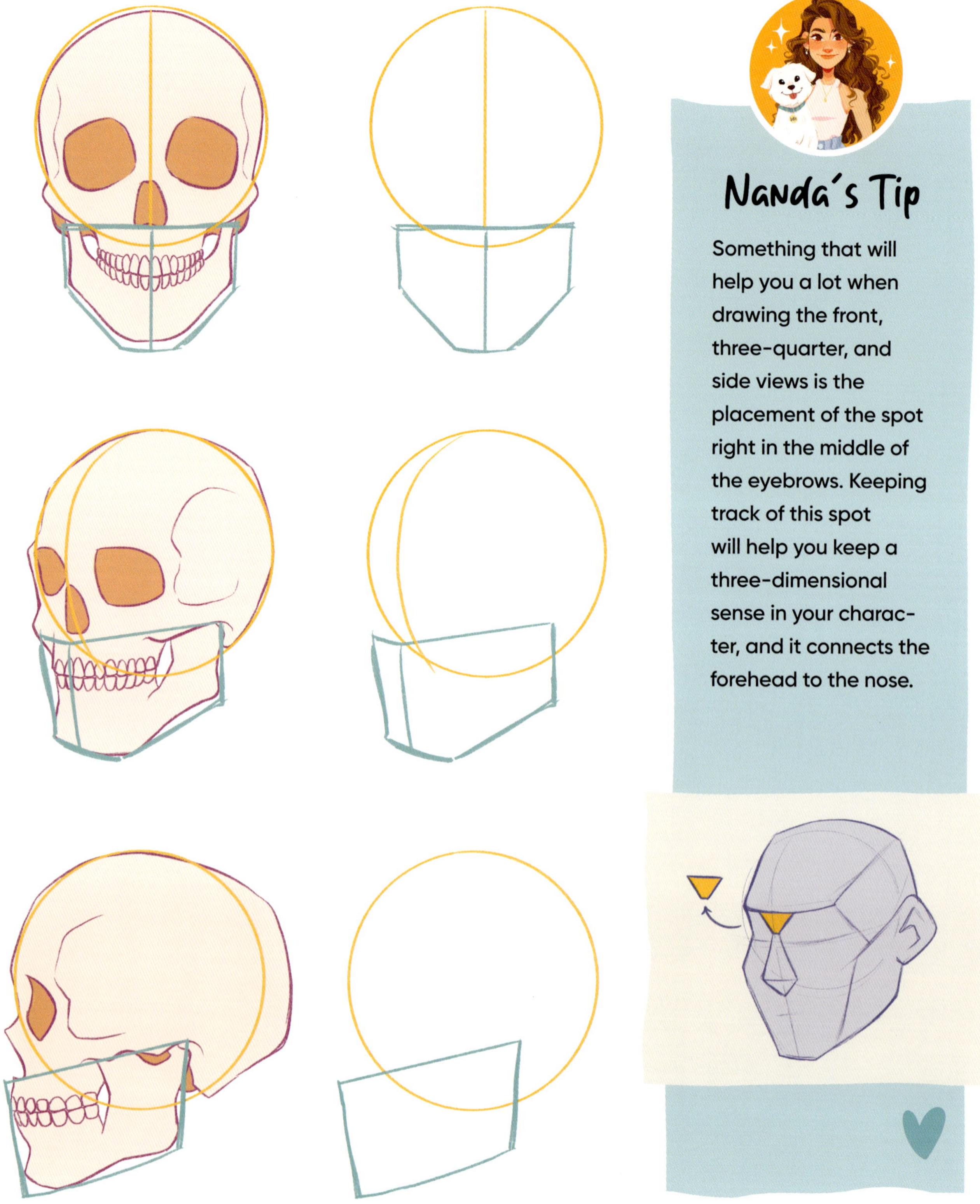

Nanda's Tip

Something that will help you a lot when drawing the front, three-quarter, and side views is the placement of the spot right in the middle of the eyebrows. Keeping track of this spot will help you keep a three-dimensional sense in your charac-ter, and it connects the forehead to the nose.

FRONT VIEW

When drawing the front view of the head, you need to define the basic reference shapes of the head using the skull drawings as a guide. I know we already have gone through how to draw a face from the front view, but now we will focus on what to keep in mind when drawing to more easily draw that same face from different perspectives later on.

It's important first to divide the face into two simple shapes. Doing that will help you build the same face later on from different angles and add the details and facial features in the correct places.

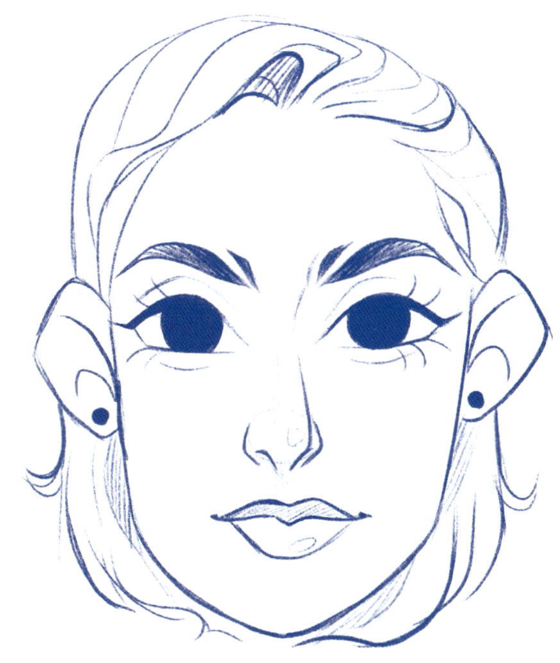

These shapes are a **circle** that will represent the cranium and the **jawline** attached to it. Here the basic reference shapes of the skull drawing are going to help you with the proportions of the head and the jawline.

Also, you are going to place the vertical and horizontal guidelines to help you locate the eyes, eyebrows, nose, and mouth. These lines will stay in the same place to assist in placing the facial features in other angles.

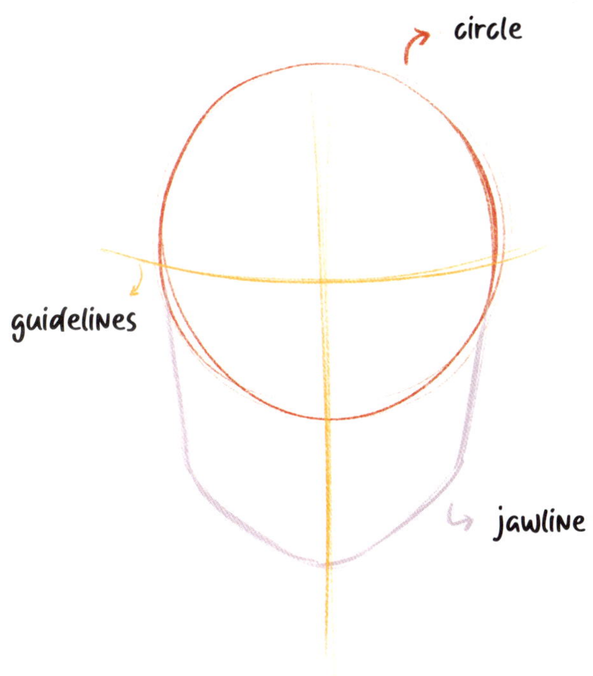

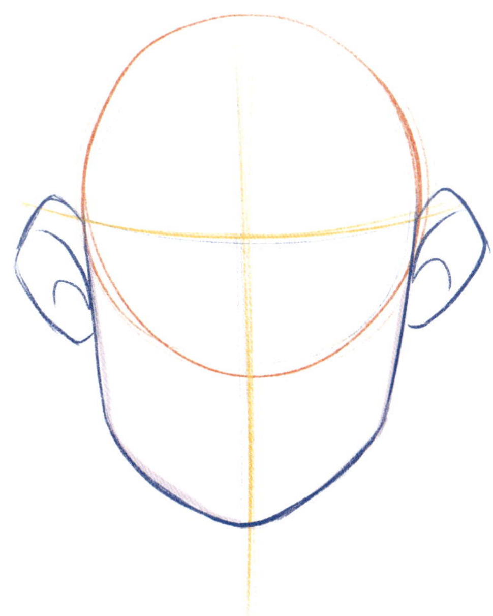

FACIAL FEATURES

When adding facial features in the front view,
you are going to apply what you learned earlier
in this chapter. Like you did when drawing
the head, you are going to keep in mind the
basic shapes that form the facial features so
you can draw those same facial features in
other perspectives.

1. Eyes and Eyebrows

Place the eyes and eyebrows on top of the
horizontal guideline. Pay attention to the shape
of the eye and eyebrows you are choosing
here (arched, circular, straighter, etc.). Remember
the shape you've used here when drawing the
other perspectives, to keep the same shape
in every view.

2. Nose

For the nose, try to visualize it in a three-
dimensional perspective. I like to imagine it
with the shape of two little pyramids.

   This will help you keep the same shape for
your character's nose when drawing other
perspectives.

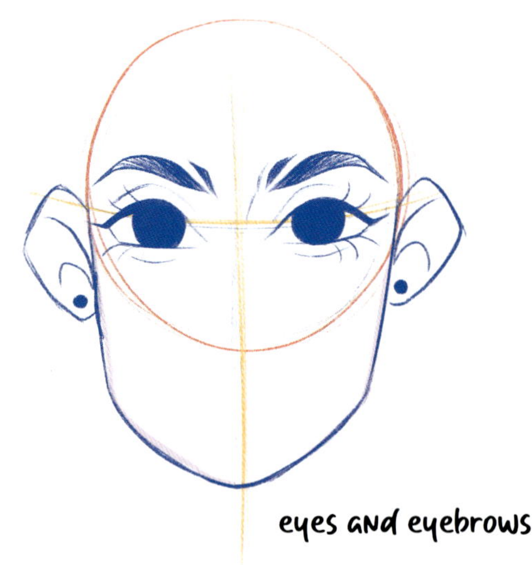

eyes and eyebrows

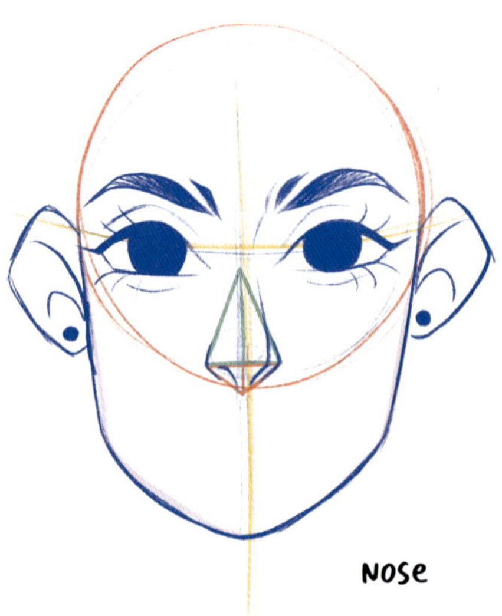

nose

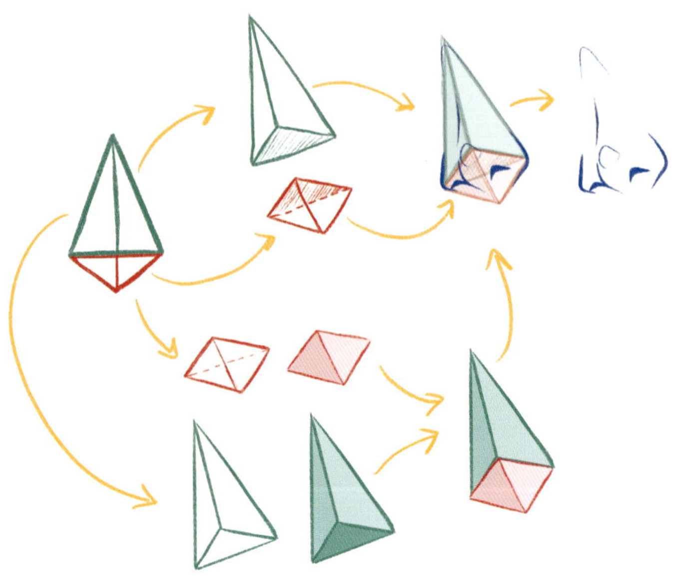

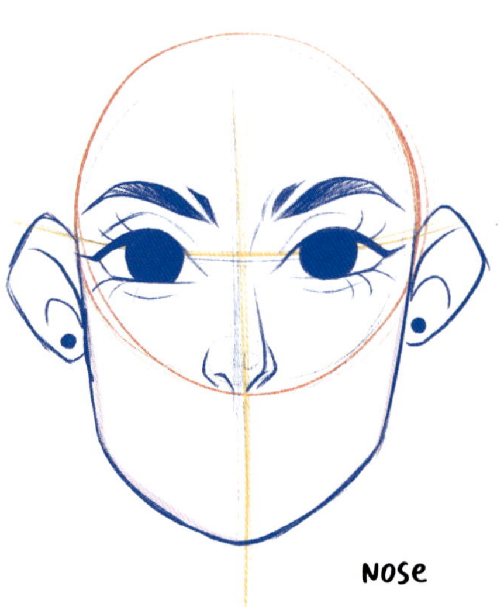

nose

3. Mouth

Like you did for the eyes, eyebrows, and nose, always pay attention to the shape that you've chosen. Keep the same shape, and build your mouth on the top of that.

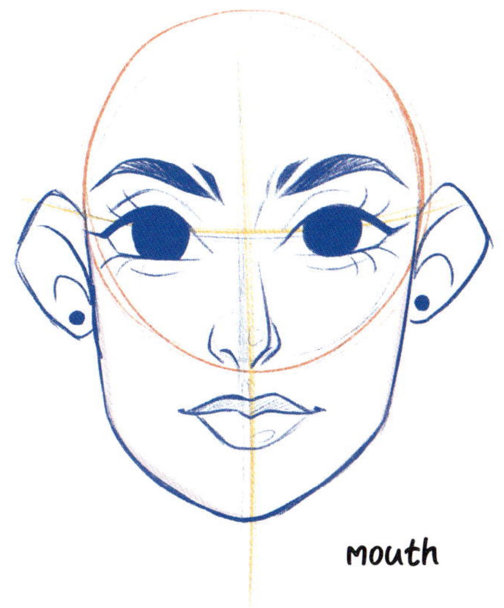

THREE-QUARTER VIEW

Now we are going to talk about the three-quarter view. This angle is probably the one I struggled with the most during my artistic career. But when I understood the basics of this angle, drawing it became a much easier task for me.

Like the other angles, keeping the ratio of both shapes that make up the head (the cranium and the jaw) is the key to making your character recognizable and drawing the three-quarter view correctly.

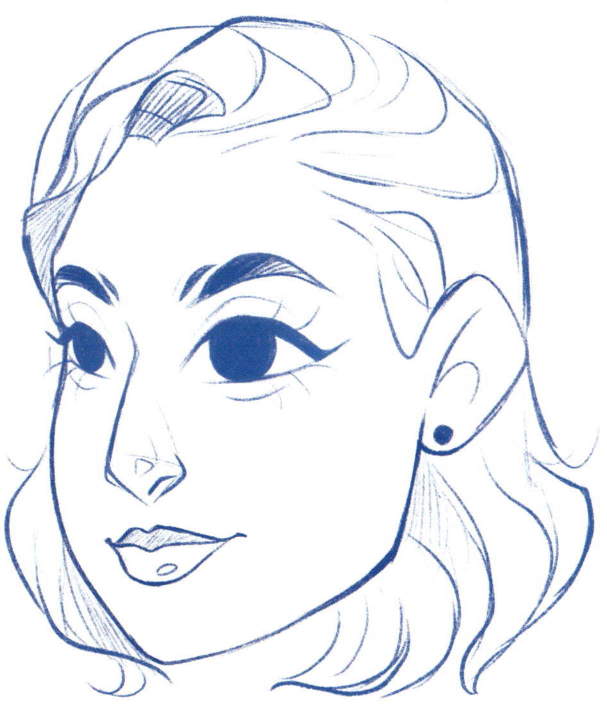

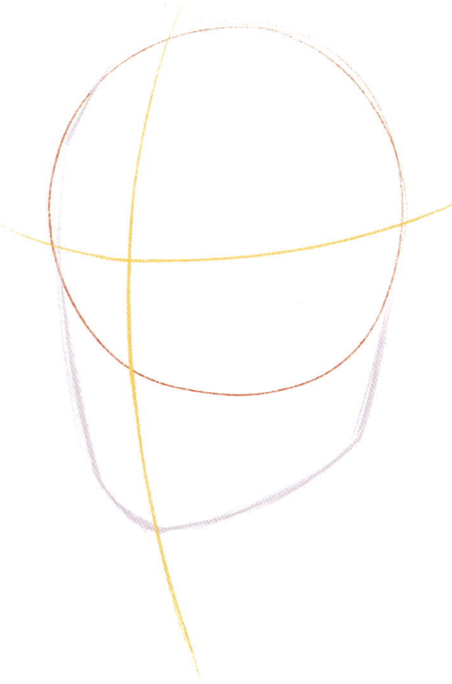

So no matter at what angle you draw, the circle of the cranium stays basically the same, but the jaw and the line that delimits the face will define the viewing angle of your character—in this case, the three-quarter view.

Always place the horizontal and vertical lines to guide you when locating the facial features later on. These lines will follow the position of your character and help you build a three-dimensional perspective.

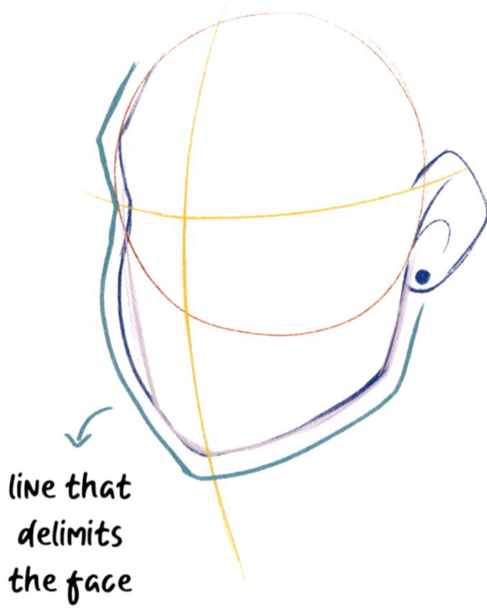

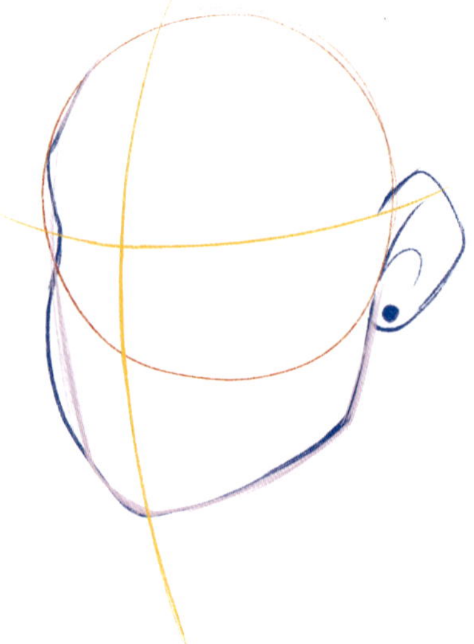

FACIAL FEATURES

Now that we have already gone through how to draw facial features in the front view, it is going to be much easier for you to build those same features in the three-quarter view. The principles are the same, but the shapes that form the features will change a little bit because of the new perspective.

1. Eyes and Eyebrows

When drawing the eyes and eyebrows for the three-quarter view, it's really important to follow the vertical and diagonal lines and use that spot right in the middle of the eyebrows to help place the eyes correctly.

The eye that is behind is a bit more arched and narrower than the one that stays closer to the viewer.

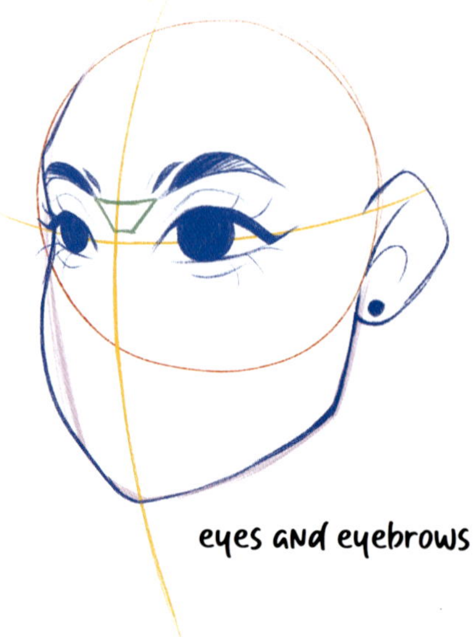

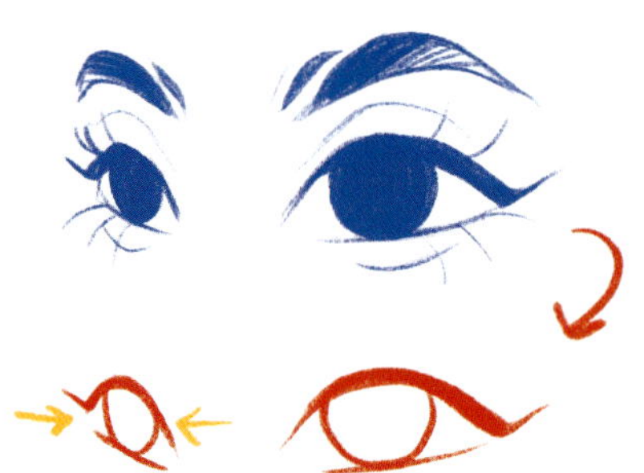

2. Nose

For the nose, you are going to use the triangular shape you've built for the front view and apply it here, rotating the pyramid to the corresponding three-quarter position. This will help you visualize the nose in a three-dimensional way.

3. Mouth

When drawing the mouth from this perspective, try to visualize it in two parts. This will help you play with those shapes to create a three-dimensional mouth that is in harmony with the three-quarter view. The side of the mouth that is farther back is more squished and narrower than the side that is closer to the viewer, just like the eye.

Remember to place the middle of the mouth in the middle of the vertical line to make the face more harmonic and centered.

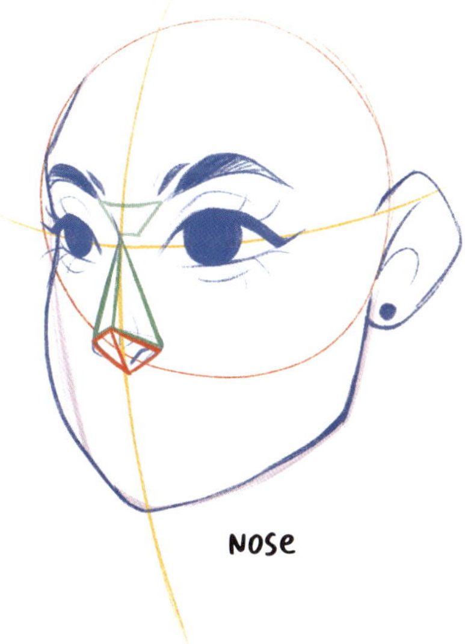

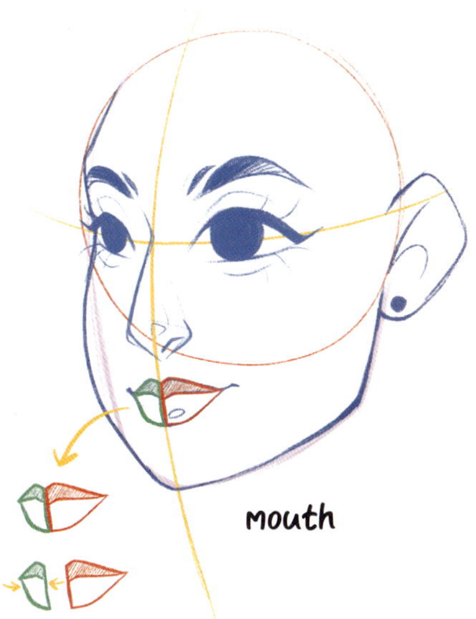

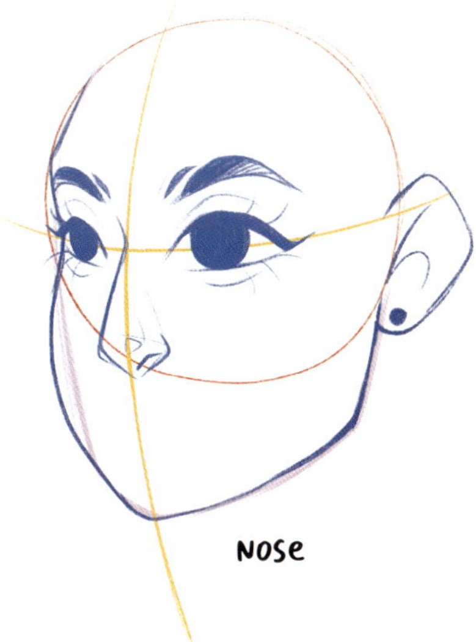

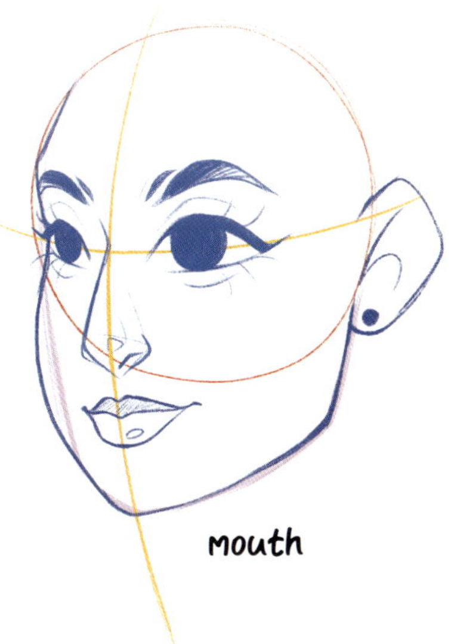

SIDE VIEW

The side view, also known as the profile angle, is one of my favorite perspectives to draw and has some special characteristics because just one side of the character will be shown.

I like to start by drawing the head circle and then the jawline. Don't worry about placing the facial features yet. The only thing that I use at this stage is a line to guide me later when I draw the shape of the profile and add the facial features.

After that, I start to draw the line that will define the profile, being careful to place the facial features where they need to be and following the guidelines I've made to keep my character recognizable. I also follow the shape of the skull, using that to help me place the facial features and build the profile.

The key is to identify the line that shapes the face when seen from the side.

Remember that the circle that forms the cranium won't be perfectly circular, since you are viewing it from the side.

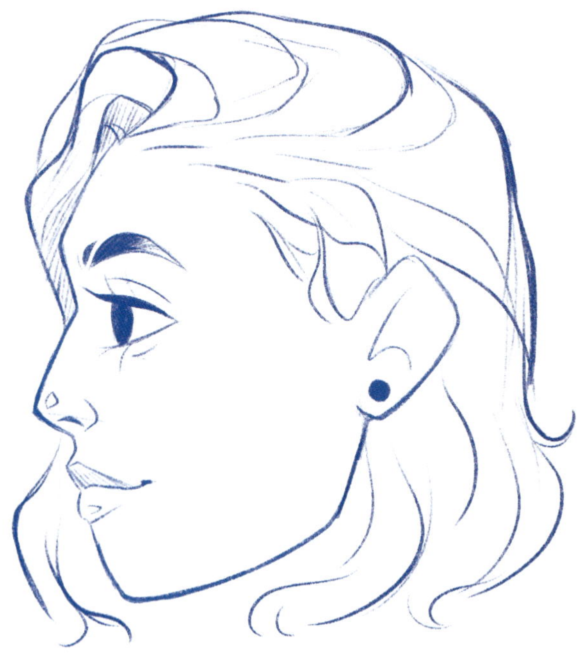

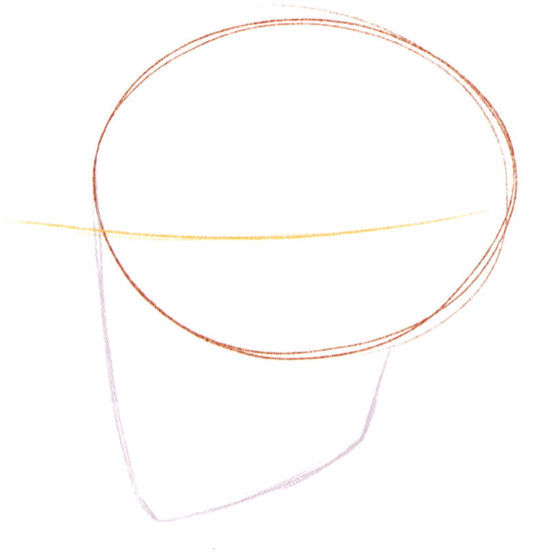

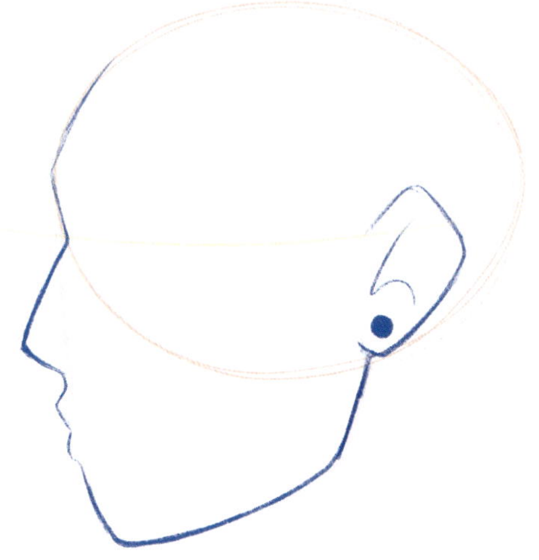

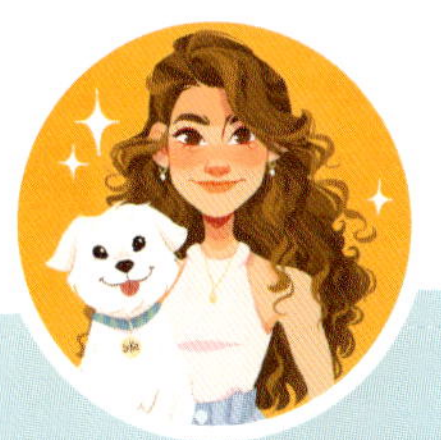

Nanda´s Tip

In the side view, the ears are placed almost in the middle of the head, not on the back side of it, close to the head limit.

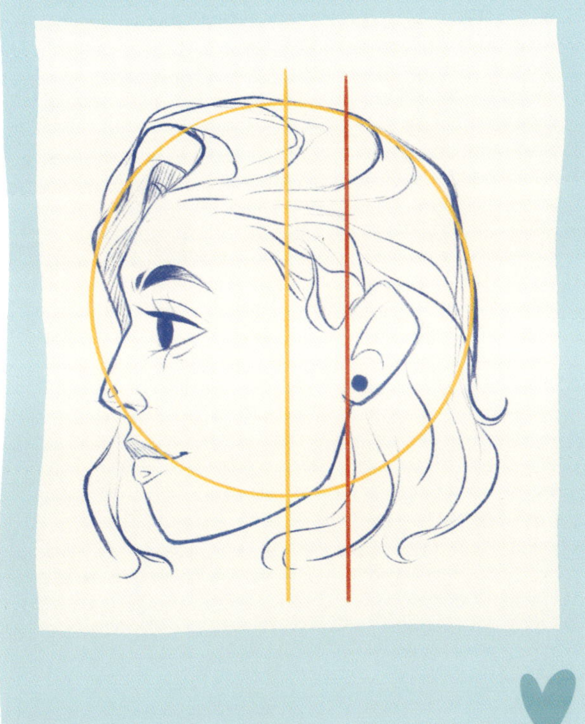

FACIAL FEATURES

1. Eyes and Eyebrows

To make the eye look natural and proportional from the side view, consider its size and form beyond the eyelid. Your main shape of reference will be a circle, but as you can see in the image below, the eyelids will be placed outside this circle and the eye globe inside the circle.

I drew a circle as a reference shape for the eye, and then I added the eyelids to form the external shape of the eye.

For the eyebrows, the shape for this profile angle doesn't change much from the front perspective. The main difference is that it looks a little bit more compressed.

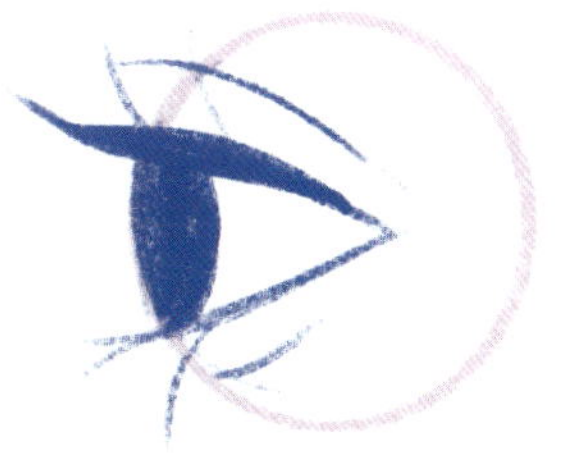

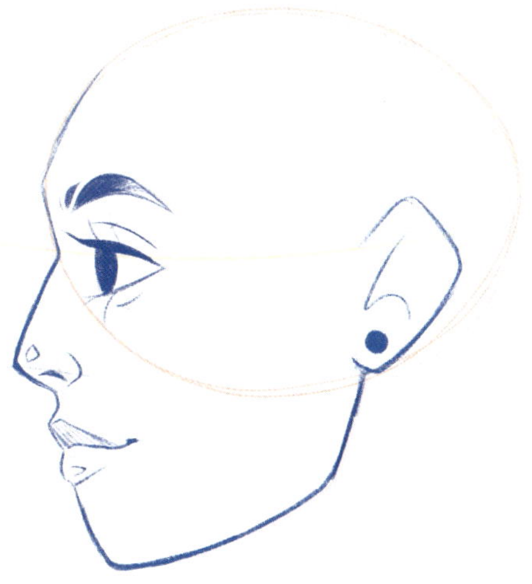

2. Nose

For the nose, use those pyramid shapes that you did for the front view to help you keep the ratio of the facial features the same.

3. Mouth

Next, define the shape of the mouth while drawing the line that will delimit the profile of the face. Then you can add the lips and some details to it.

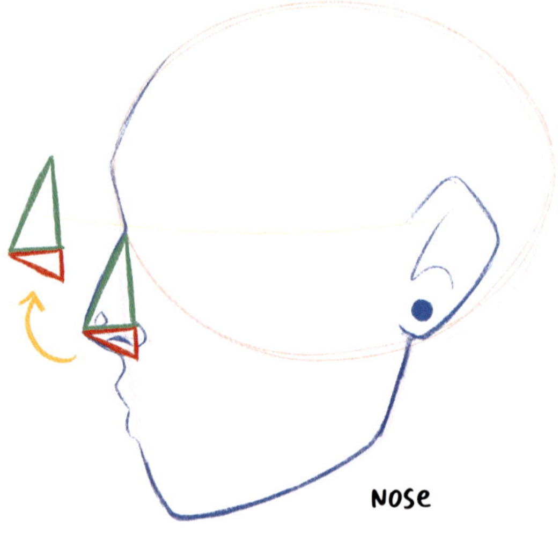

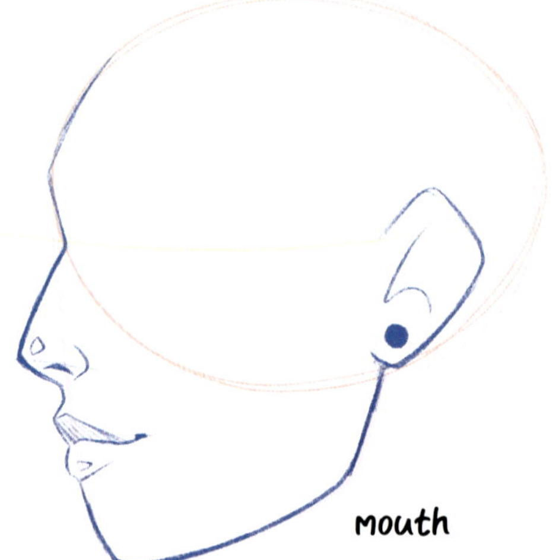

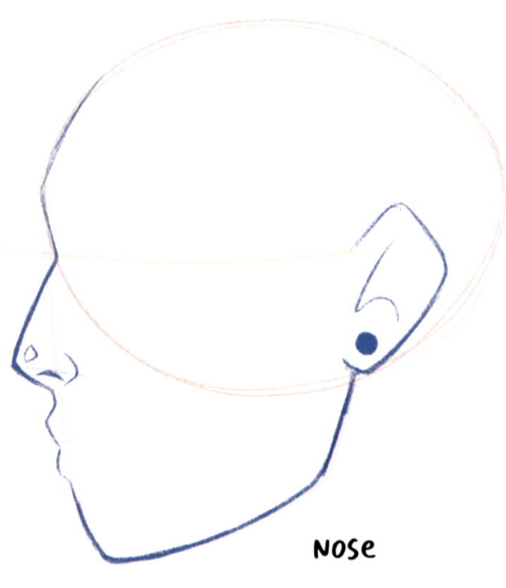

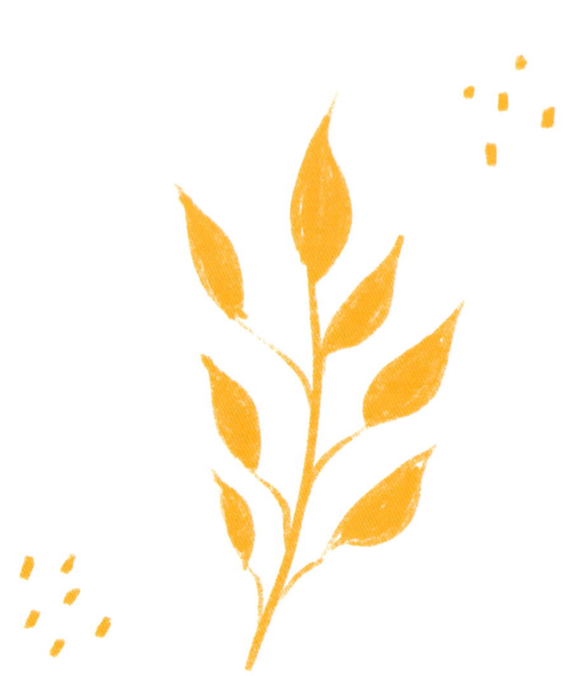

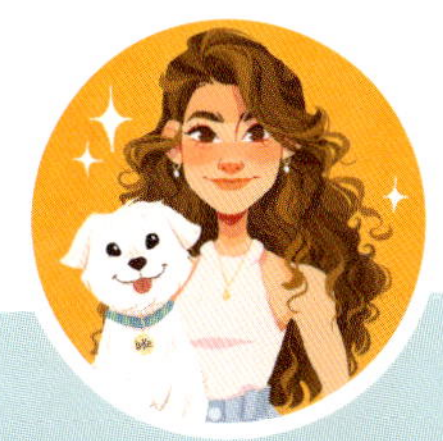

Nanda's Tips

• Remember to allow enough space for the back of the head.

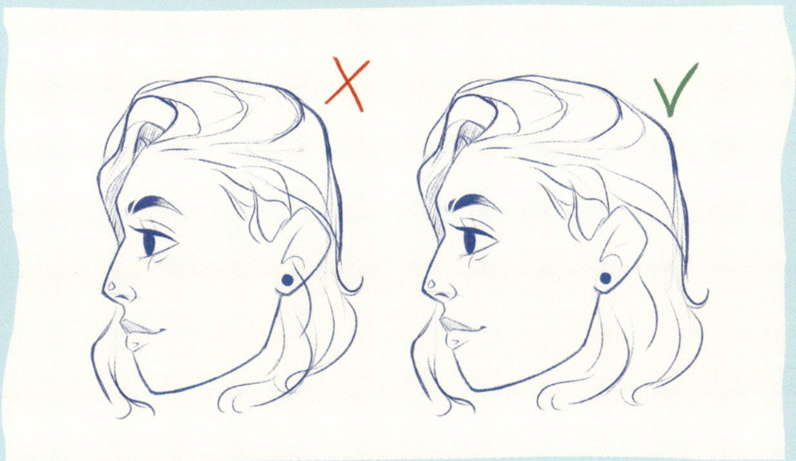

• There is another angle between the three-quarter and side views, closer to the profile view. In this perspective, you will be able to see a little bit of the eyelashes, eyebrows, and mouth that would be covered in the profile angle. You can do this angle by slightly turning your character from the profile position to show just a little bit of the covered side.

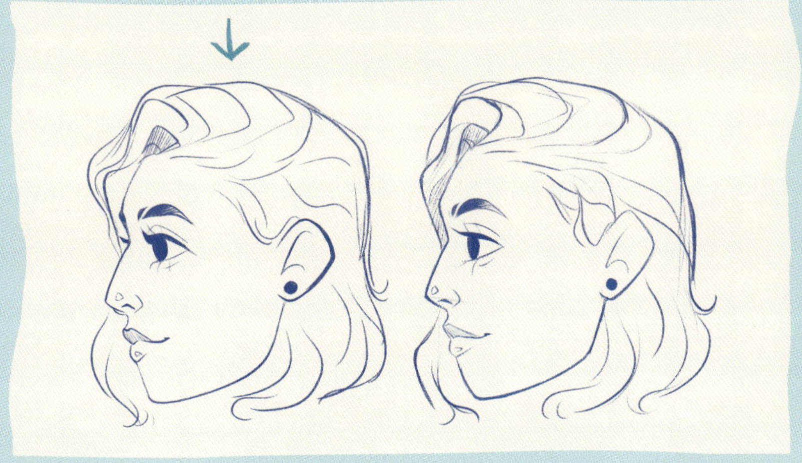

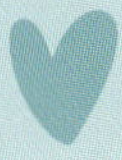

Characters from Different Angles

Now that you have an idea of how to draw faces from different angles, you are going to adjust the basic shapes (the circle that builds the cranium and jaw) in many different combinations to create innumerable kinds of characters.

We will later go into more detail about how you can play with proportions to make unique characters. For now, we'll cover how to change the shapes that build the face to create different characters and make them recognizable from different angles.

Let's begin with this example.

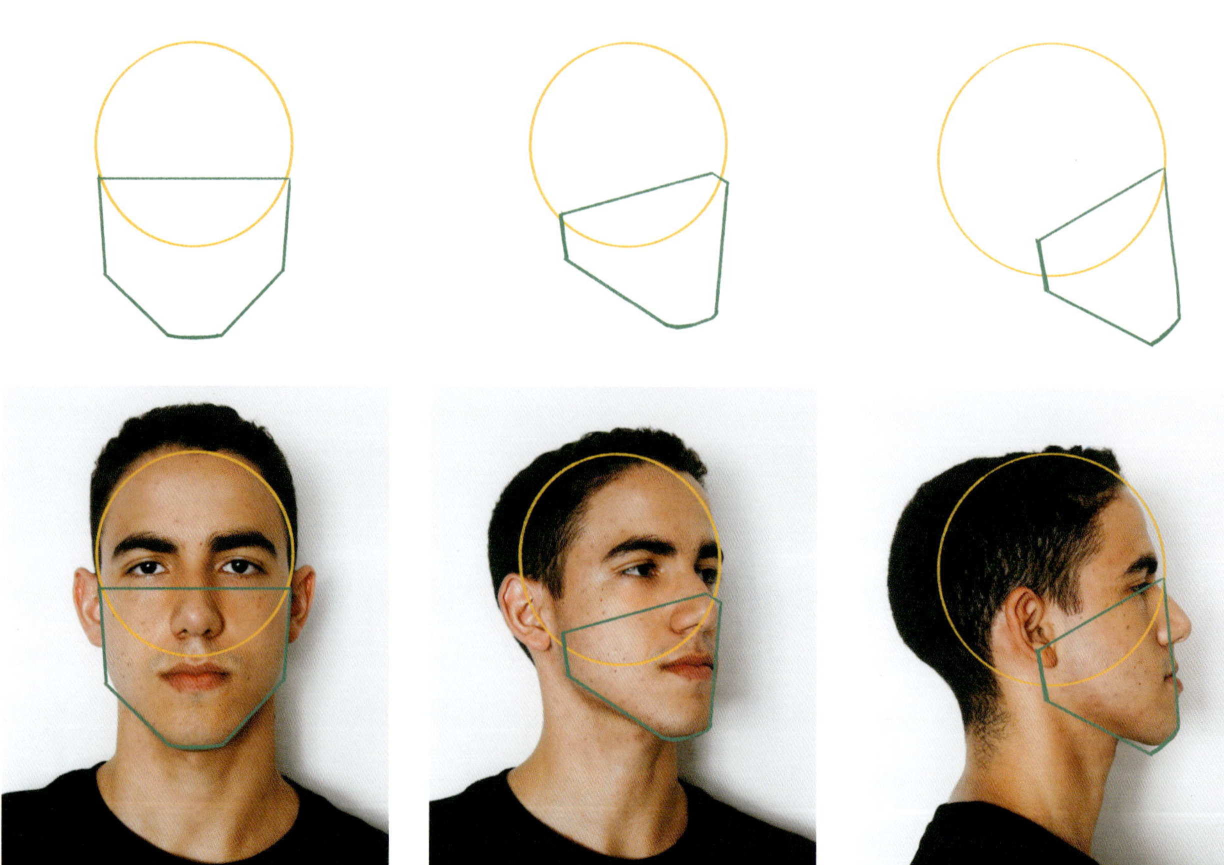

When drawing characters
from different angles using
a reference photo, I take my
reference as an inspiration
and identify the shapes that
build the face in every angle
(circle and jaw) so I can turn
it into a drawing. The reason you know that it is the
same person in every angle
is because I kept the proportions and shapes the same.
Pay attention to the fact that
each shape changes a little bit
depending on the angle and
adapts to the perspective
from which you're looking at
your character.

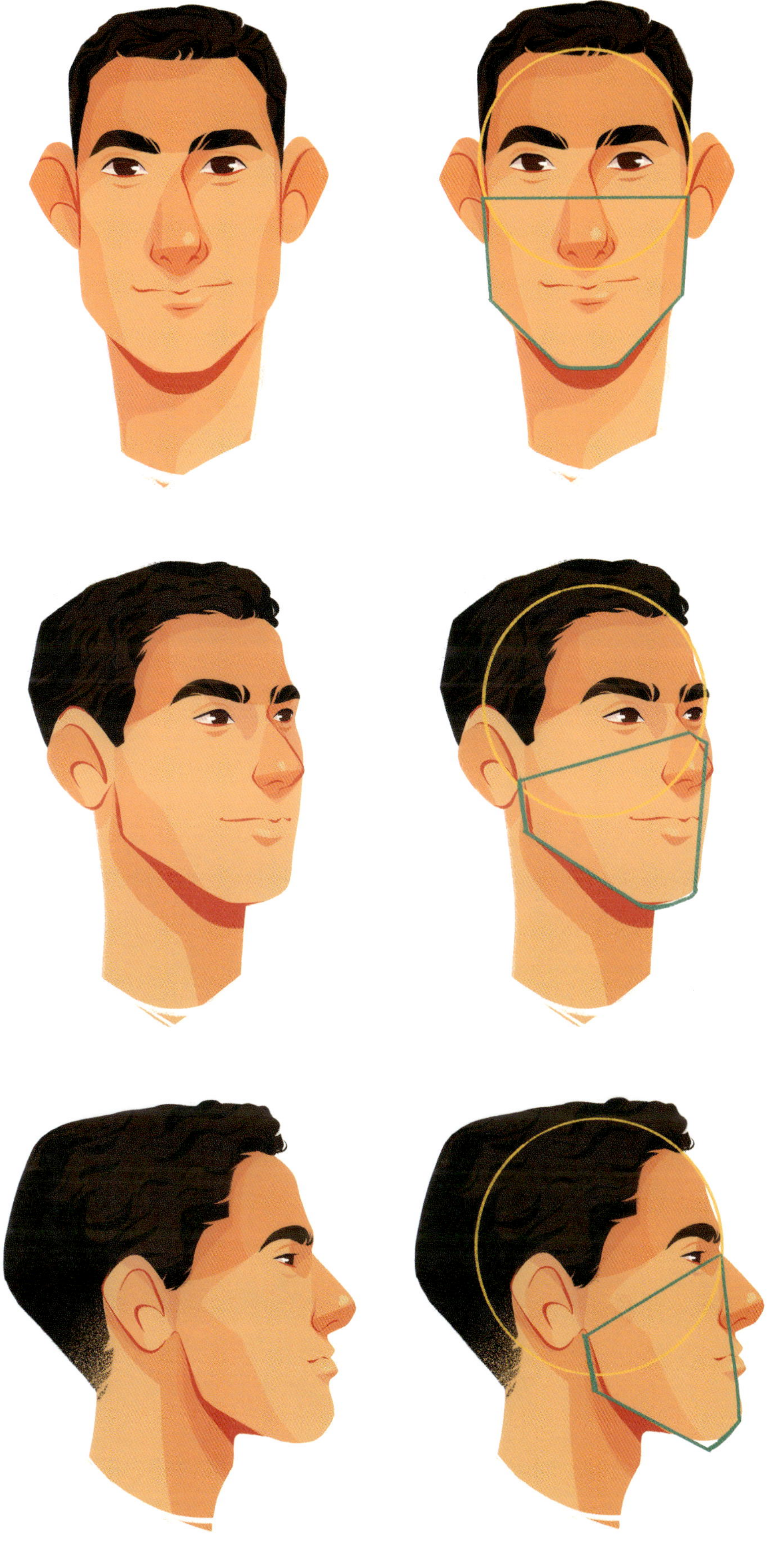

To create variations of characters without having to use a reference photo, change the shapes that build the face (the cranium and the jaw). This will help you create a lot of variations of characters.

In a nutshell, creating characters from different angles and making them recognizable is only a matter of changing the shapes that build their face and facial features, keeping the proportions equal, and maintaining the same shape for every angle, adjusting to the perspective that you are looking to your character. You don't need a reference photo; you can create characters from your imagination just by changing the shapes.

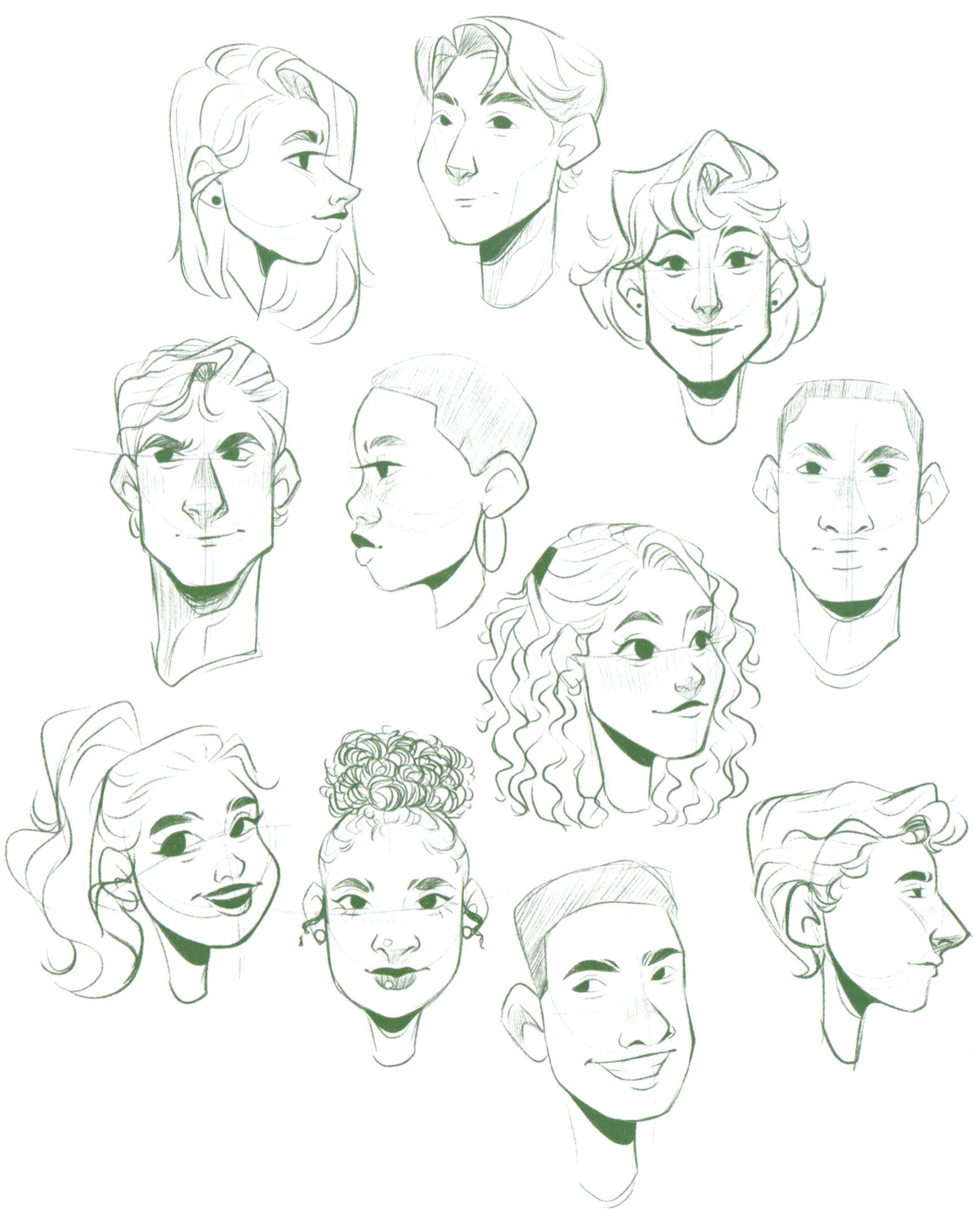

Facial Expressions

You probably don't want every character you draw to have the same facial expression. You also don't want to avoid drawing a character who is angry, for example, just because you don't know how to draw that facial expression. Knowing how to convey what your character is feeling through your drawings is an important ability that every artist should have. Learning what and how you can change each facial feature, where to exaggerate some shapes, and what to emphasize and highlight is what will make your character able to show emotions.

In this section, I'm going to teach you how to draw the seven most-used facial expressions so you can convey your character's feelings through your drawing. Keep in mind that the fundamentals you will learn about what to change in each facial feature or what to emphasize in your character can be applied to drawing many facial expressions. So you're not restricted to only these facial expressions, experiment with other facial expressions, or even mix them up.

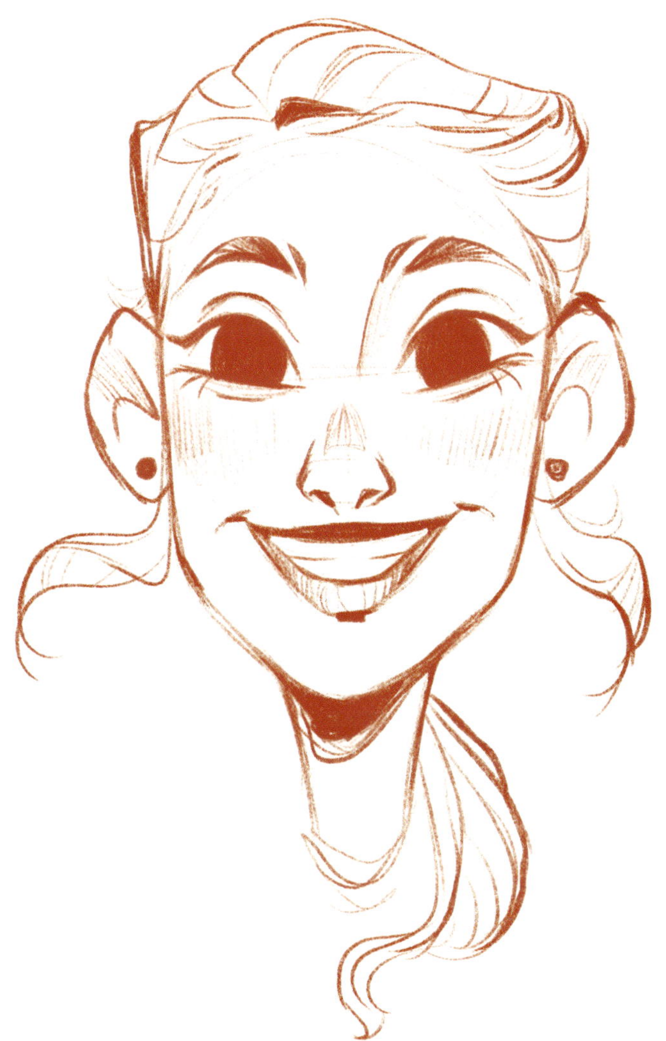

MY MOST-USED FACIAL EXPRESSIONS

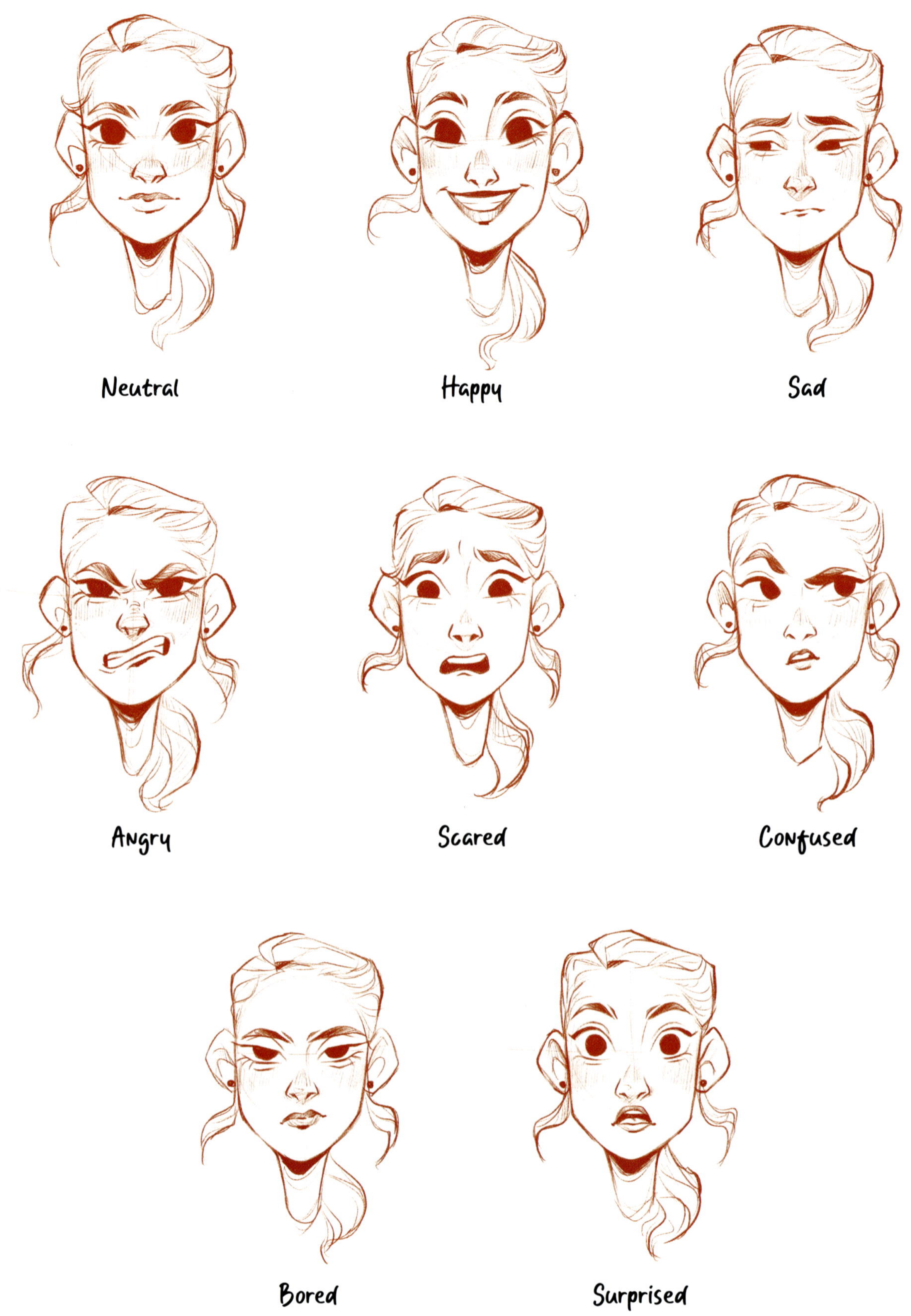

I usually choose to draw my characters in the happy or neutral expressions, but this is just a personal preference. I also challenge myself sometimes to draw specific expressions that I normally don't draw because that can expand the possibilities of the combinations I can make with the traits of my characters and allow me to create even more variations on them.

Combining all the elements that compose your character's face will result in those facial expressions, and mastering these combinations will lead to better results. In addition to the examples opposite, here are some important tips!

1. Although face elements change a lot, the shape of the face stays basically the same. This will help you keep the correct placement of all the facial elements.

2. As you can see, the construction of a facial expression sometimes requires altering the size of an eye (a bit more open, for example) or the length of a mouth. Even when doing that, you want to keep the proportions for a cohesive result. Therefore, although I can open an eye or reduce the length of a mouth, they will be the same mouth and eye of my neutral face expression, just showing this new element in a way that can help you understand the desired expression.

3. You have a little bit more freedom with the eyebrows. In some expressions, like the confused one, they will be placed at different heights (left and right), but they are still proportionally harmonic even when the height and format are different.

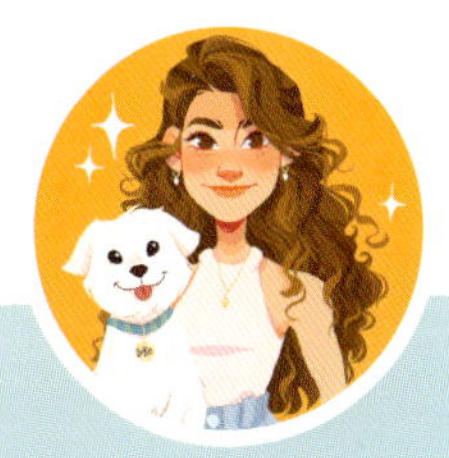

Nanda's Tip

Remember that the more you emphasize each facial feature, the more of a cartoonish look your character will have.

Finally, for a more advanced version, you could use other elements like hair or ears to help compose these facial expressions. But for now, we are working just with the most important elements that you will have to combine to express your character's emotions.

Playing with Proportions

Now that you have the knowledge about facial features and have played with it, you will be able to develop your drawing skills by experimenting with the proportions and sizes of your characters.

When creating a character, you must choose what personality, traits, and characteristics you want them to express. And, when doing that, you are going through a process of constructing and combining each facial feature in a distinct way to make your character unique.

Combining different shapes and playing with the proportions and sizes are how you can create many characters with different styles. They can vary depending on their age, gender, ethnicity, and so on. You'll learn how to modify each specific trait of your characters to create innumerous variations.

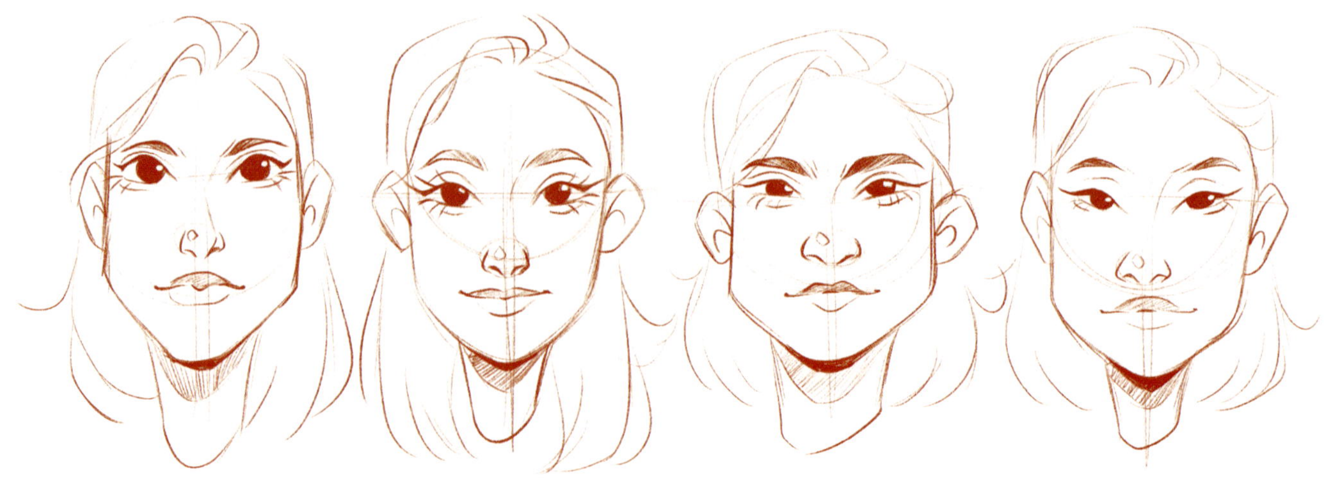

HEAD SHAPES

Whenever you start an illustration of a character, begin with the shape of the head. The most common head shapes are round, heart, diamond, square, and oval.

As you can see, you can create many different characters just by changing head shape. It is such a distinct characteristic that stands out a lot in a drawing.

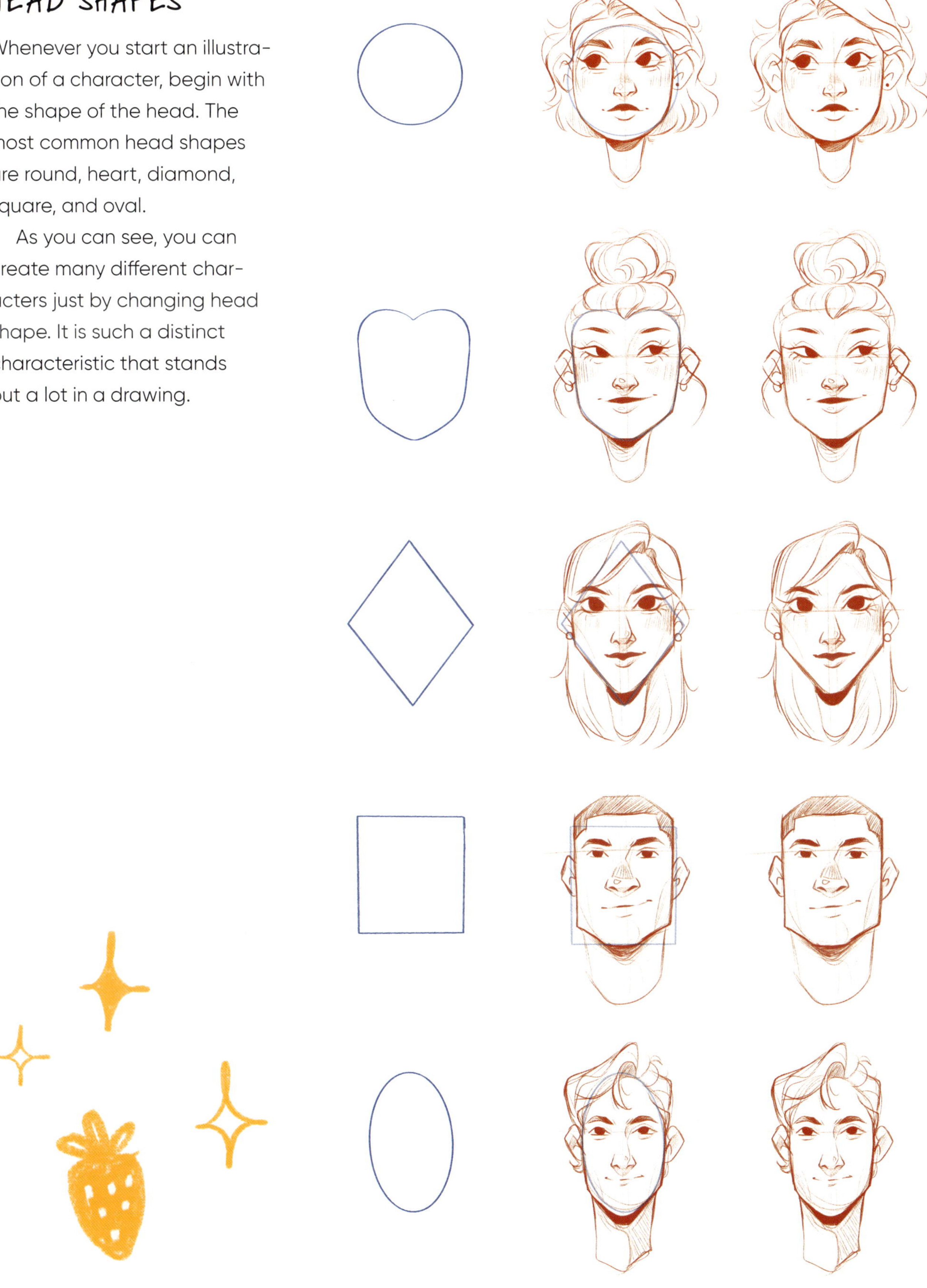

Usually, I like to choose the round shape for kids. And for men, I often use the square shape. Obviously that doesn't mean that all kids have round-shaped heads and all men have square-shaped heads. They are just more commonly seen on those characters.

While I've listed the most common head shapes, there are variations. Not everyone in the world is going to fit one of those five. For example, a person or character can have a face shape that's a combination of the oval and square.

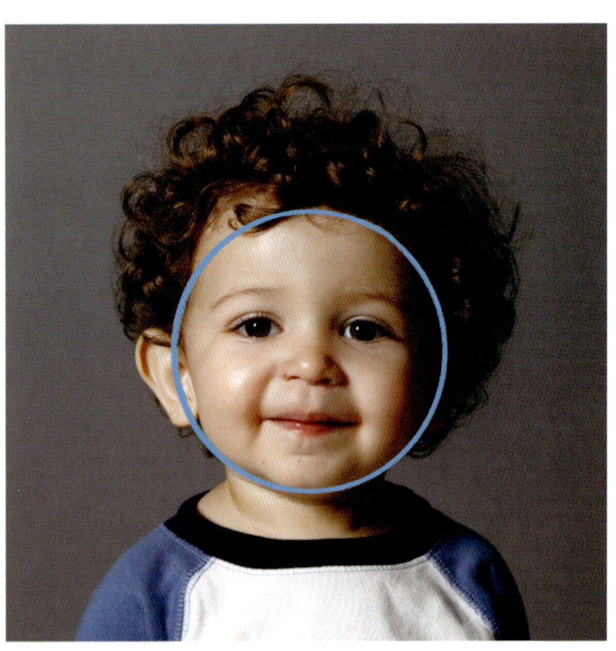

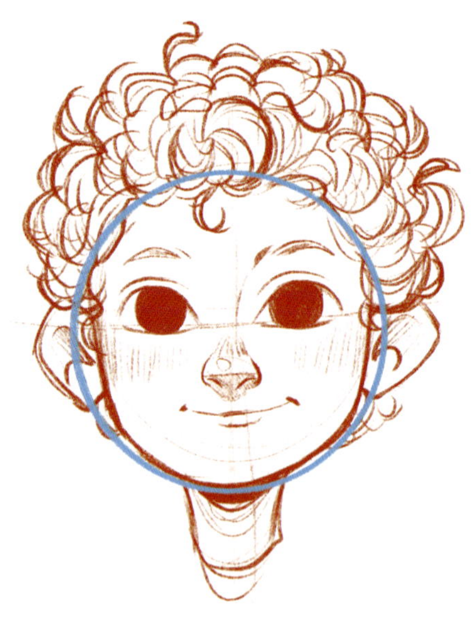

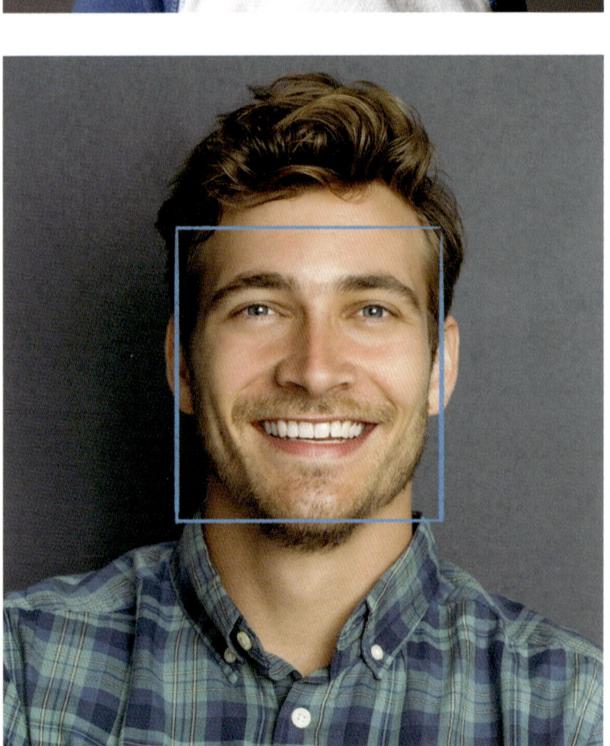

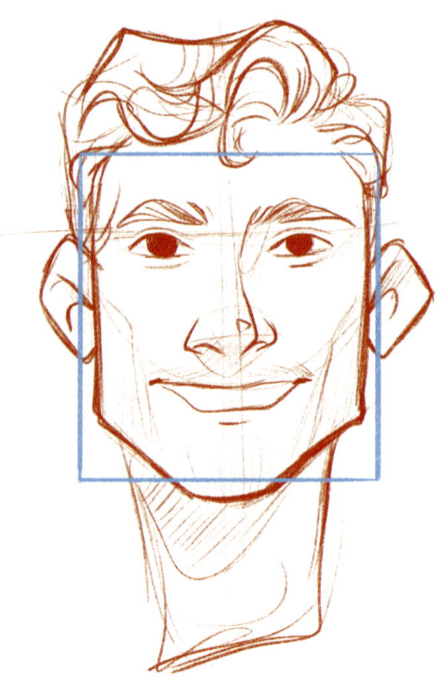

EXAGGERATING SHAPES

You can exaggerate some lines and shapes to reinforce the feature that you want to stand out. By doing this, you are also building the personality you want your character to have. This will prevent all your characters from looking too much alike.

In these next images, I did a few characters that have somewhat exaggerated features to illustrate what changes you can make to build a character with personality and unique traits.

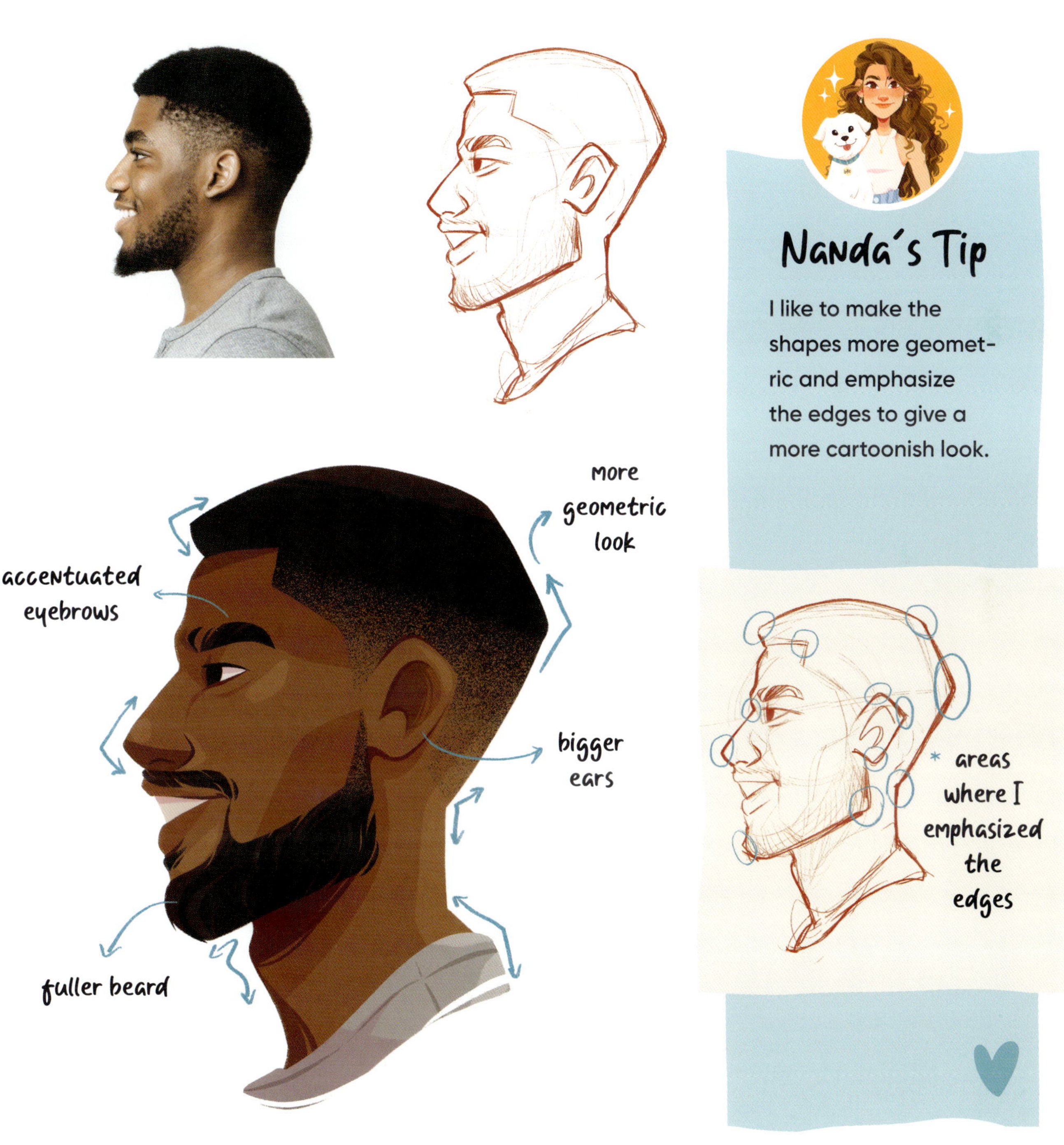

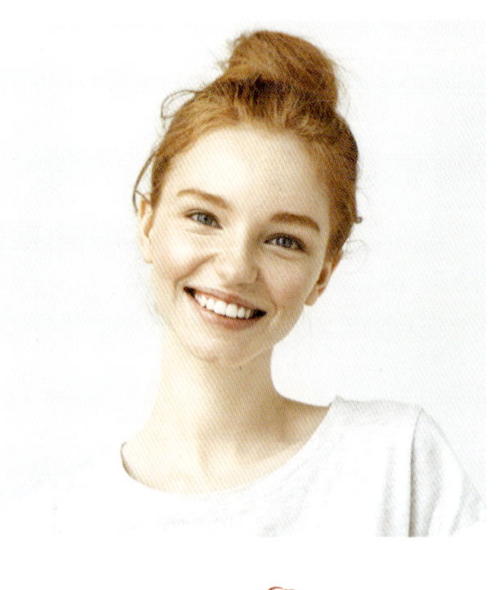

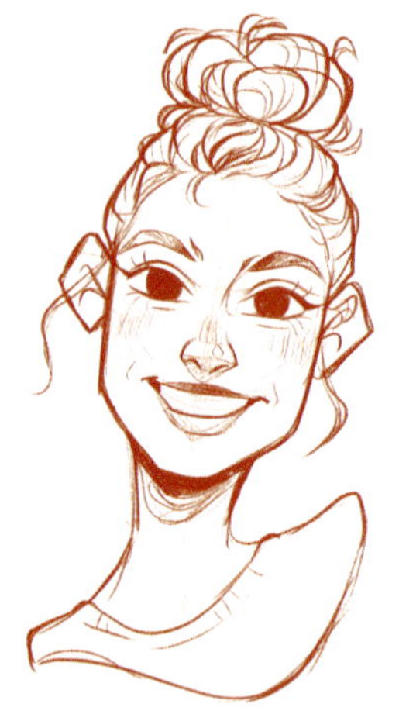

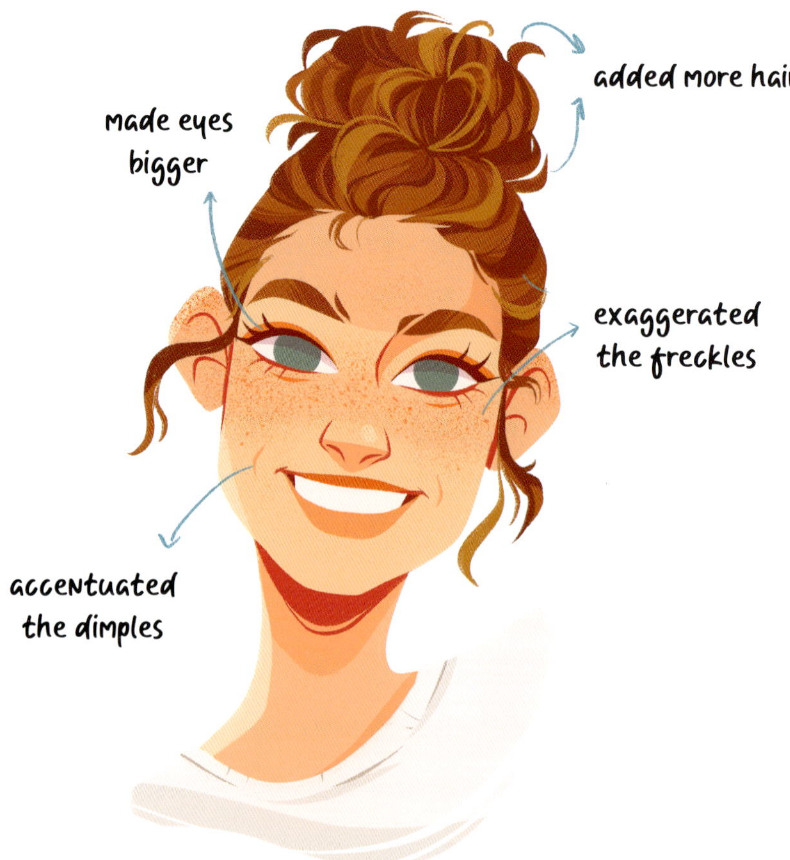
added more hair
made eyes bigger
exaggerated the freckles
accentuated the dimples

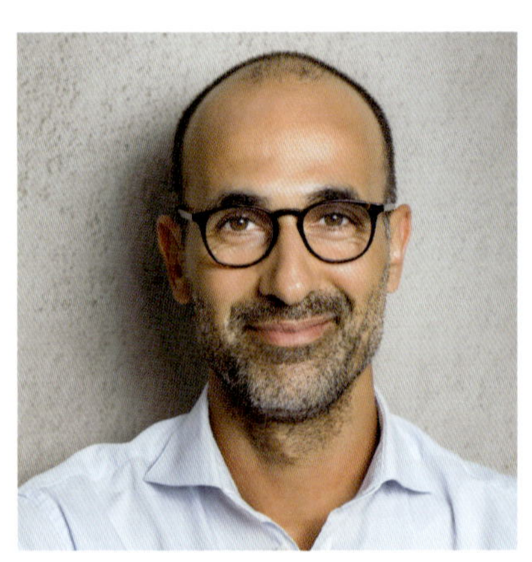

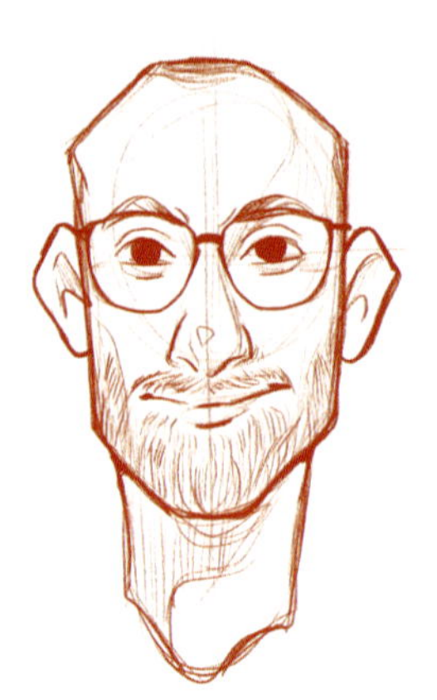

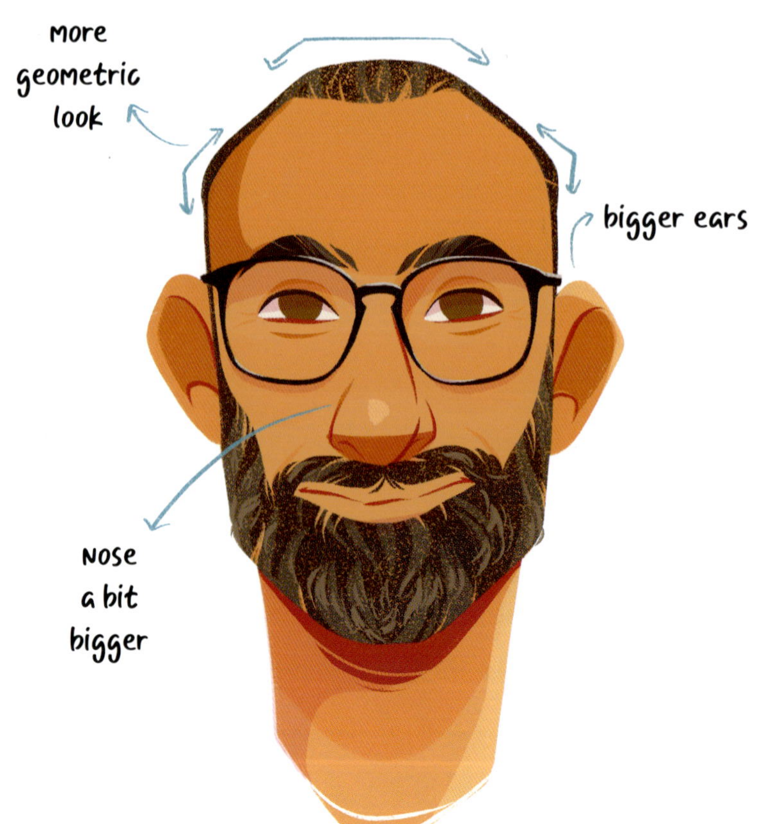
more geometric look
bigger ears
nose a bit bigger

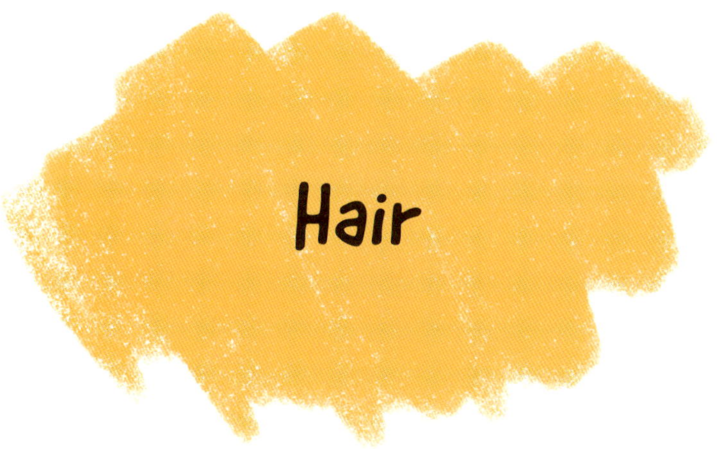

Hair

There are a few different types of hair that you can choose when drawing your character, including straight, wavy, curly, or coily hair.

You can play with these types of hair and make different combinations. For instance, you may divide your character's hair into two parts, the first one being wavy and the other being curly. Don't be afraid of trying different combinations and testing variations! The drawing is yours—you can do anything you want with it.

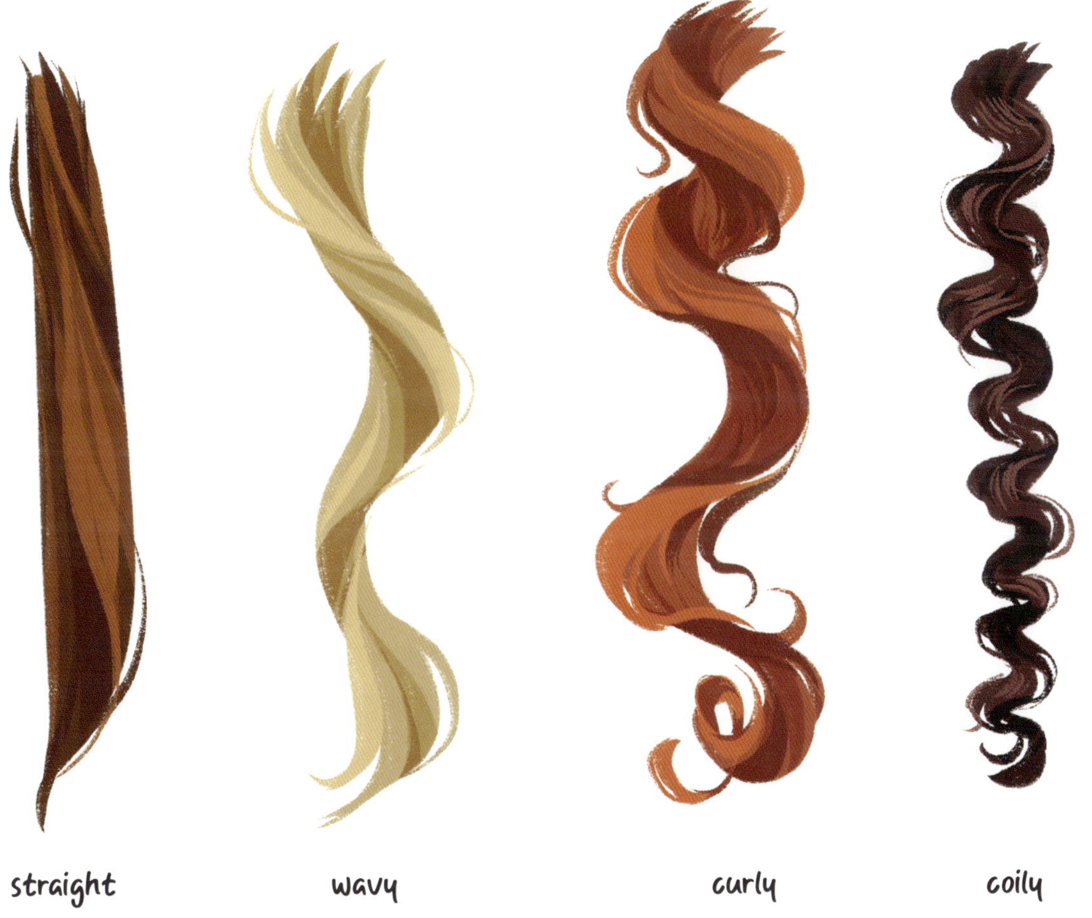

Try different combinations for the color of the hair too! The colors also play a big part in adding individuality and uniqueness to your character's personality. So be bold, and don't be afraid of giving your character a different hair color too.

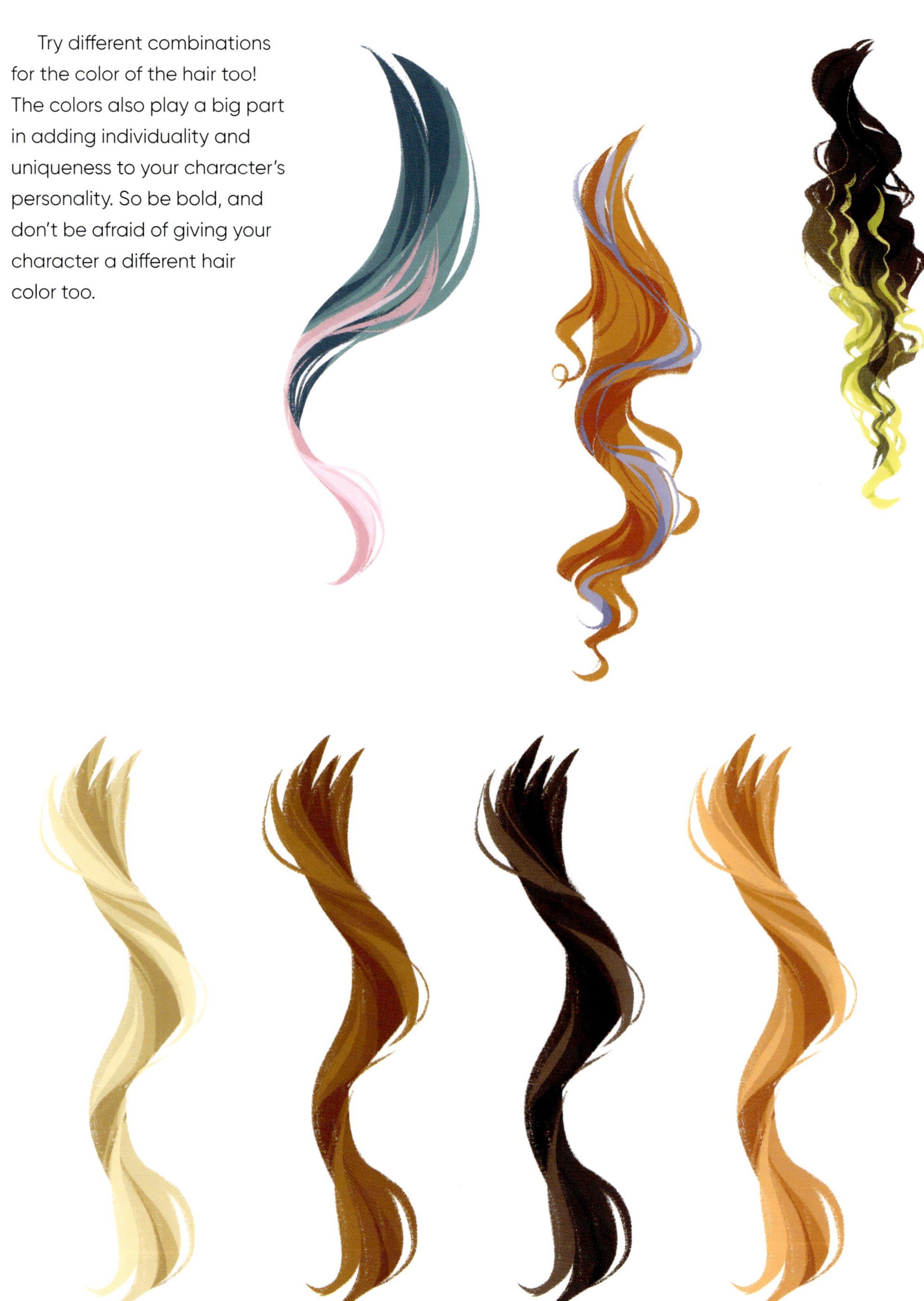

HOW TO MAKE HAIR FLOWY AND DYNAMIC

Now that you have an idea of the types of hair you can choose when drawing your character, I'm going to teach you how to add a sense of dimension and movement to their hair.

Before we go any further, I'm going to help you visualize how to identify the dynamic shapes that build the hair and turn it into a drawing.

As you can see, I took the format that the hair naturally has and exaggerated it, emphasizing a few parts.

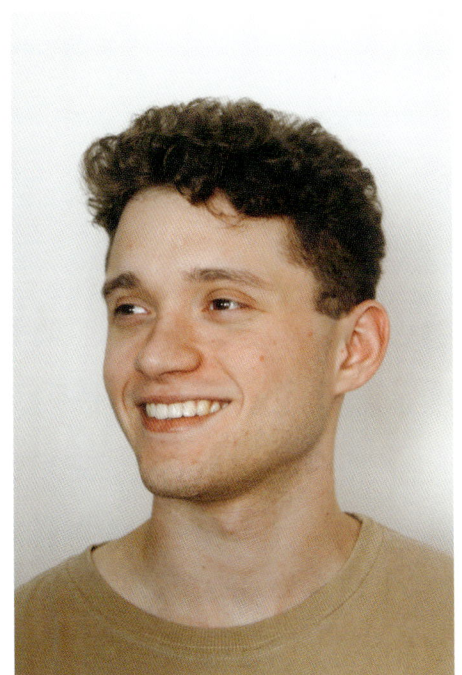
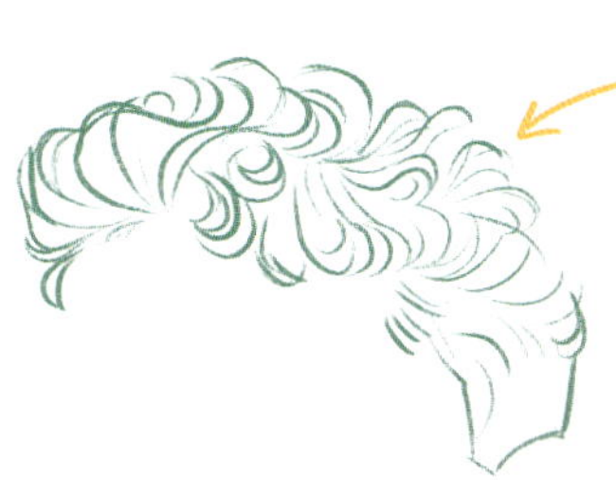
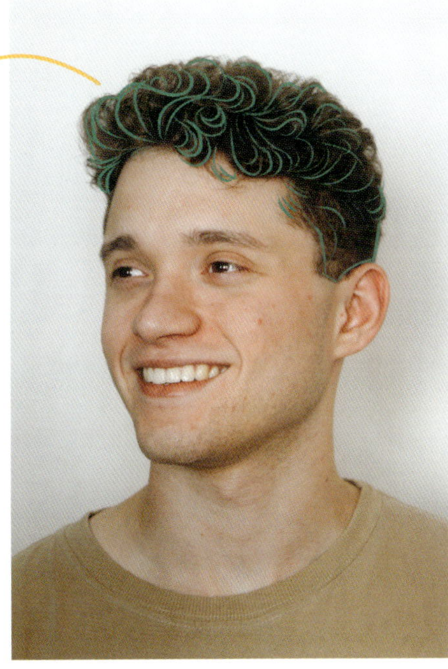
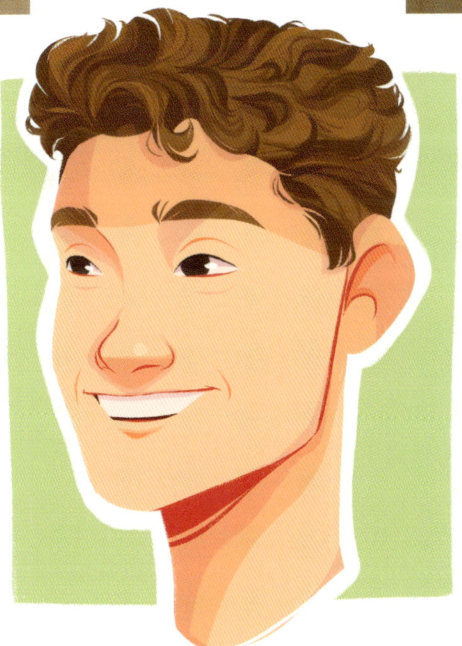

The first thing to keep in mind is to draw the lines and hair strands following the shape and movement of your hair. Try to draw the lines in harmony with the way the hair goes so you can build hair that looks like it is moving.

Take a look at this example.

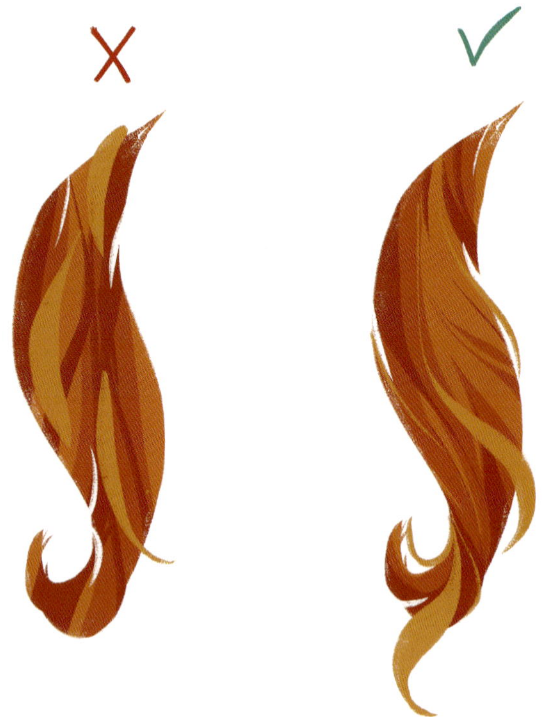

In the first drawing, I didn't follow the hair strands when drawing the hair's movement. In the second drawing, though, I did them in harmony with the flow of the hair. The second drawing has much more life and gives a sense of "flowyness" and movement to your character.

In addition to drawing the hair strands following the shape and movement of your hair, to give it a flowy and dynamic look, you also must be careful about where you are adding the details and lines. If you add it all over the hair, it is going to create a buzzy drawing, and you are going to be kind of confused about where to look or what to focus on. It's essential to learn where to add the details.

Something that helps me is to visualize the hair as hair chunks, not as one piece. For each chunk, you may work on the details that you want to add and the movement that piece is going to have.

Add them wherever you want more attention to be drawn. Draw more dark lines and strands where it is going to be darker and other lighter lines in the lighter places to give it a beautiful shine.

As you can see, I've added details on just a few parts of the hair. By doing that, I control where I want to draw more attention so I don't over-detail some parts of it.

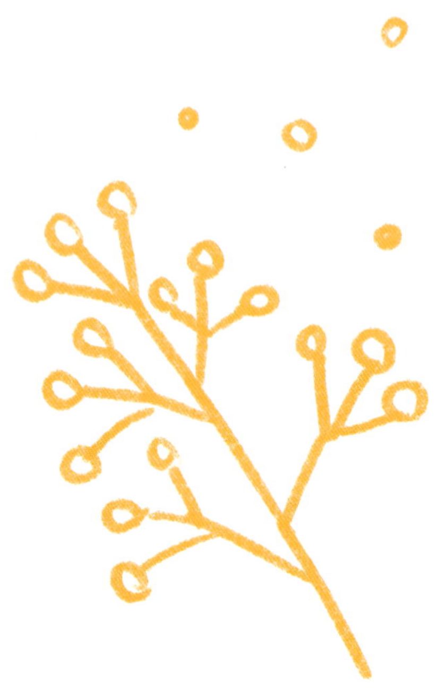

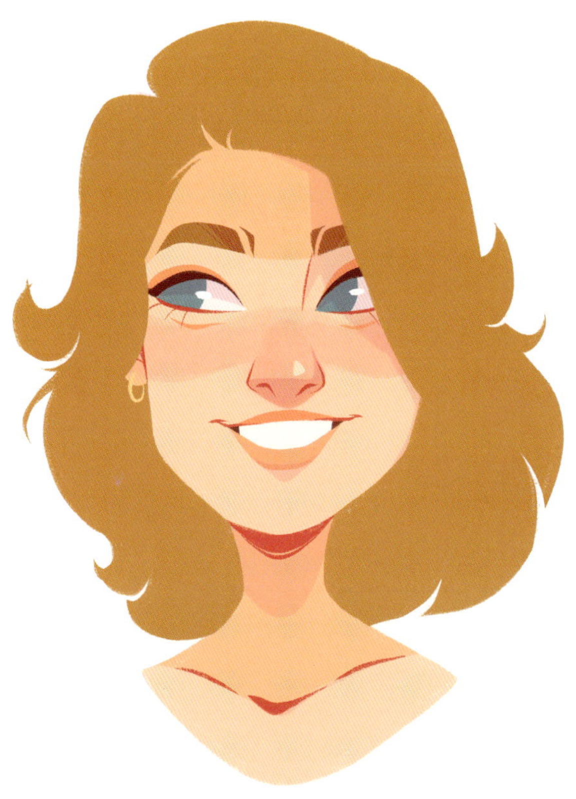
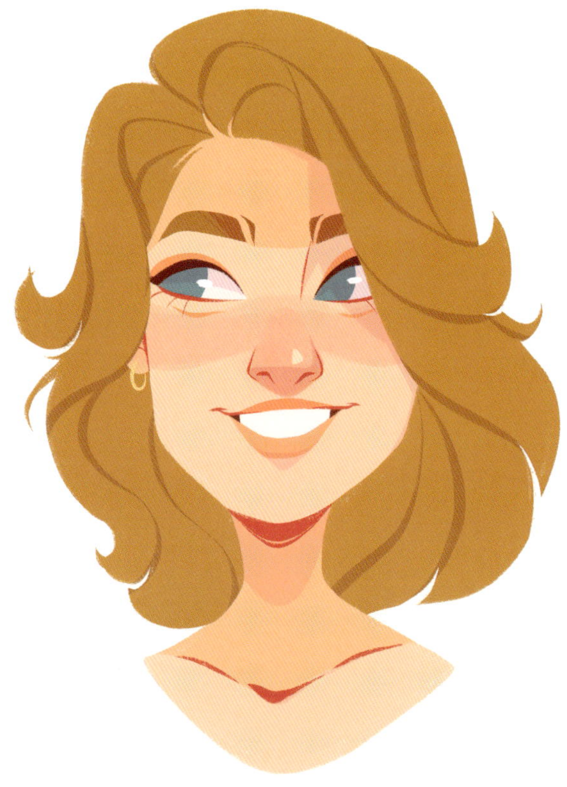
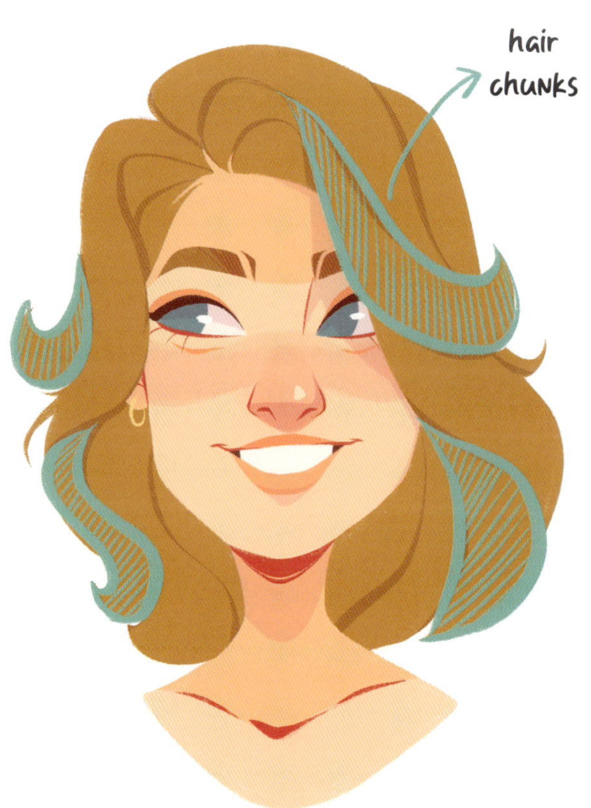

hair
chunks

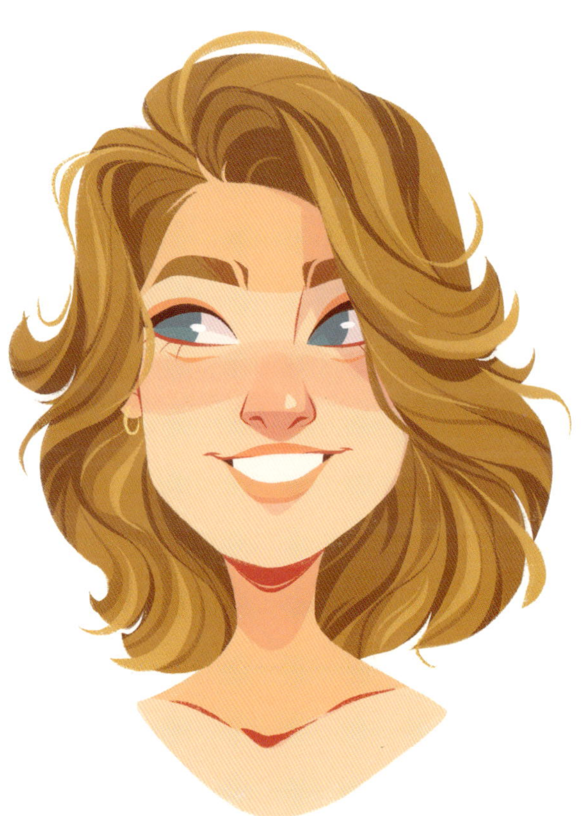

ADDING COLOR TO HAIR

When coloring hair, I follow these steps to make it very flowy and with lots of movement. I use about five colors in the hair.

Remember to always make the brushstrokes follow the movement of the hair.

1. Add the first shadow. The color is not that dark compared to the base color of the hair. I also draw bigger shapes with this color.

2. Add darker brushstrokes to give the hair more movement and depth.

3. Then I choose a lighter color based on the main color of the hair to add some highlights and lighter hair locks. I draw this step on a separate layer to make it easier if I want to make any changes.

4. Finally, I add a few extra hairs in a lighter color than the last one I chose for that extra final glow.

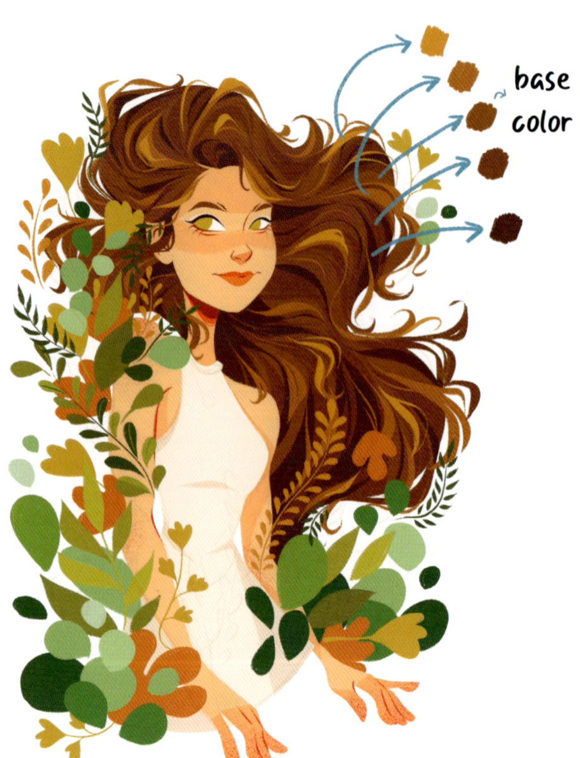

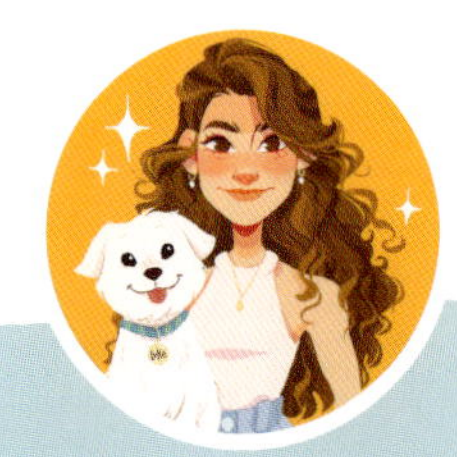

Nanda's Tip

You can vary the pressure that you put on your pen while drawing to build up a sense of dimension and give more life to your character. You can use this tip for drawing other things too!

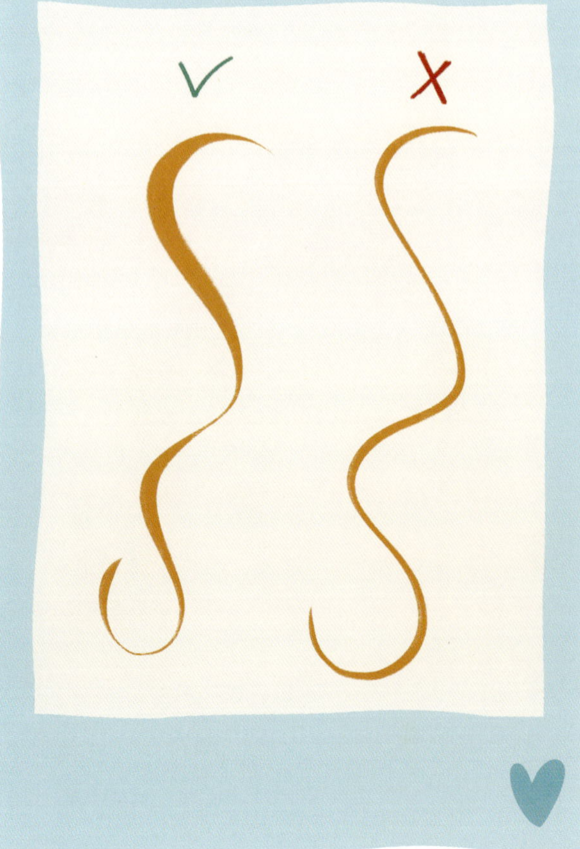

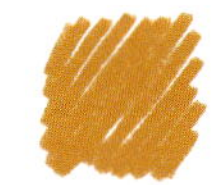 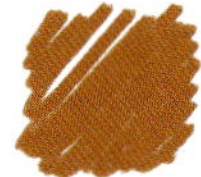 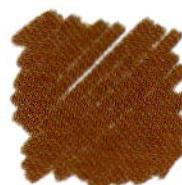 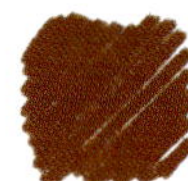 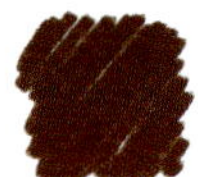

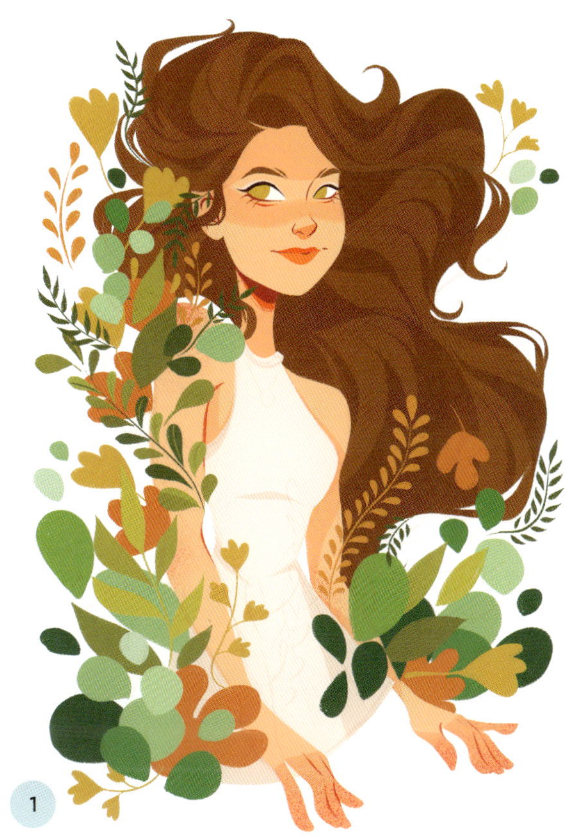

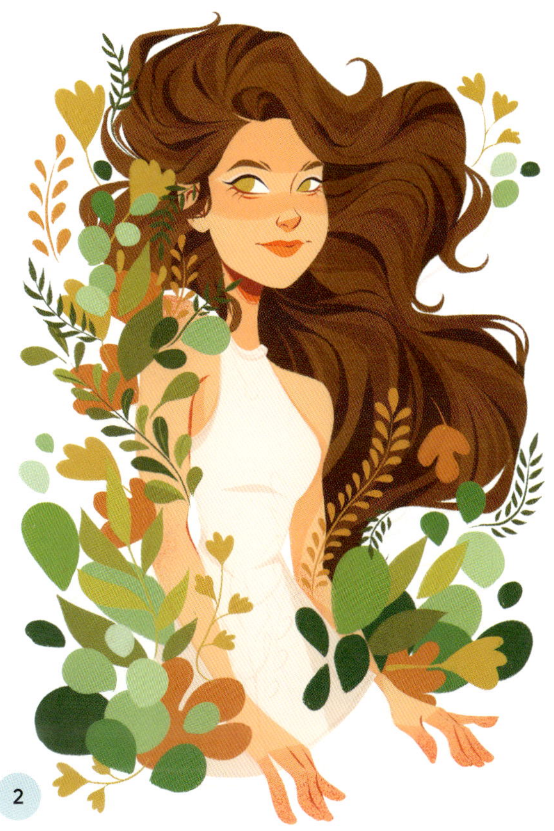

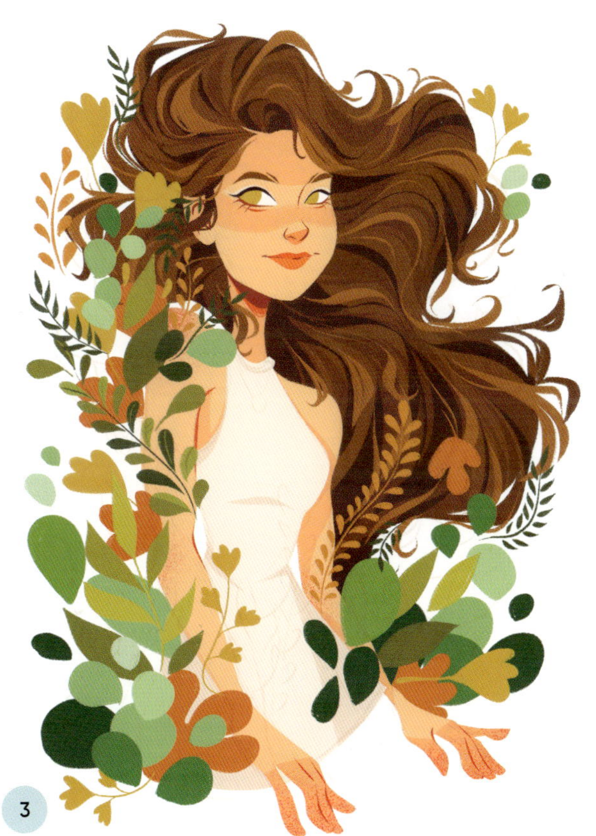

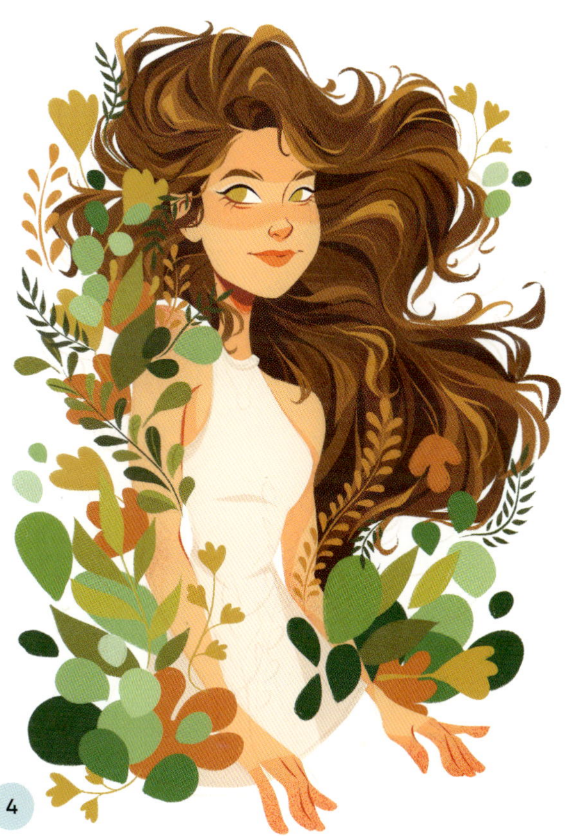

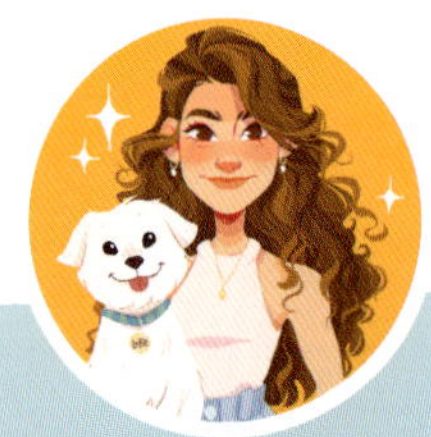

Nanda's Tip

Here is a quick step-by-step on how to draw braids.

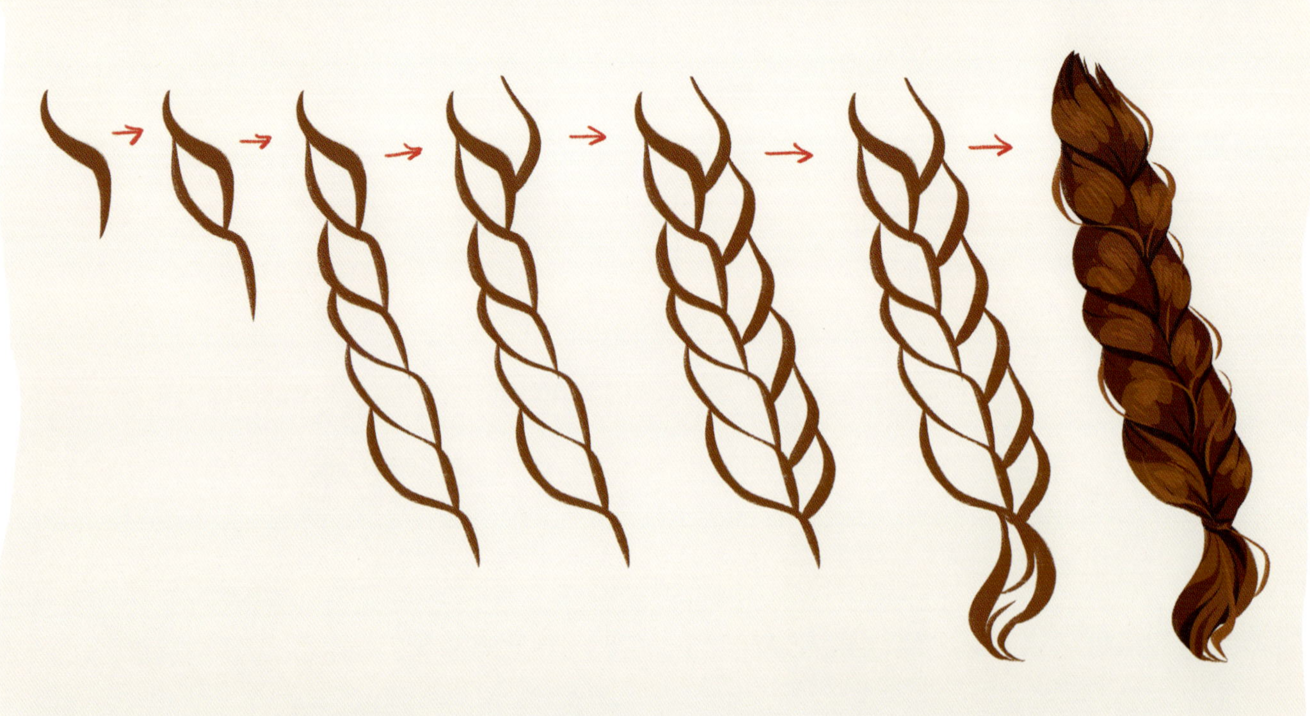

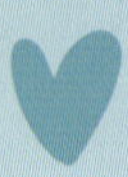

Now that you know about the different types of hair and how to draw it in a flowing and dynamic way, you can start to play with everything you learned to create different variations. Combine different elements, experiment with hair accessories, and add details and personality to your character.

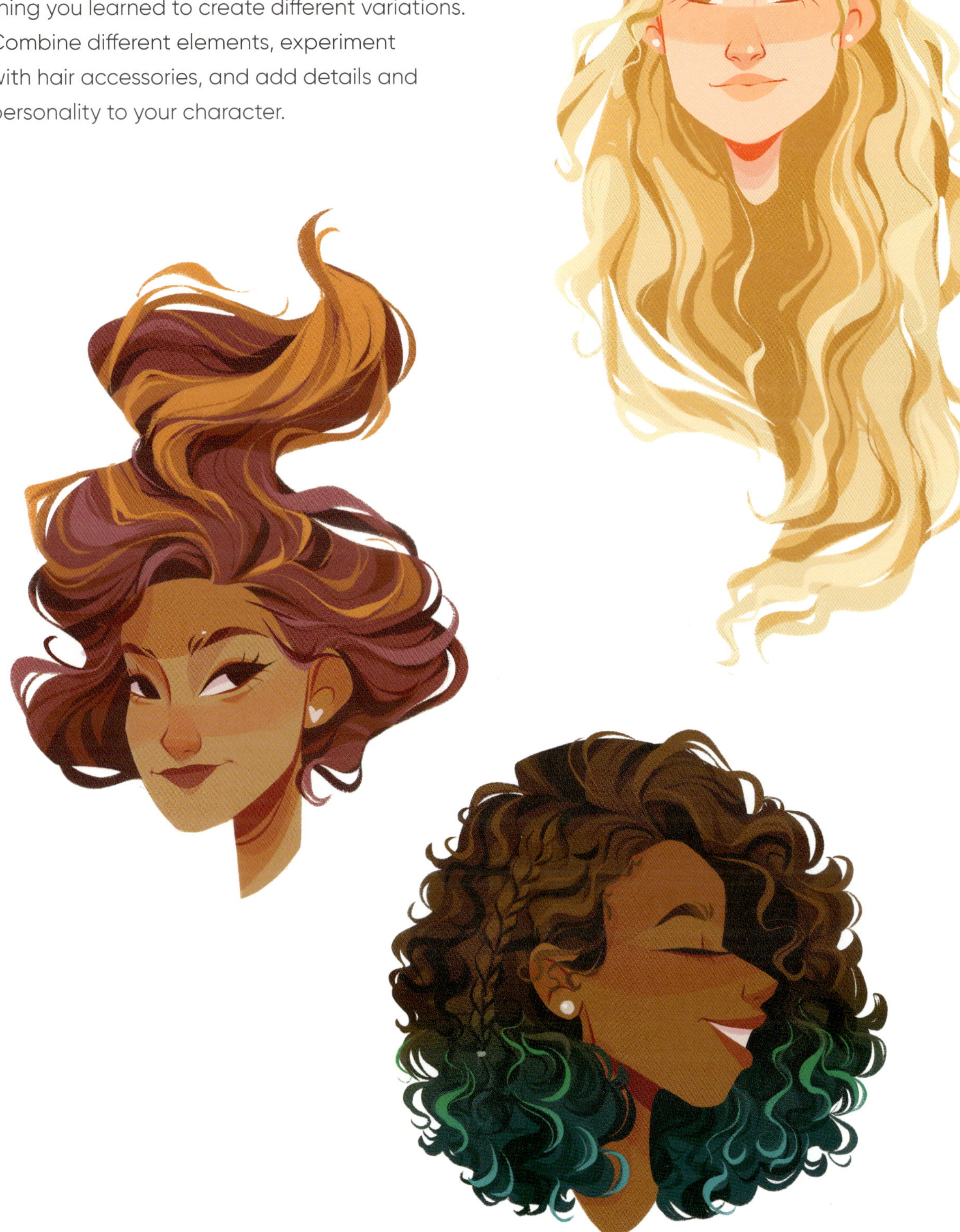

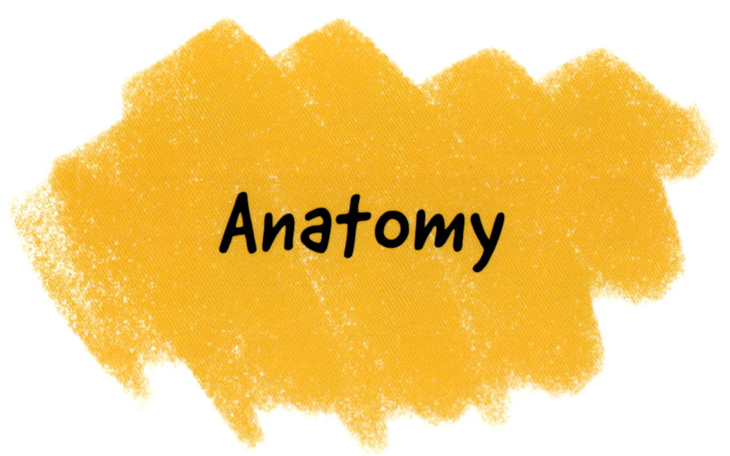

Anatomy

Learning to draw the anatomy of your character is an important skill that every artist should have. But before we go any further, I want to make a quick disclaimer about this topic. Since this book is not aimed at teaching how to draw anatomy but rather aimed at teaching how to draw characters, I will not go into many details and techniques about anatomy. I'm just going to go over the most basic and important things to help you build your character and create different variations of them.

The anatomy that I'm going to teach you is not 100 percent realistic—it is a bit exaggerated and cartoonish. So you must keep in mind the ratio of your characters but exaggerate and play with their proportions.

Another thing that is very important when drawing anatomy is practice! Practice, practice, and practice as much as you can. Take some time to study the anatomy of the human body, even if your drawing style is more cartoonish and less realistic.

Remember that you must learn how to draw characters in a realistic way to have a better idea of what you are drawing and how to stylize the anatomy to make it more cartoonish. The more studying you do, the more you are going to be able to control what shapes and features you can change or exaggerate to make your drawing more stylized.

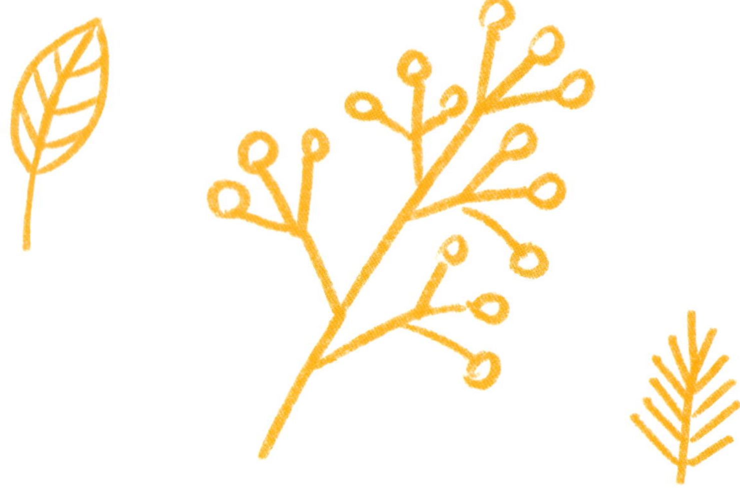

1. BASIC SHAPES

When drawing the anatomy of your character,
start by simplifying the human body into basic
shapes and lines. For this topic, I'm going to
draw a female anatomy, but this works for the
male anatomy too. Always start with the simplest
version, and then go to the most complex and
detailed one. In this stage, you are going to focus
on the proportions and life of your character,
defining if they are going to be in a dynamic or
a static pose. Don't worry about the details here,
but make sure that the ratio is correct.

2. CONSTRUCT THE ANATOMY

Here you are going to combine simple shapes
to make the body of your character. Now that
you have the proportions and pose of your
character to guide you, it's going to be much
easier to construct the human anatomy. I choose
to do a static pose so it's easier to learn the
step-by-step.

3. FINAL TOUCHES

Finally, you are going to fix any mistakes that you
made, define the lines, add details and shading
to your character, and make the final adjustments, putting it all together.

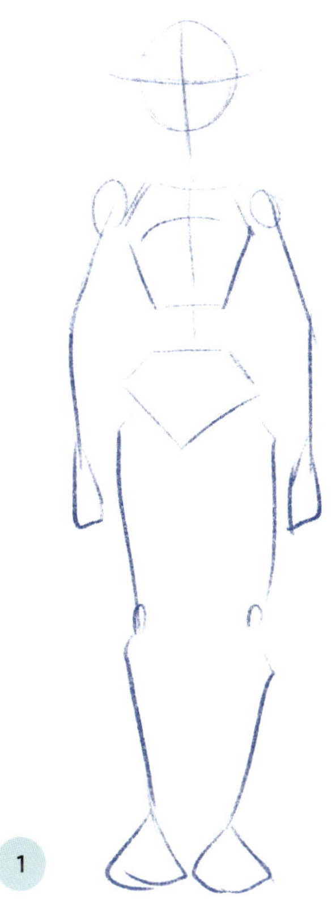

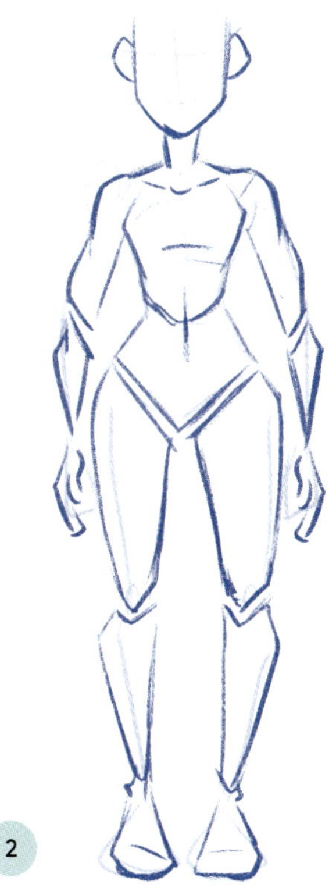

MALE AND FEMALE ANATOMY

Now that you've learned how to construct the body, I want to go a little bit further and show you about the male and female anatomy and their main differences. Obviously, every man and every woman is different, and not everyone is going to look like the examples I show here.

These examples will help you learn the main differences between the basic male and female anatomy, but it doesn't mean that everyone is going to fit into these examples. This is just another tool to improve your drawing abilities.

First, look at the drawings of the male and female anatomy side by side to the right so you can better visualize their dissimilarities. As I said before, not every male and female are going to have these body types—this is just an illustration to show you the main differences.

One of the main distinctions between the male and female anatomy is that women usually have wider hips than men. In addition, men normally have no waist, and the torso is straighter and more square. Women are often drawn with a more accentuated waist, and their torso is more curved. Men are also usually drawn with more visible and defined muscles than women. Another thing to notice is that usually women have heart-shaped faces while men's are more square-shaped.

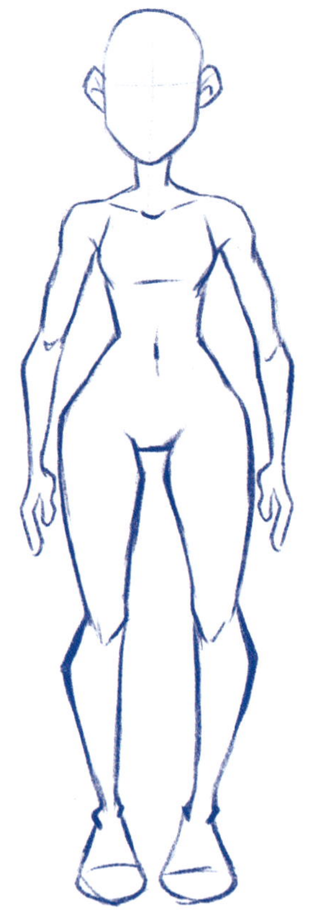

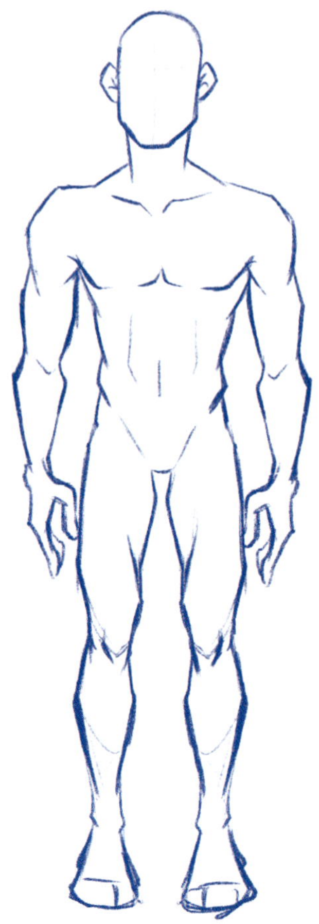

Body Types

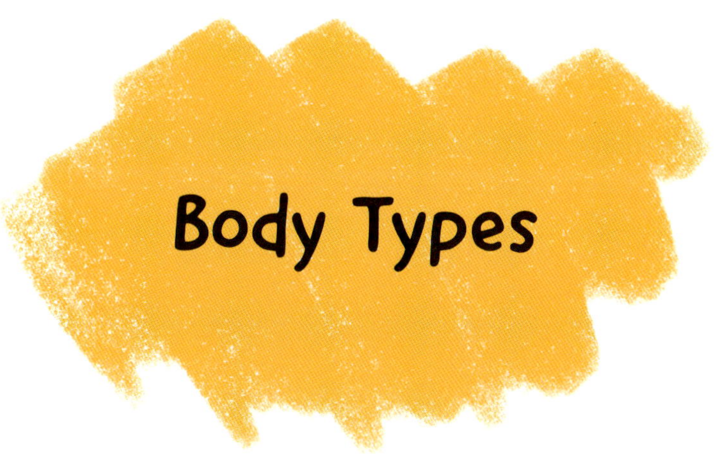

In the previous sections, I've talked about how to create the anatomy of your character and the main differences between the male and female anatomy. Because everyone is differ-ent, there are a lot of body types that you can choose for your character. They can have a more rectangular shape, be curvier, slimmer, fatter, stronger, and so on. Every body type is beautiful, so experimenting and exploring different body types for your character is something that will give more variety to it and also give you the tools to create many characters.

As examples, I will go through five common body shapes for women and men. For women, these include oval, inverted triangle, hourglass, rectangle, and pear. For men, the examples include triangle, rectangle, trapezoid, inverted triangle, and oval.

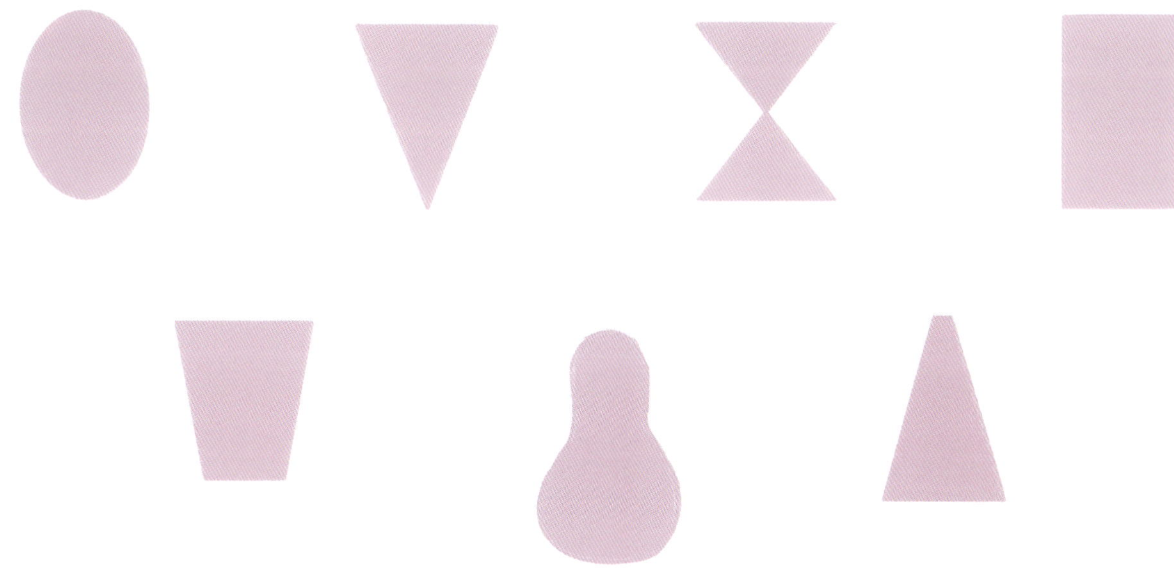

WOMEN'S BODY TYPES

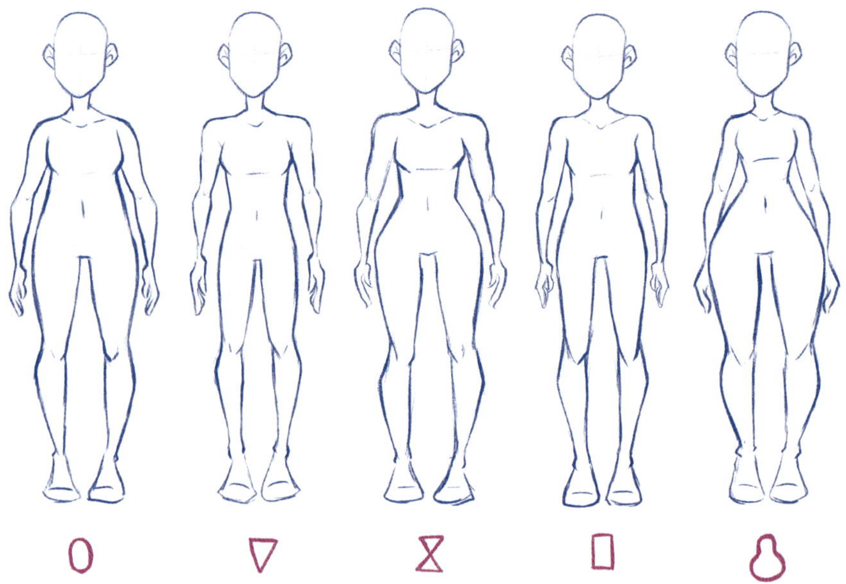

OVAL

In this body type, the bust is larger than the hips and the rest of the body, with a wider midsection and larger waist.

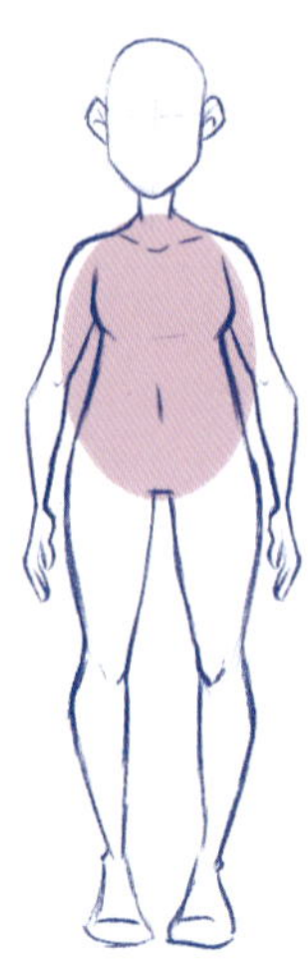

INVERTED TRIANGLE

The inverted triangle means the bust is larger than the hips.

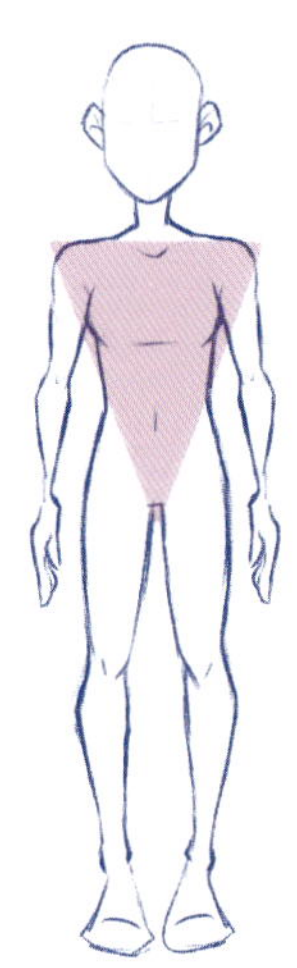

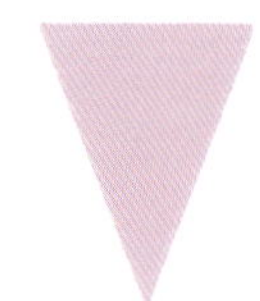

HOURGLASS

Like the rectangle body type,
this body type has equal hip
and bust measurements,
but the waist is smaller.

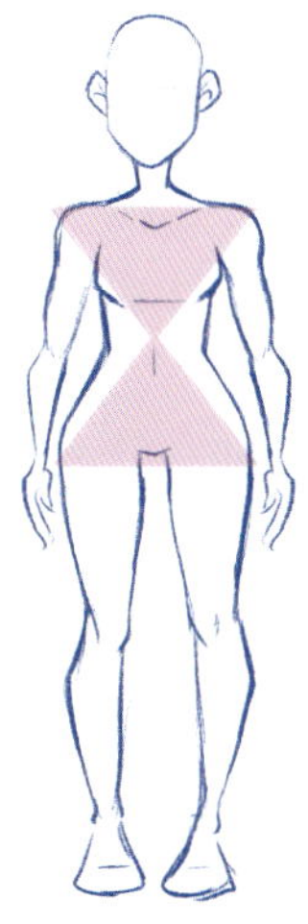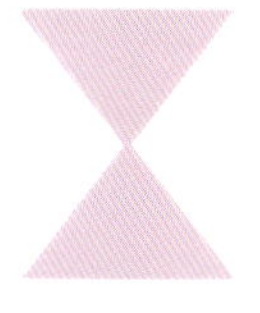

RECTANGLE

In this shape, the shoulders
are the same width as the hips
and bust. There are fewer body
curves and no defined waist.

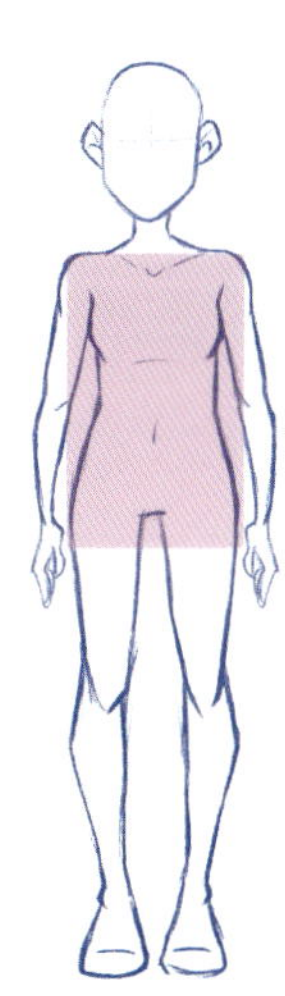

PEAR

In the pear body shape, the
waist measurement is larger
than the bust and is defined.

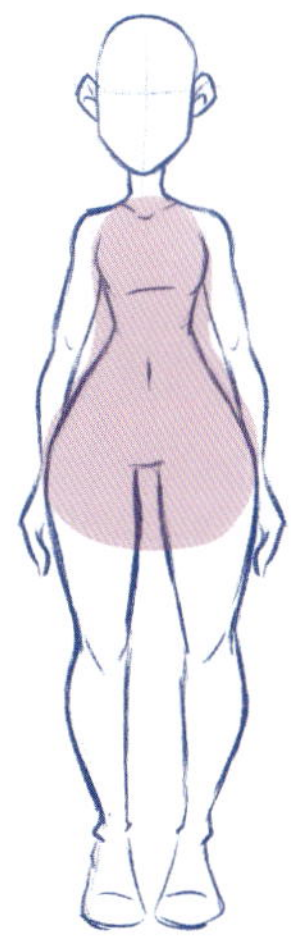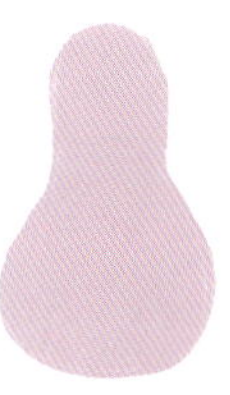

MEN'S BODY TYPES

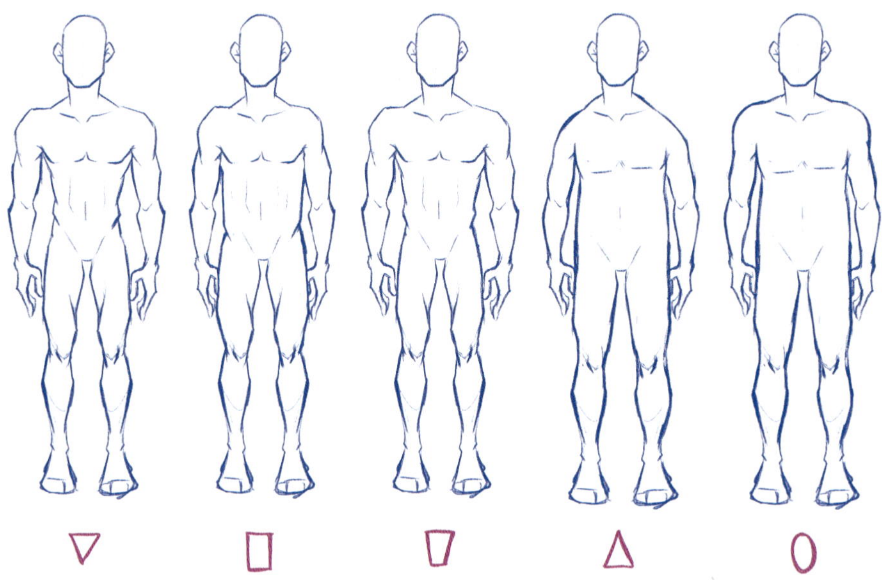

TRIANGLE

The triangle body shape follows almost the same characteristics as the women's pear body shape. The middle section is wider, with a larger waist and hips compared to the chest.

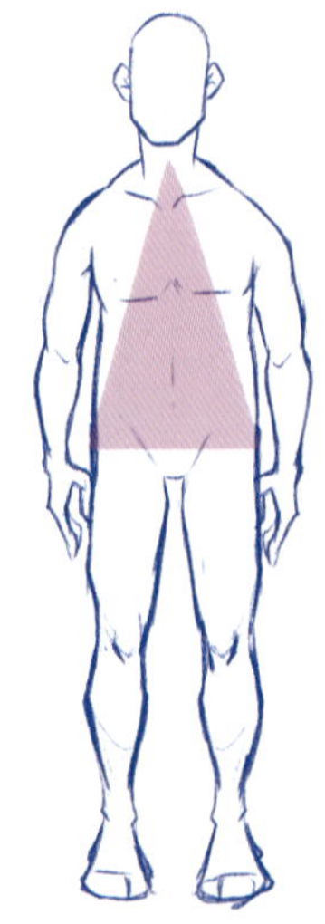

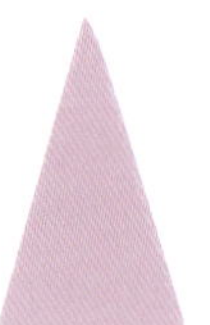

RECTANGLE

For the rectangle, the shoulders are as wide as the waist, like the women's rectangle body shape.

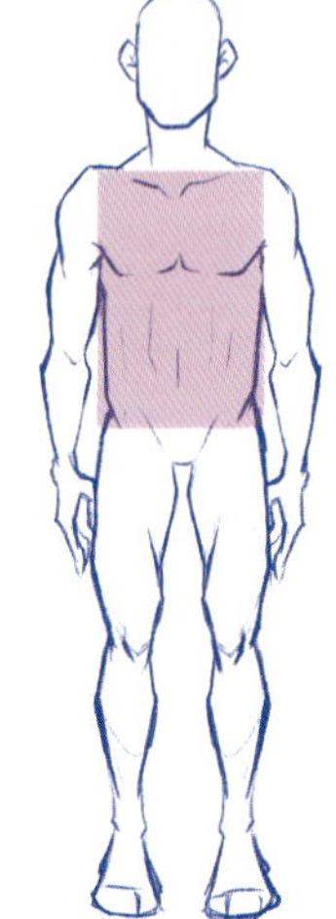

TRAPEZOID

The trapezoid is like the
inverted triangle body shape.
The waist is a little bit bigger
than the inverted triangle,
but it is still narrower than
the shoulders.

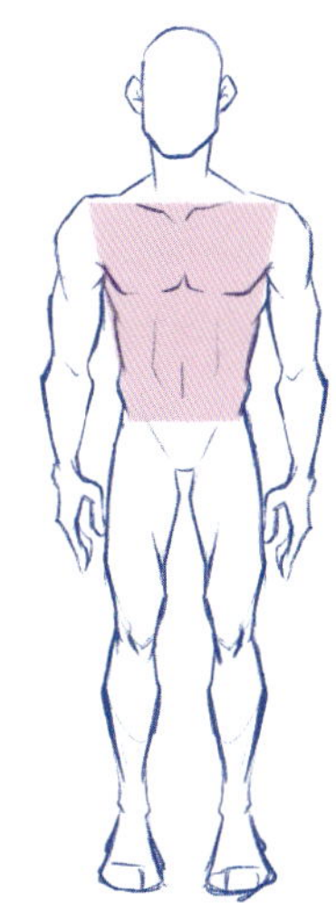

INVERTED TRIANGLE

Opposite of the triangle body
shape, the inverted triangle
means wider shoulders and
chest compared to the hips
and waist.

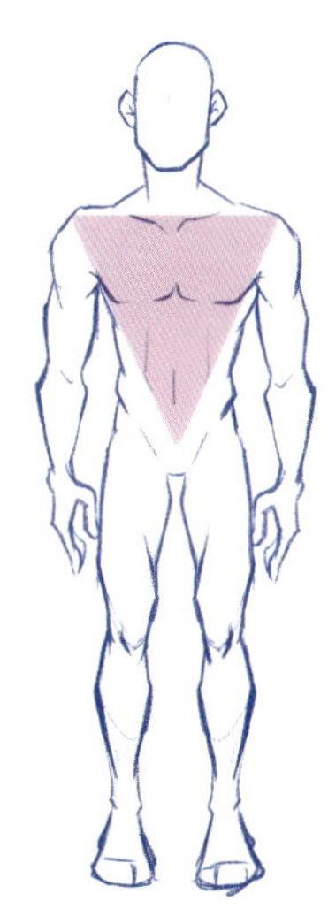

OVAL

Make the center of the torso
bigger compared to the hips
and shoulders for the oval
body shape.

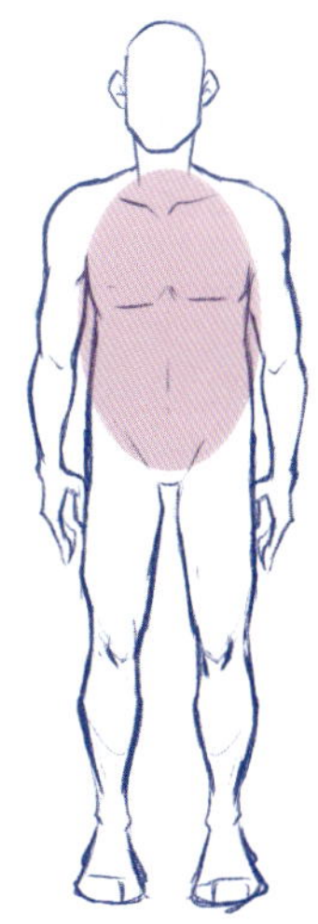

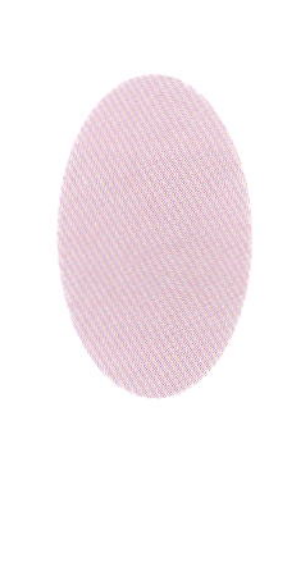

Remember that these are just examples of the different body types. By taking what you've learned here, you can further explore each body type and experiment with them, creating characters that are shorter or taller and thinner or bigger, with longer legs or bigger torsos.

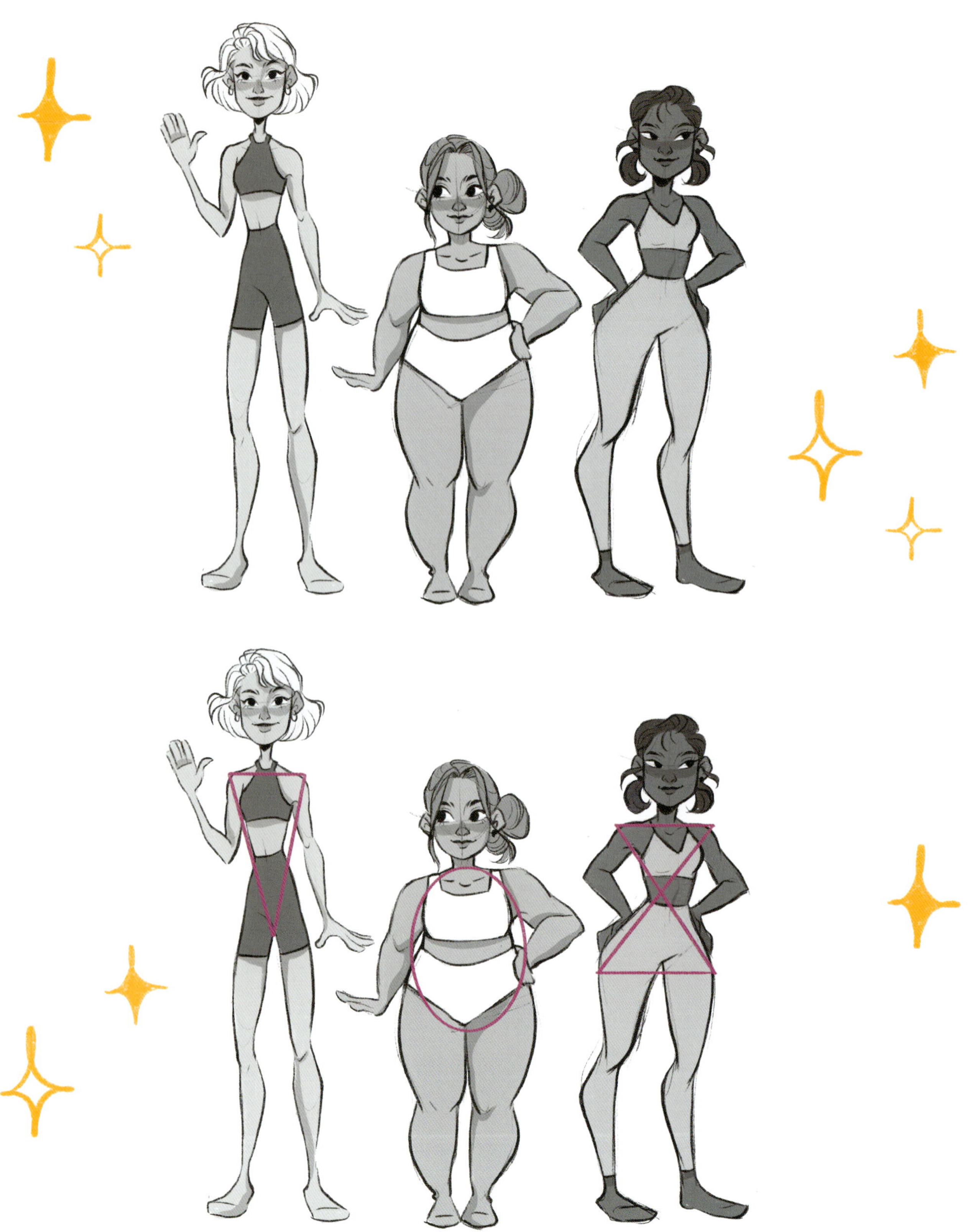

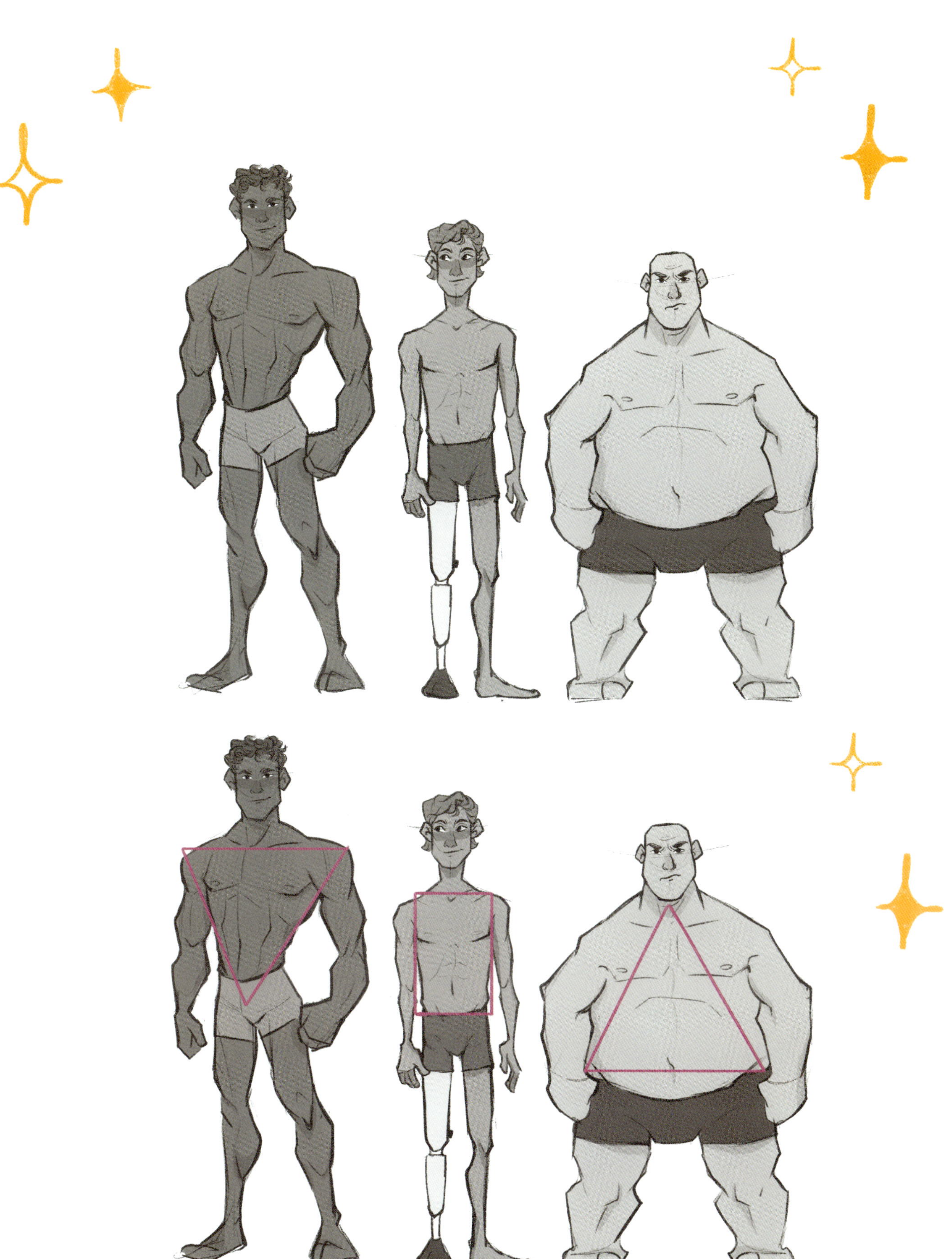

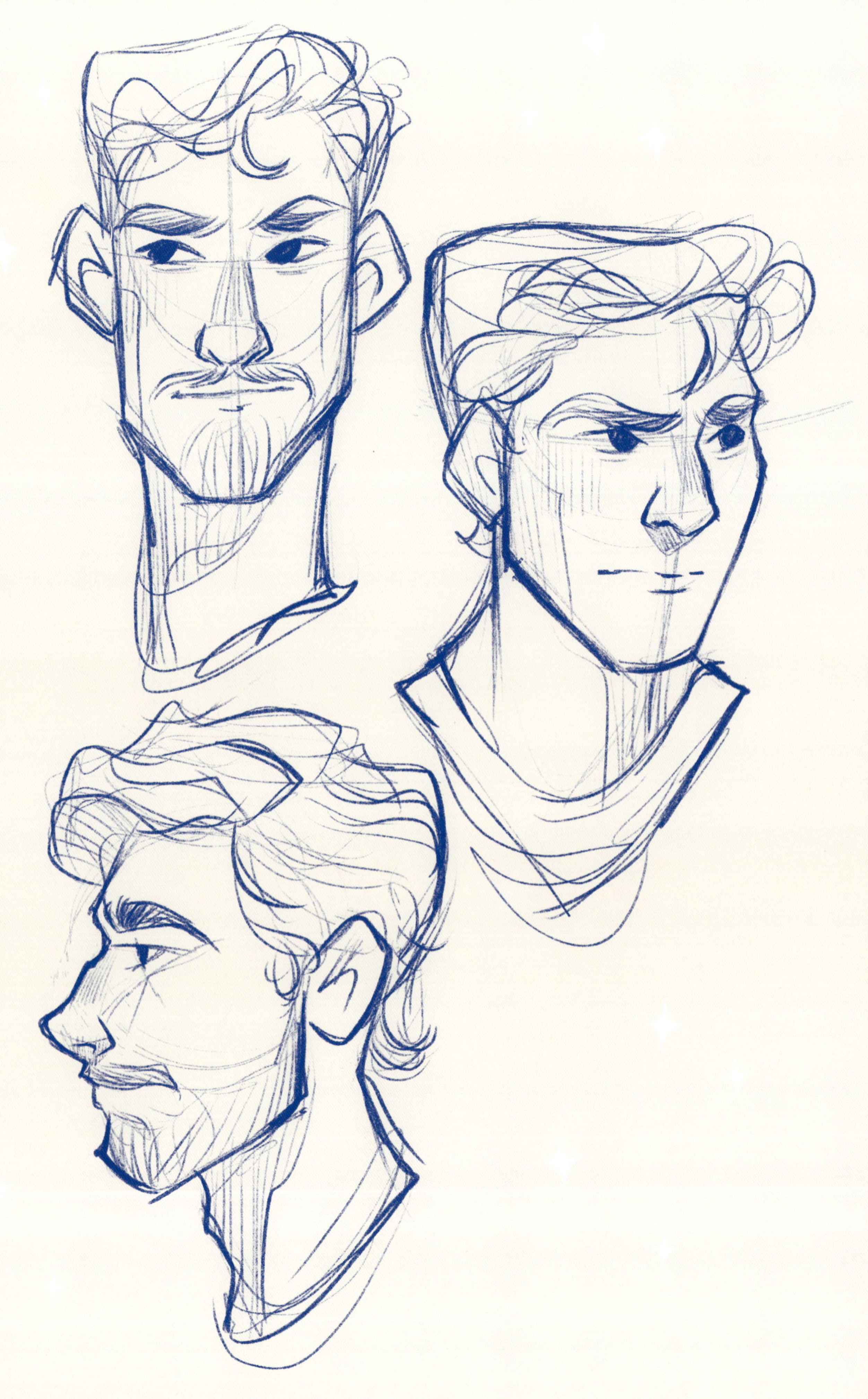

Sketching

For me, sketching is one of the most important techniques that every artist should use. You can sketch to brainstorm ideas, to practice, to develop a new character, or maybe just to have fun.

This chapter covers subjects ranging from the importance of sketching to ideas of what to draw. Learn how to sketch with colored pencils and draw monochromatic characters. In addition, I will teach you how to turn a realistic image into a creative drawing.

This is probably my favorite chapter because sketching is something that I love to do, and I hope you like it too!

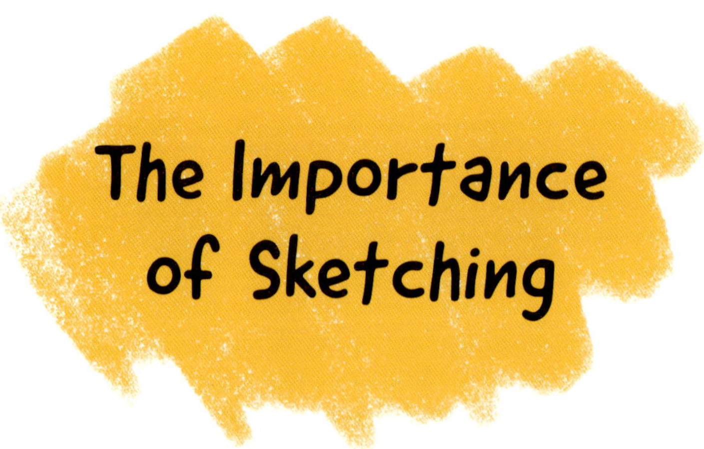

The process of turning a photo into a drawing is an experiment that can lead to countless different results. How you interpret a picture will affect how you transfer what you see to the paper, and the way you interpret what you see is something really personal.

I don't know if you have seen those challenges of two artists drawing the same image, but they end up drawing two completely different drawings while looking at the same reference picture. That's what I'm talking about—this is real art!

Each person has a unique interpretation of what they see. And that's what makes your art special. You can turn reality into a beautiful piece of art in which each pencil stroke carries a little bit of you.

The main thing about the semi-realistic/cartoonish style is that you are inspired by your reference, without copying it.

In this chapter, I will teach you how to look at reality, interpret it, and transform what you are seeing into a stylized drawing, keeping in mind that the style that I'm teaching is not realistic but an interpretation of reality, made with a lot of imagination and creativity.

To begin, I'm going to do a simple drawing of a leaf so you can have an idea of what stylization is all about.

Comparing the photo and the drawing, you can see that I didn't exactly copy the picture. That would be like placing transparent paper over the image and following the exact lines. So, the first thing that you must have in mind for stylized drawing is that you are not drawing it to be exactly like it is in real life. Let go of the idea that everything must be a perfect match to your reference. Learn how to see the shapes and exaggerate them. Overemphasize the beautiful features and special characteristics of what you're drawing. Try to move with the image, seeing it not just like a leaf but understanding the movement and the life that is behind the moment that the picture was taken. I added lines, shapes, and movement to the drawing, and it isn't exactly 100 percent realistic, but it's good.

And this advice applies not only to this leaf but also to all the drawings that you do. Styling a drawing is much more about the way you interpret what you see than a step-by-step way by which you must follow to copy something.

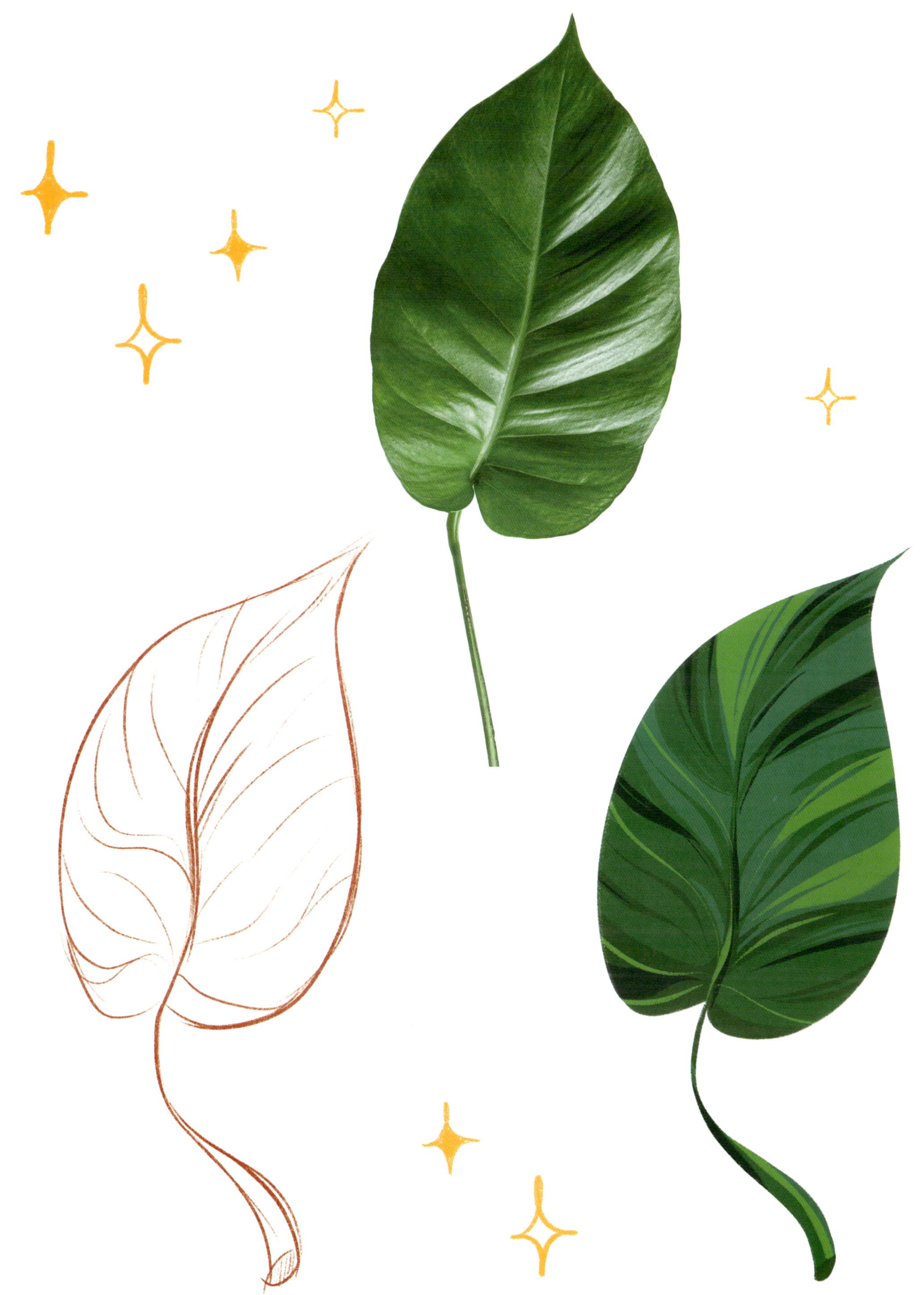

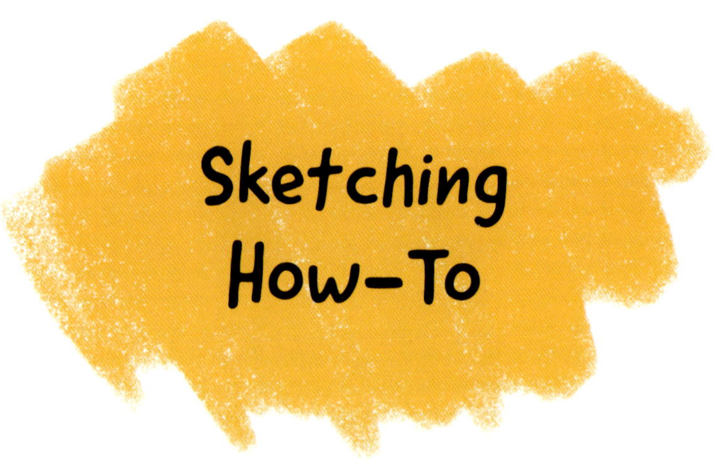

INTERPRETING AN IMAGE

Now that you understand that styling a drawing is more about how you interpret what you see rather than following a "yes and no" tutorial of how to do it, I'm going to teach you how to have that artistic vision and how to turn reality into art.

For this lesson, I'm going to use a picture of a face and go through all the thoughts I have during the creative process and how to identify what you can exaggerate and stylize to make it cartoonish and less realistic but also aesthetically beautiful.

IDENTIFYING SHAPES AND LINES

Identifying shapes is an important step to start stylizing your drawing, so next, I'm going to use this image as a reference to teach you to identify them.

As you can see in this drawing, I've tried to convert the three-dimensional image to two-dimensional line art. And when I isolate the pencil layer, we have a "realistic" type of drawing. I did this to help you visualize the shapes and lines that exist in your reference, but remember, this type of drawing is not what we are looking for.

With time, this step will become automatic for you. You are not going to need to do it because, with practice, your eye is going to be trained to identify those shapes and automatically stylize them.

Now that we have identified the shapes and lines, we are going to start the fun part: the stylization.

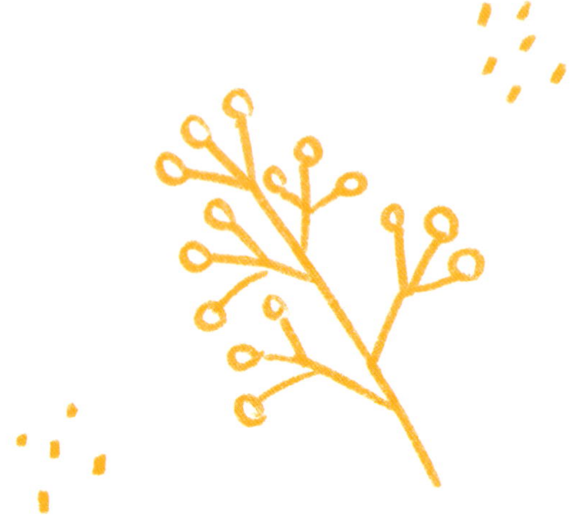

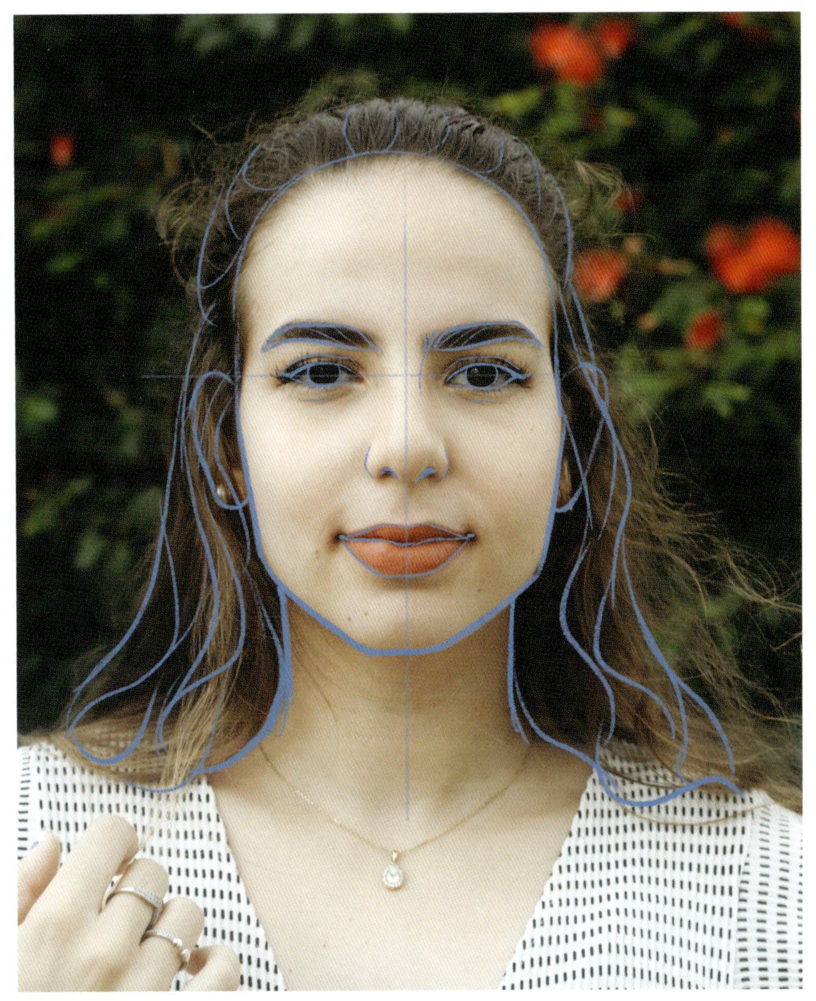

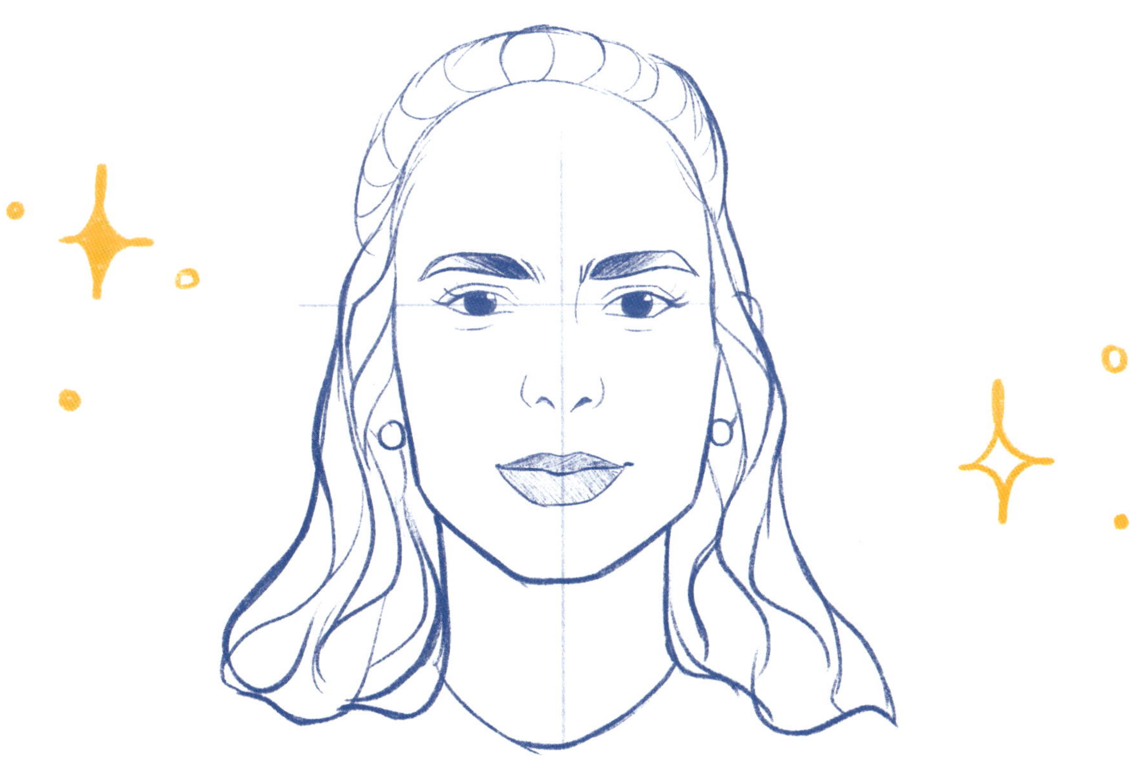

START TO STYLIZE IT

Like I said before, stylization is all about interpreting reality, exaggerating shapes, and being
inspired by what you see, not copying it.

After interpreting the image and stylizing it,
you are going to have something like this.

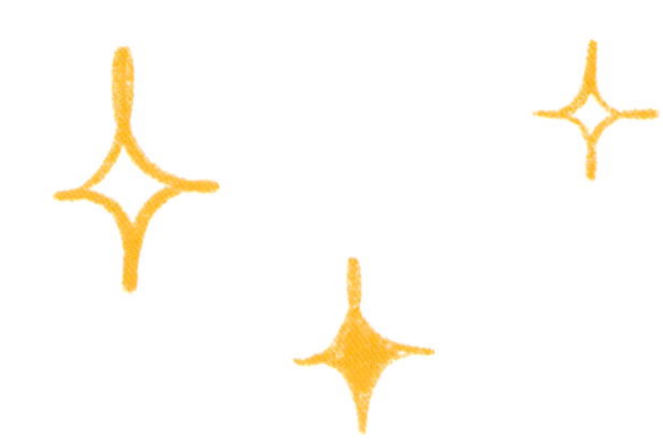

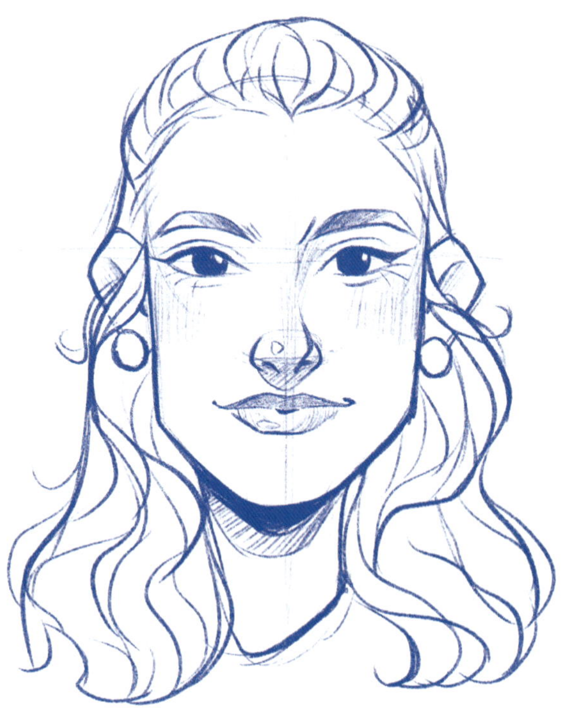

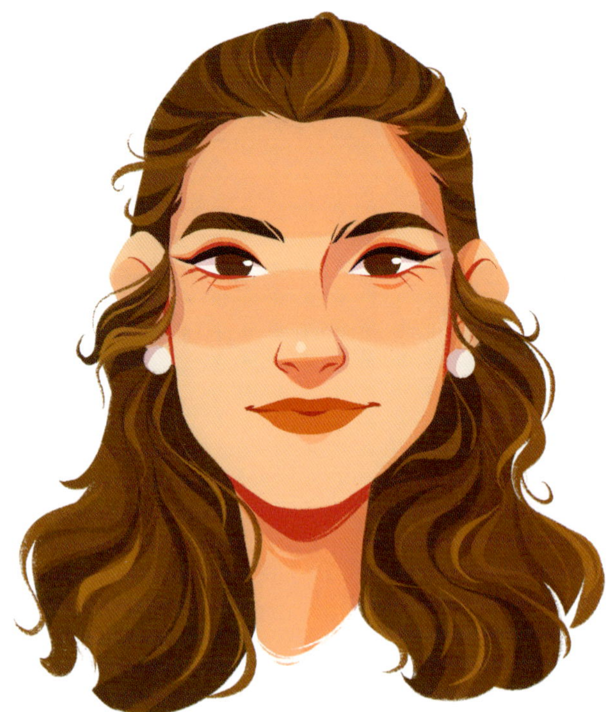

This step is all about identifying that original
shape and transforming it into an artistic vision.
Be inspired by that original realistic image, but
try to interpret it in a different way. Choose what
inspires you and what makes sense to you, and
then make the decisions that reflect your personality—that's how you can transmit yourself
through your drawings. Sometimes I don't even
look at the picture for a few moments to let my
creativity flow and so I don't get attached to
the image but to my imagination.

As you can see in this drawing here, I exaggerated the size of the eyes, mouth, and eyebrows, made the nose a bit smaller, and added
more movement and volume to the hair. These
choices are really personal to each artist and
to what style you are trying to achieve.

For example, I could have made the nose
bigger instead of smaller, or I could have
exaggerated even more the size of the head
and the eyes.

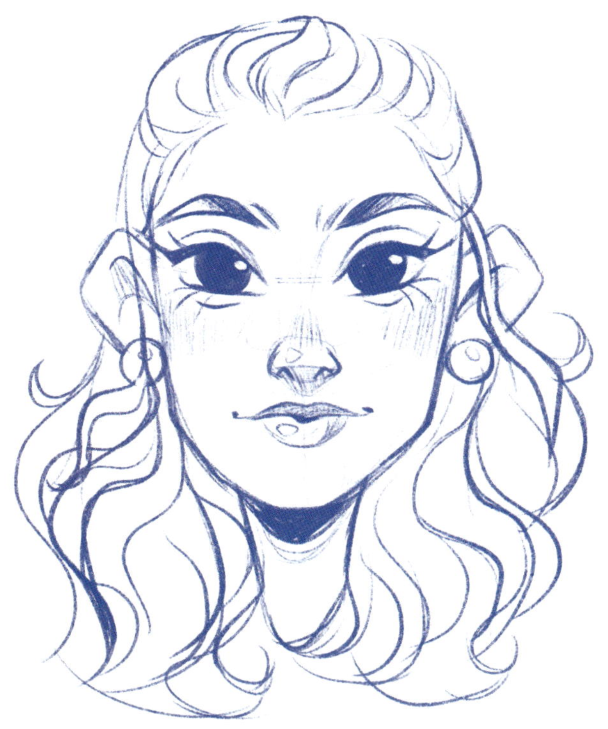

Here's an example of another drawing based on the same picture in which I changed my choices during the process, including making the eyes bigger.

As you can see, although it's based on the same picture as the other two drawings, it's unlike the others because of the different interpretations of the shapes I made in the process of making each piece.

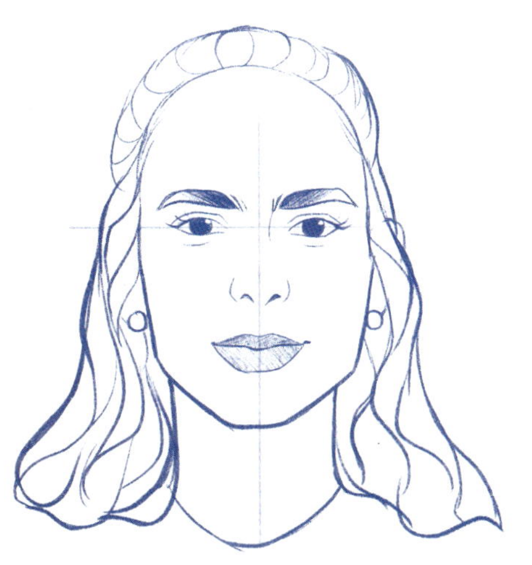

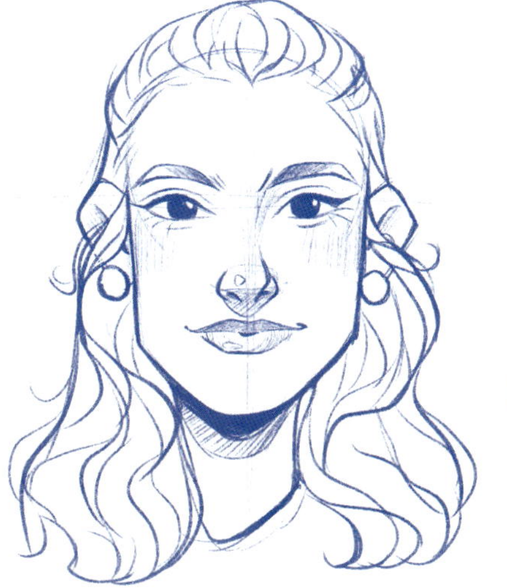

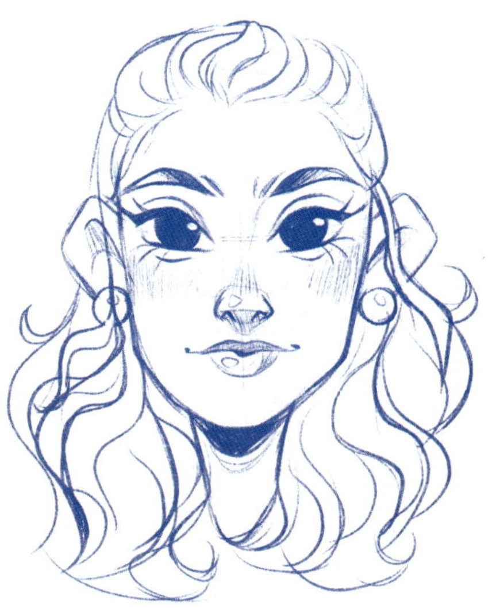

This first drawing shows a realistic type of drawing, but it doesn't have any interpretation of reality. It simply copies it. In this type of drawing, you don't have a lot of space to let your creativity flow.

However, the second drawing starts to interpret the shapes identified in the first drawing in a unique and different way from reality, with choices that created a new style.

Finally, in the last drawing, you can see the shapes and lines are much more manipulated and exaggerated, with bolder choices than the ones in the second drawing.

ADD MOVEMENT AND DIMENSION

Now that you've learned how to identify the shapes of your reference photo and to stylize them, you are going to start developing your style even more, adding movement and dimension to it. But how can you add movement and dimension to a static drawing?

The answer is adding lines and more shapes. Since you aren't doing a three-dimensional drawing, you must use the resources you have to give it a sense of motion and add life to your drawing.

I will demonstrate this in practice. Let's start with this drawing.

After adding the shapes and lines, your drawing is going to look something like this.

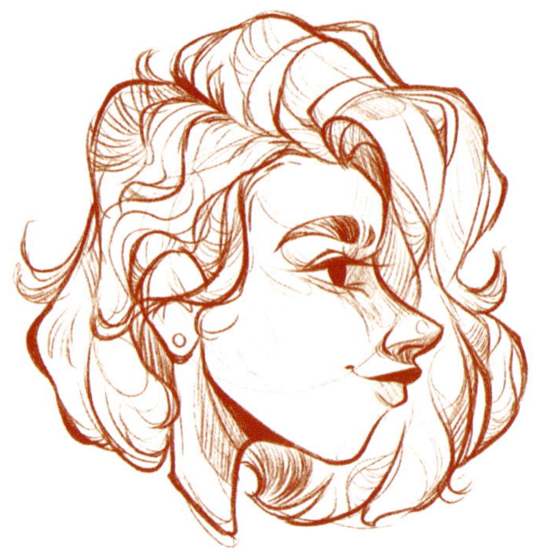

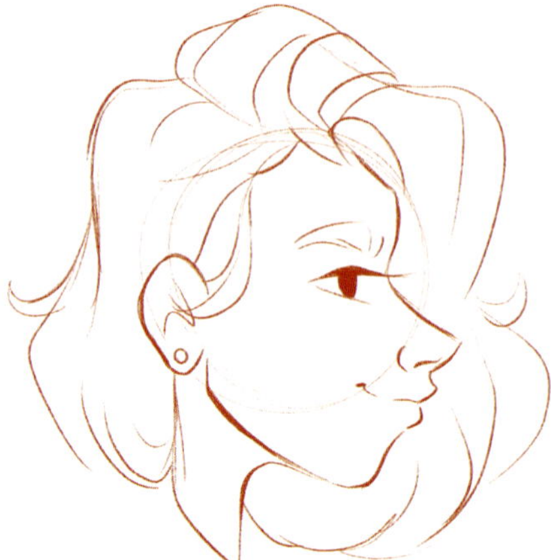

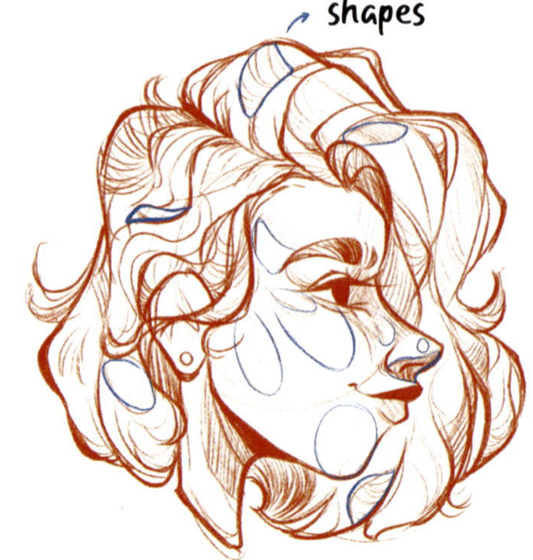

As you can see, this drawing is already stylized, but it doesn't have much movement. Yes, I changed the original shapes and made it more exaggerated and cartoonish, but it is still missing something. And that is movement.

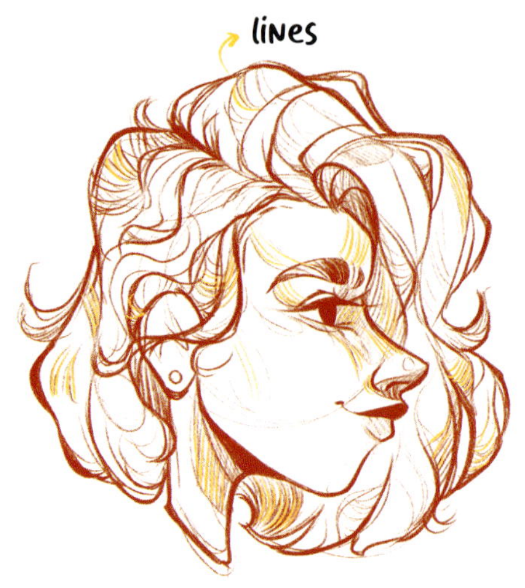

Obviously, the quantity of lines and shapes of each drawing is going to vary depending on what style you're aiming for, such as if you want it to be more clean, if there are more shadows, and so on.

Always keep in mind that your drawing is an interpretation of reality, and reality has life and movement. When you add that sense of action to your drawing, it will increase its value and quality.

LINES

Lines can have a big impact on this step of the drawing. They can add shadows and movement and can also help build the structure of your character.

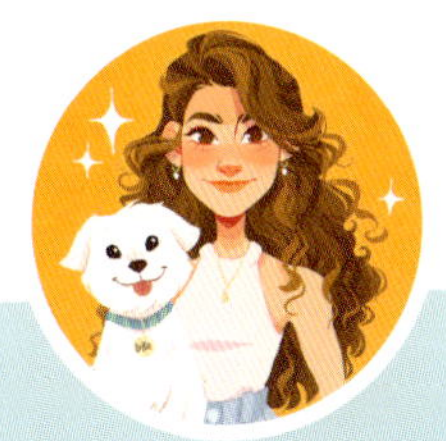

Nanda's Tip

Always remember to add lines following the shapes and the movement of your character. Don't draw them straight and with no sense of where they are going because it will only make your drawing more "busy" and "dirty."

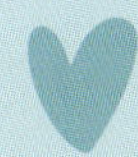

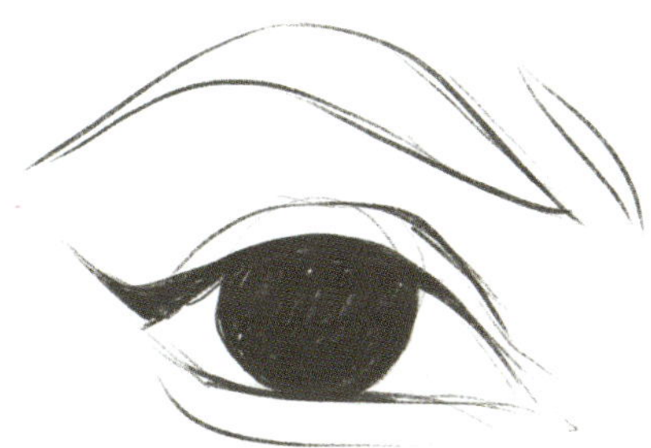

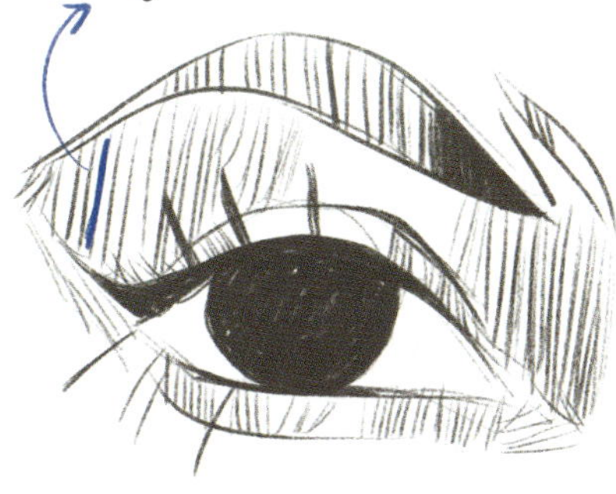

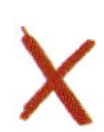

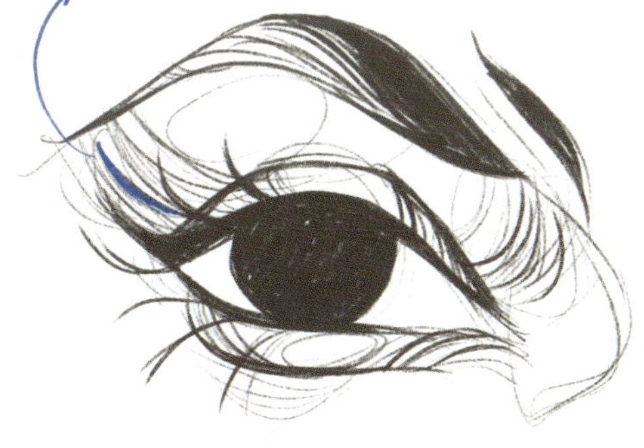

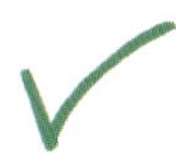

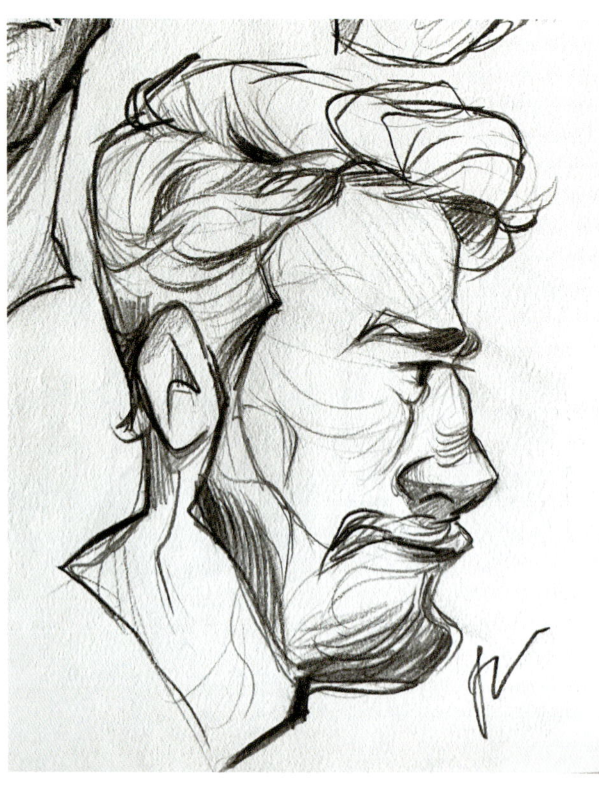

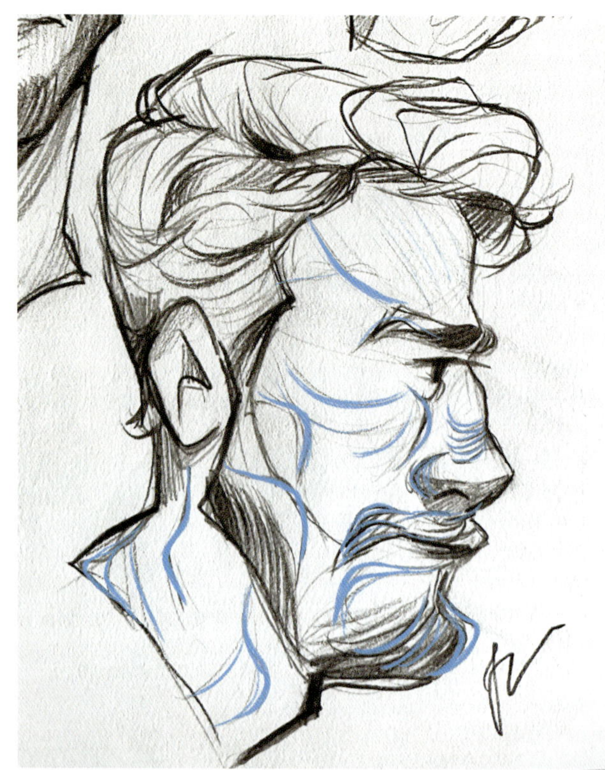

When adding lines to make the shadows, remember to go around with the shape of the face and body to give that sense of dimension and action. Flow with the shapes you originally constructed when you were stylizing. It gives more value and personality to your drawing.

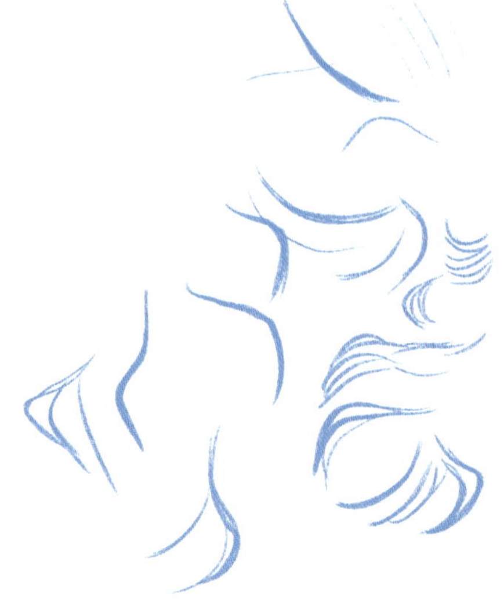

SHAPES

Adding shapes is another way to add a sense of dimension and depth to your drawing. Try to visualize the structure and the anatomy of your character, and add the shapes where you find necessary. This can be for the face, hair, plants, objects, and so on. I'm not referring to the "visible shapes," like the shape of the eyes or the mouth that you identified to stylize your drawing, but the three-dimensional shapes and shapes that are built by the shadows.

Let's start with this image below. As you can see, I identified the shapes that build her face, dividing it into areas so it will be easier to draw them later on.

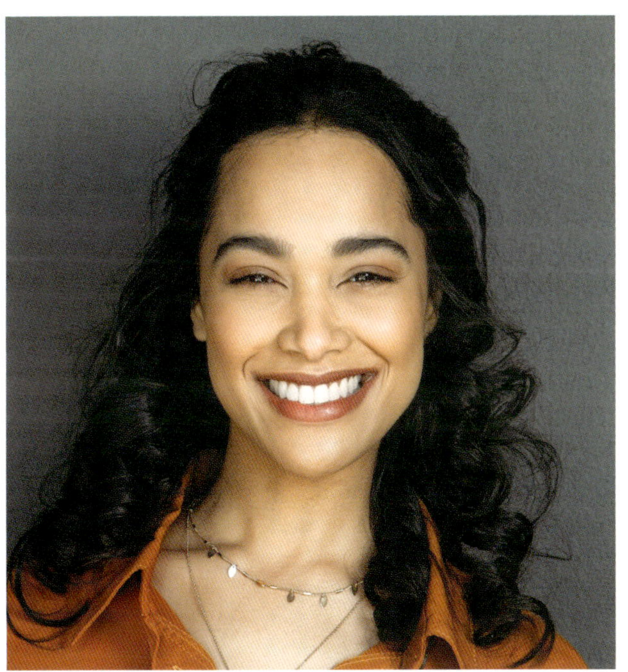

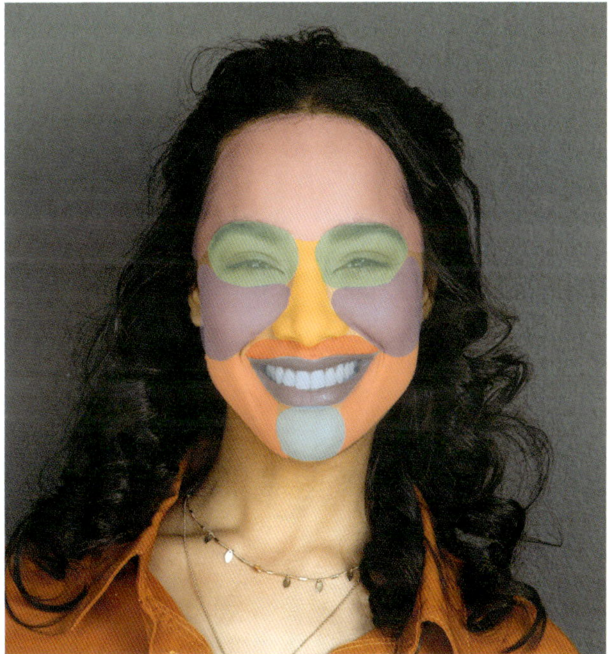

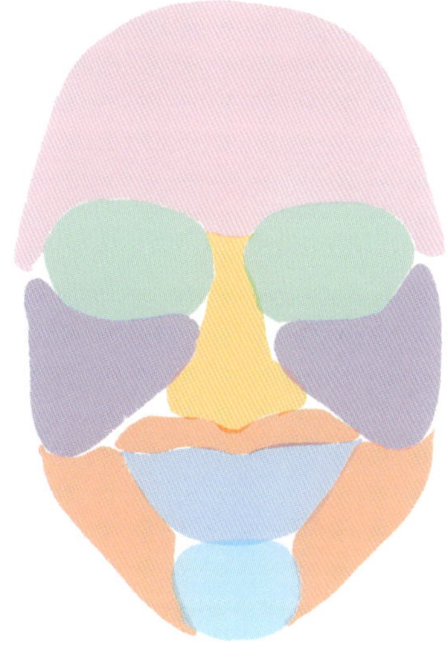

After you have identified those, you are going to start to draw shapes inspired by those ones and inventing new ones, breaking up the shapes you've created into even smaller shapes. By doing that, you're building her face structure and adding shadows with the help of the lines.

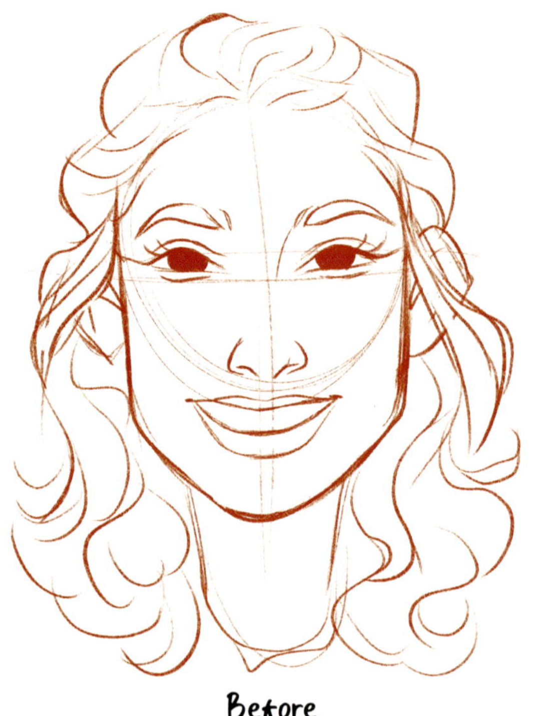

Before

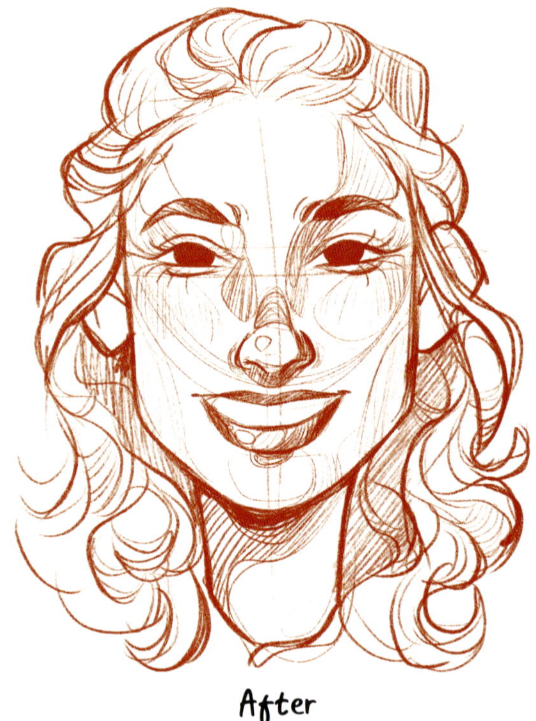

After

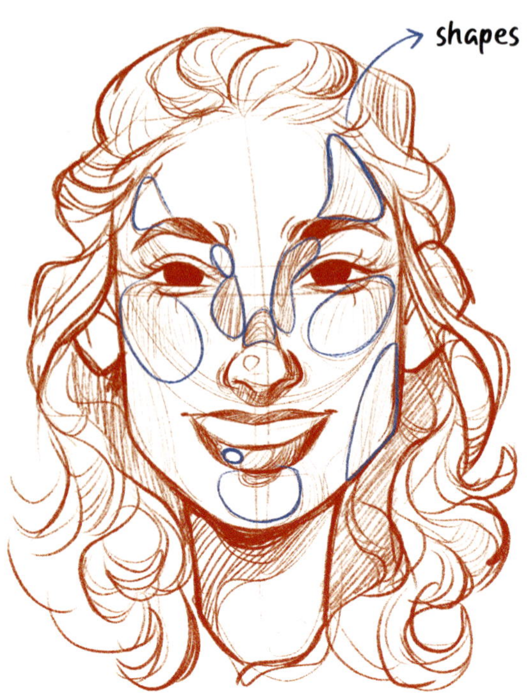

You can also identify those shapes in
this drawing.

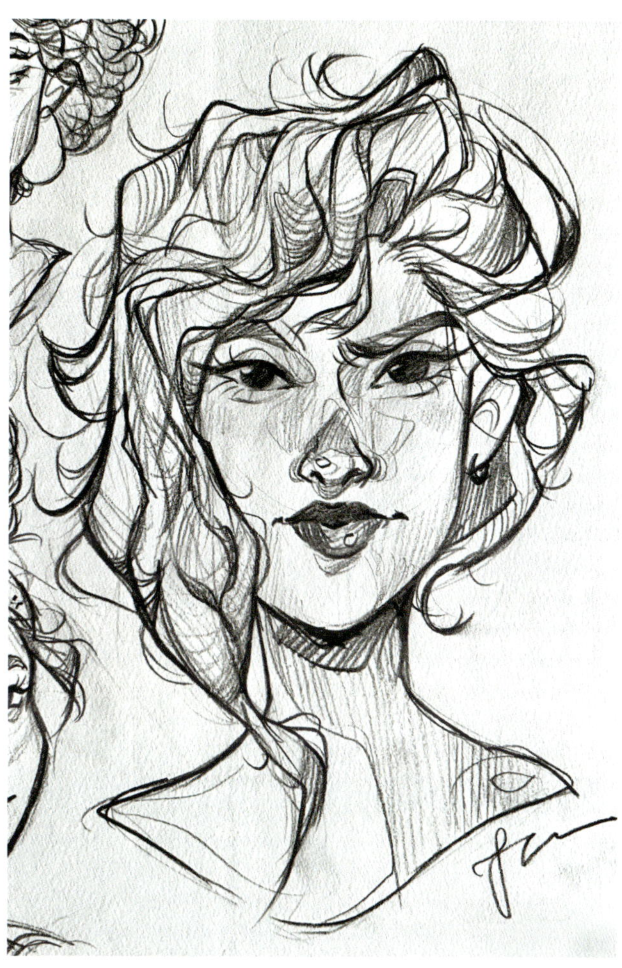

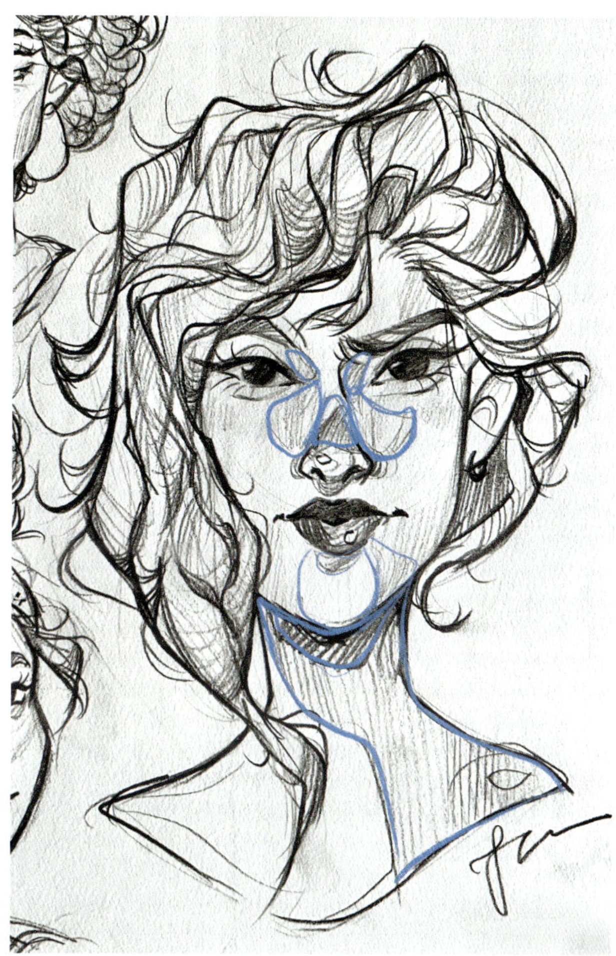

In the end, this process of adding movement and dimension to your drawing is going to
be a combination of adding lines and shapes
throughout the sketching process. It will become
intuitive for you to identify in your image what
you can transform into shapes and lines to build
a character full of movement and life.

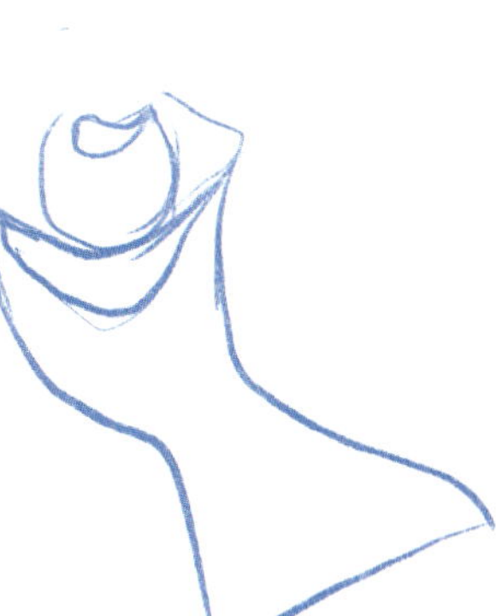

Reference Imagery

One of the greatest demands for artists is to convert a picture or another reference into a drawing. Many people would like to have their family photos or friends' images interpreted into an artistic drawing.

I'm going to show you a few examples of references versus art that I've made to give you some inspiration for and examples of this specific drawing technique.

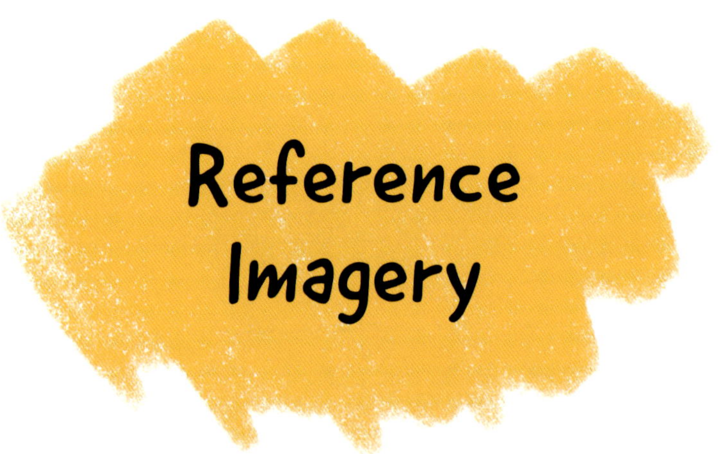

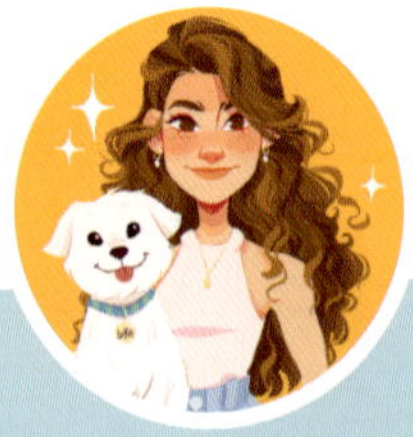

Nanda's Tip

You can combine more than one picture to create a drawing, like in this example.

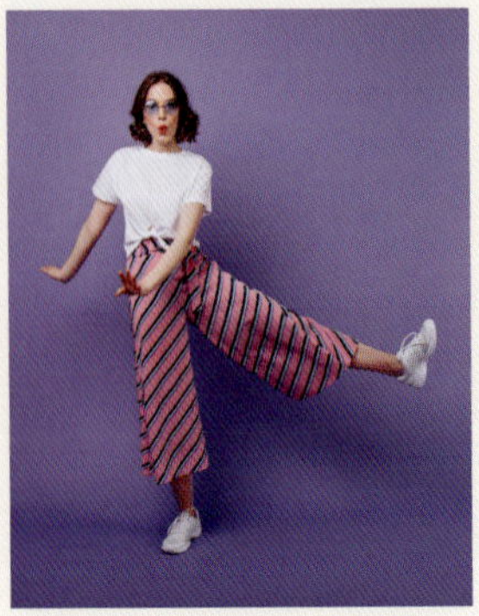

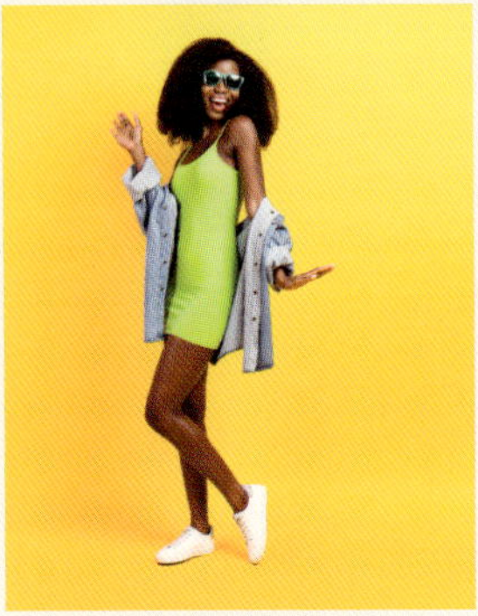

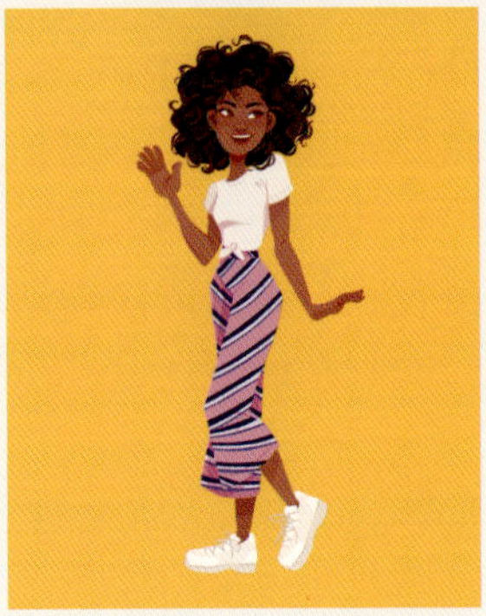

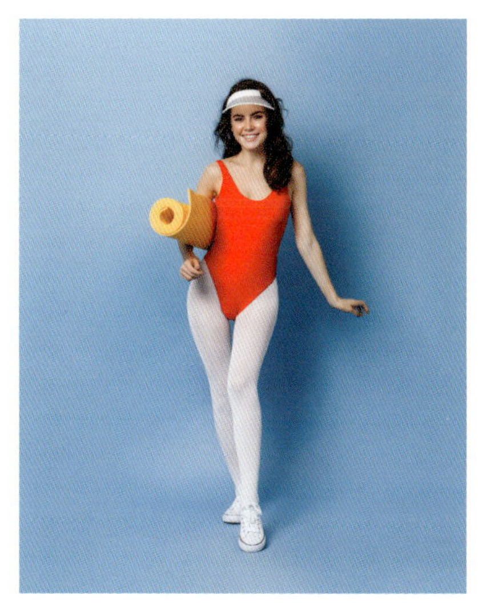
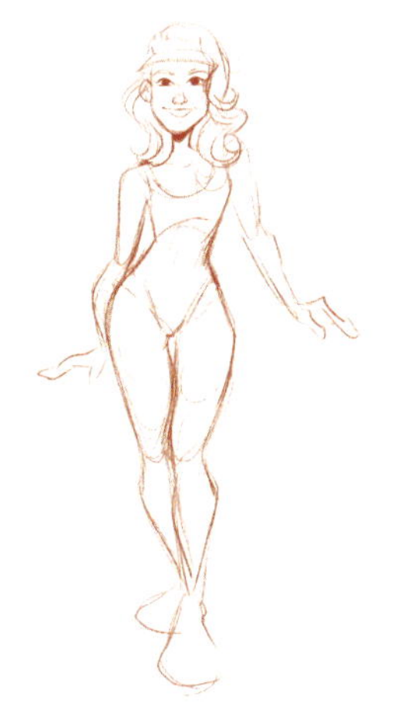
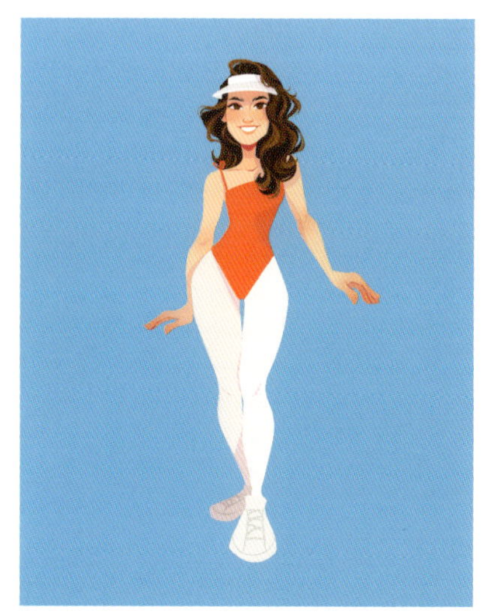
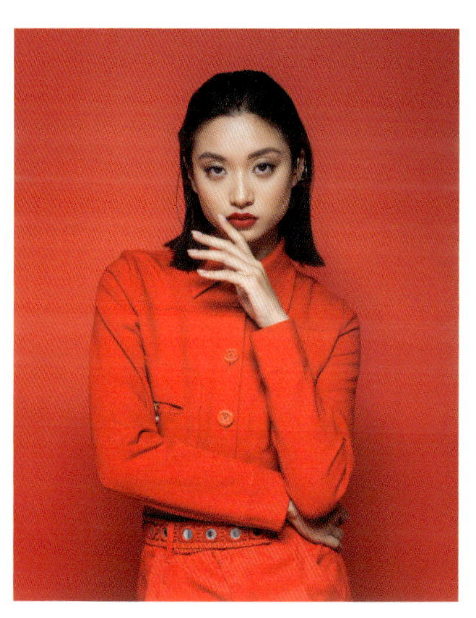
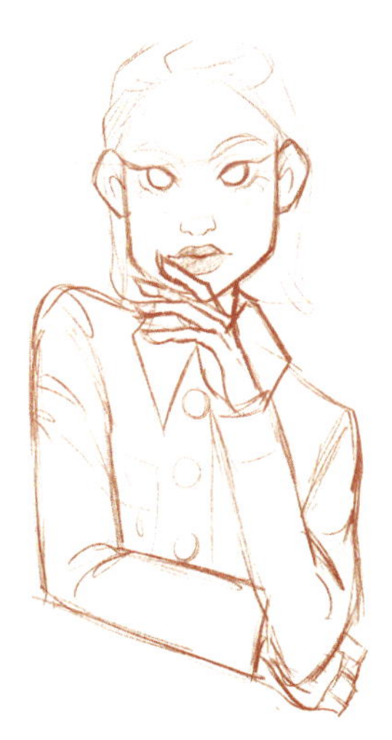
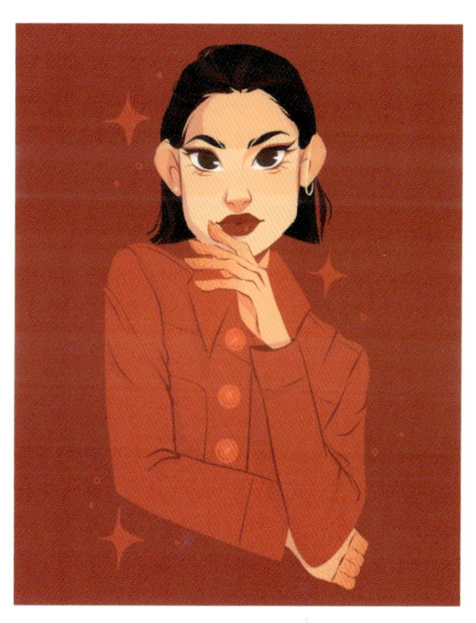
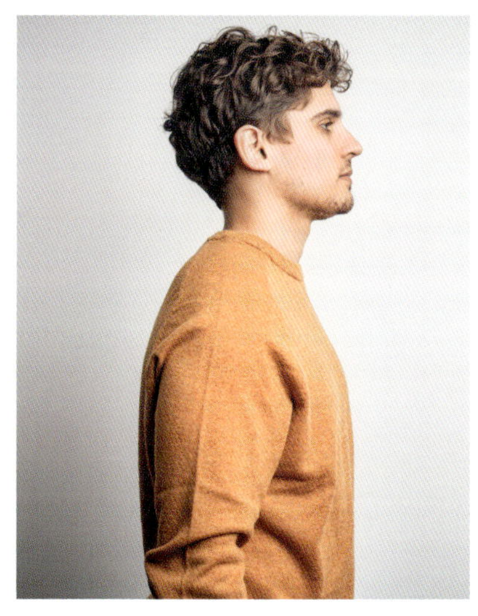
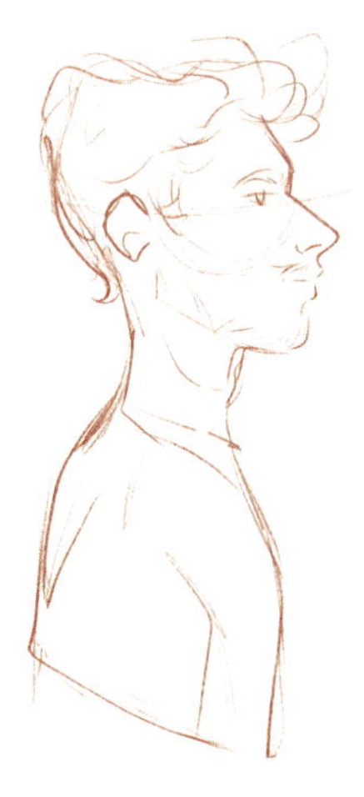
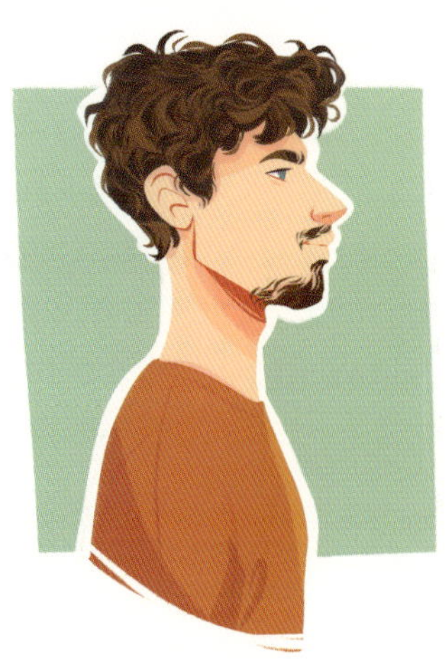

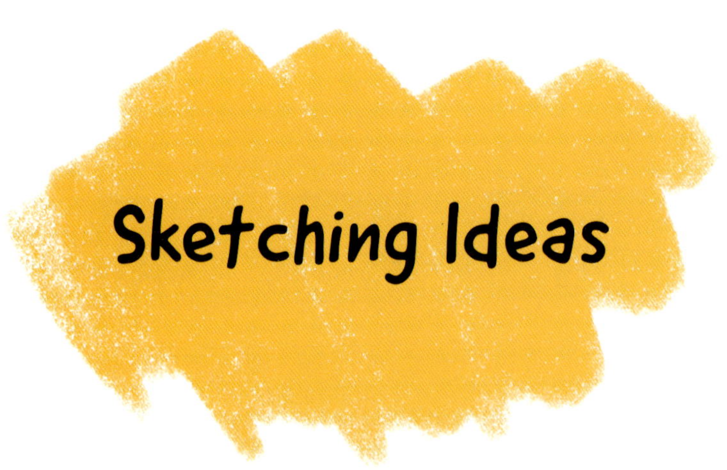

Sketching Ideas

Have you ever found yourself in front of that intimidating blank piece of paper and thought, "I have no idea what to draw"? If your answer is yes, you are not alone. I'm sure every artist has felt that way, and overcoming art block sometimes can be harder than it seems. I'm going to help you find motivation and come up with new creative ideas of what to create.

FIND INSPIRATION AROUND YOU

There are a lot of things you can do if you are stuck and have no idea what to draw. One of them is searching for inspiration around you. Look around, and try to visualize something that can be transformed into a drawing. Maybe you can find inspiration in people around you, a beautiful view, or nature, or you can even start to draw the objects you see around you. Get out of your comfort zone, and challenge yourself to draw something you have never drawn before. I know this book is about drawing characters, but drawing other things can help you improve your drawing skills and enhance your creativity.

Sometimes when I try to find inspiration around me, my perfect model is my dog. I like drawing him in different poses, trying new things and challenging myself to draw something that isn't easy for me. My dog moves all the time, so I challenge myself to capture the essentials of what I'm seeing and transform it into a little piece of art.

In addition to finding inspiration around you, you can also find it in your favorite artists and people whose artwork you admire! Study their art and art style and get inspired by it—obviously without copying it—and learn their techniques and creative processes.

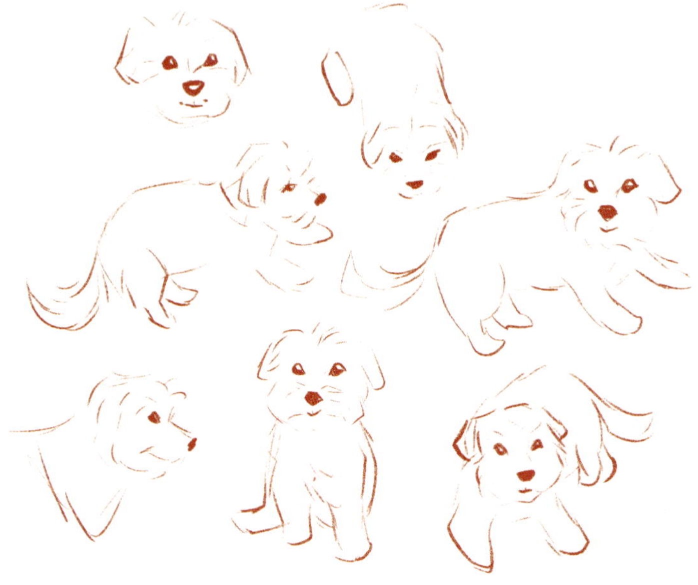

CHALLENGE YOURSELF

Another thing to try when you don't know what to draw is to challenge yourself. You can find many art challenges on the internet, so take a risk and try one of them!

One thing I like to do is to go on Pinterest and try to make a drawing with the first three images that appear on my page. Another thing you can do is redraw an old drawing to see how your art has changed with time. But remember, don't feel restricted to the challenges that already exist—try to invent a new challenge for yourself!

DRAW WHAT YOU LIKE

You don't have to always push yourself to draw something that challenges you or that gets you out of your comfort zone. Sometimes you just need to draw what you like. I can put pressure on myself to always improve my art style or to draw something different and complex, but sometimes drawing a simple character or doing a fan art is what I need to relax and enjoy my time. Just because you are not pushing yourself to draw something elaborate and different doesn't mean that you are not a good artist who doesn't try to improve. It's okay to draw things that are easy for you, and sometimes that's all we need.

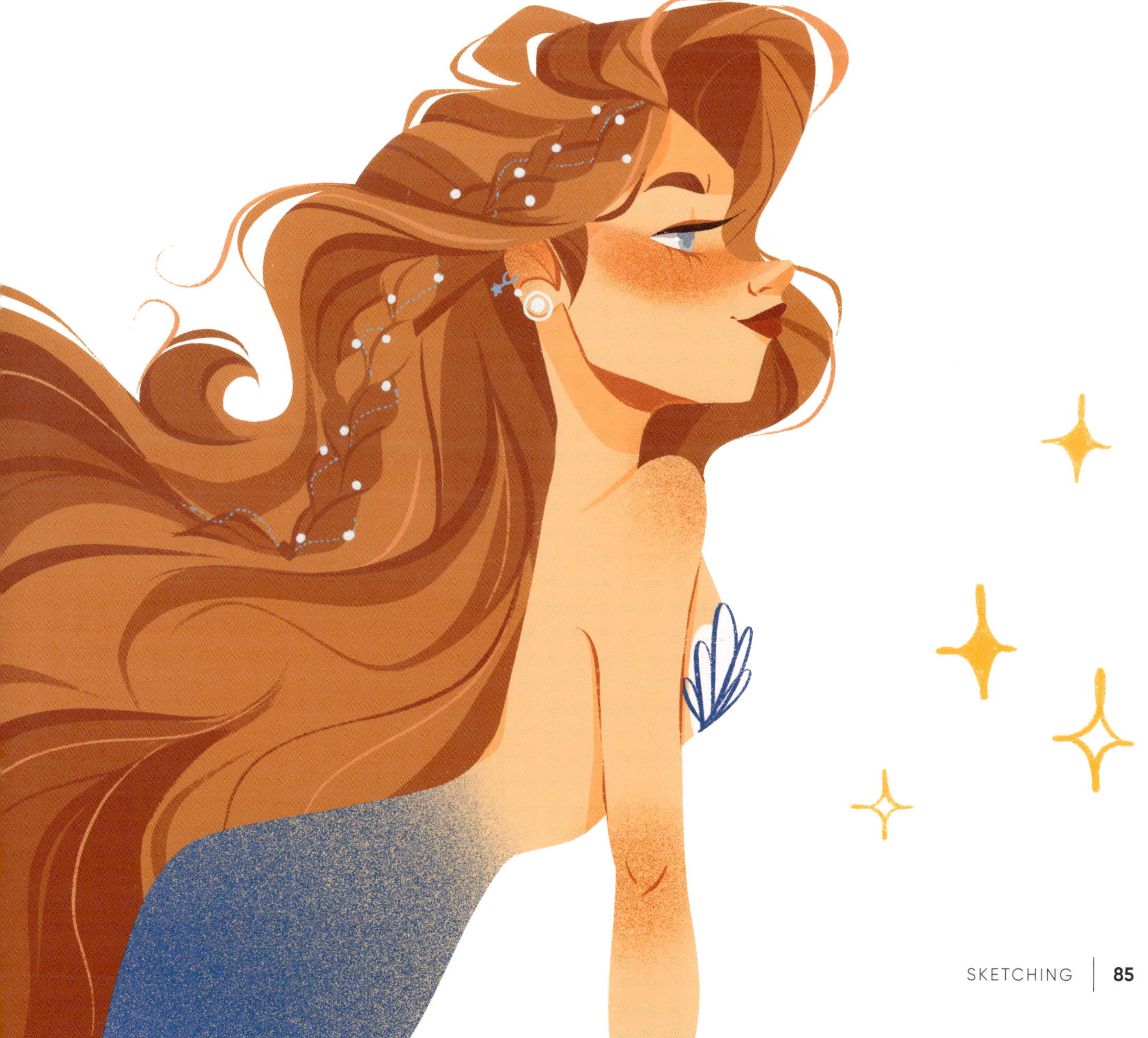

TRY SOMETHING NEW

Sometimes even drawing something that we like to draw feels a little bit off. So if you are feeling inspired, try something new! Maybe try a different media or a different style. You can also try to draw something that you've never drawn before. If you are used to drawing landscapes, try to draw a character! Don't limit yourself to the things that you already know; try to push yourself to draw different things. It can depend on how you are feeling that day, but when you're feeling more experimental, try something new.

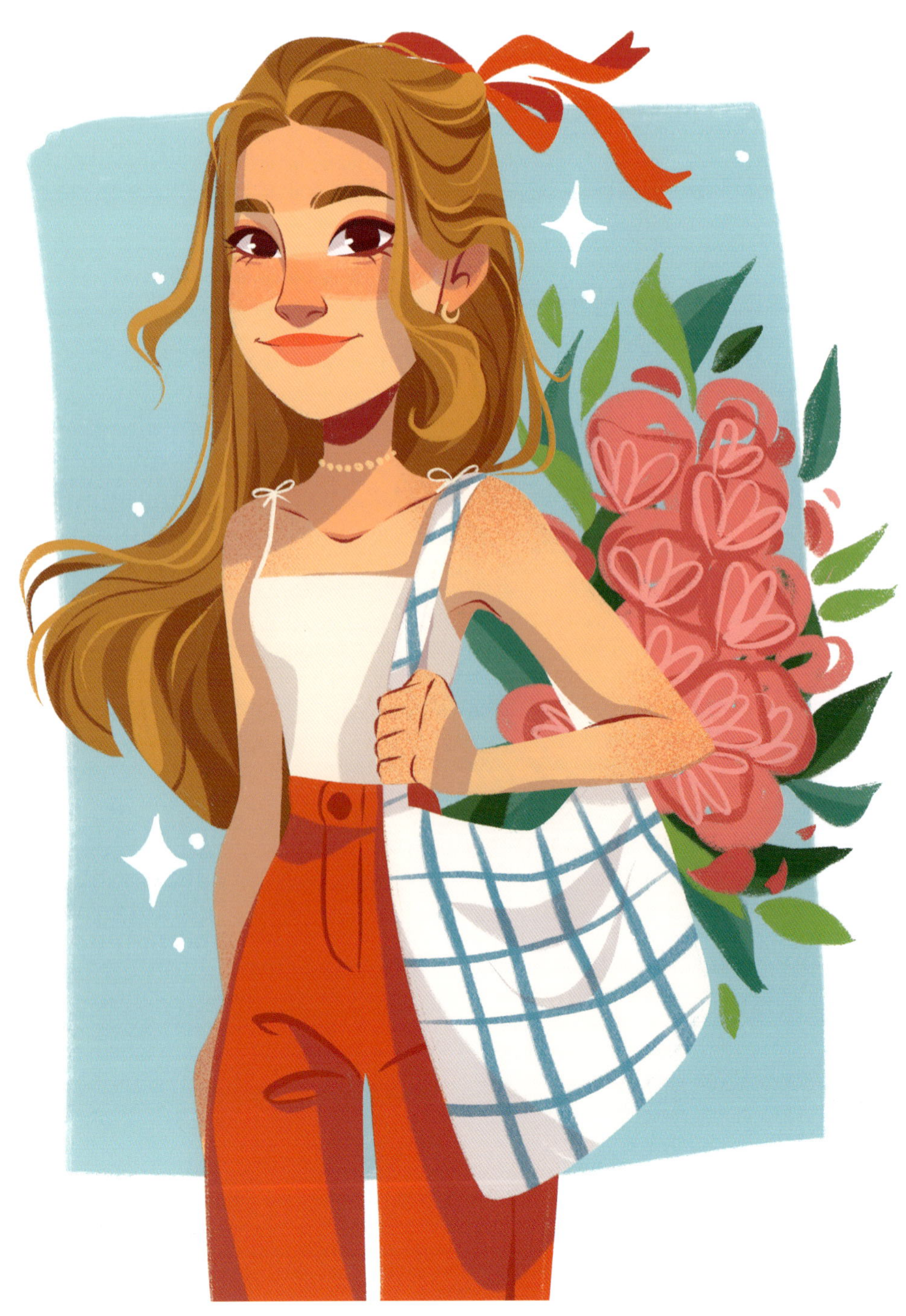

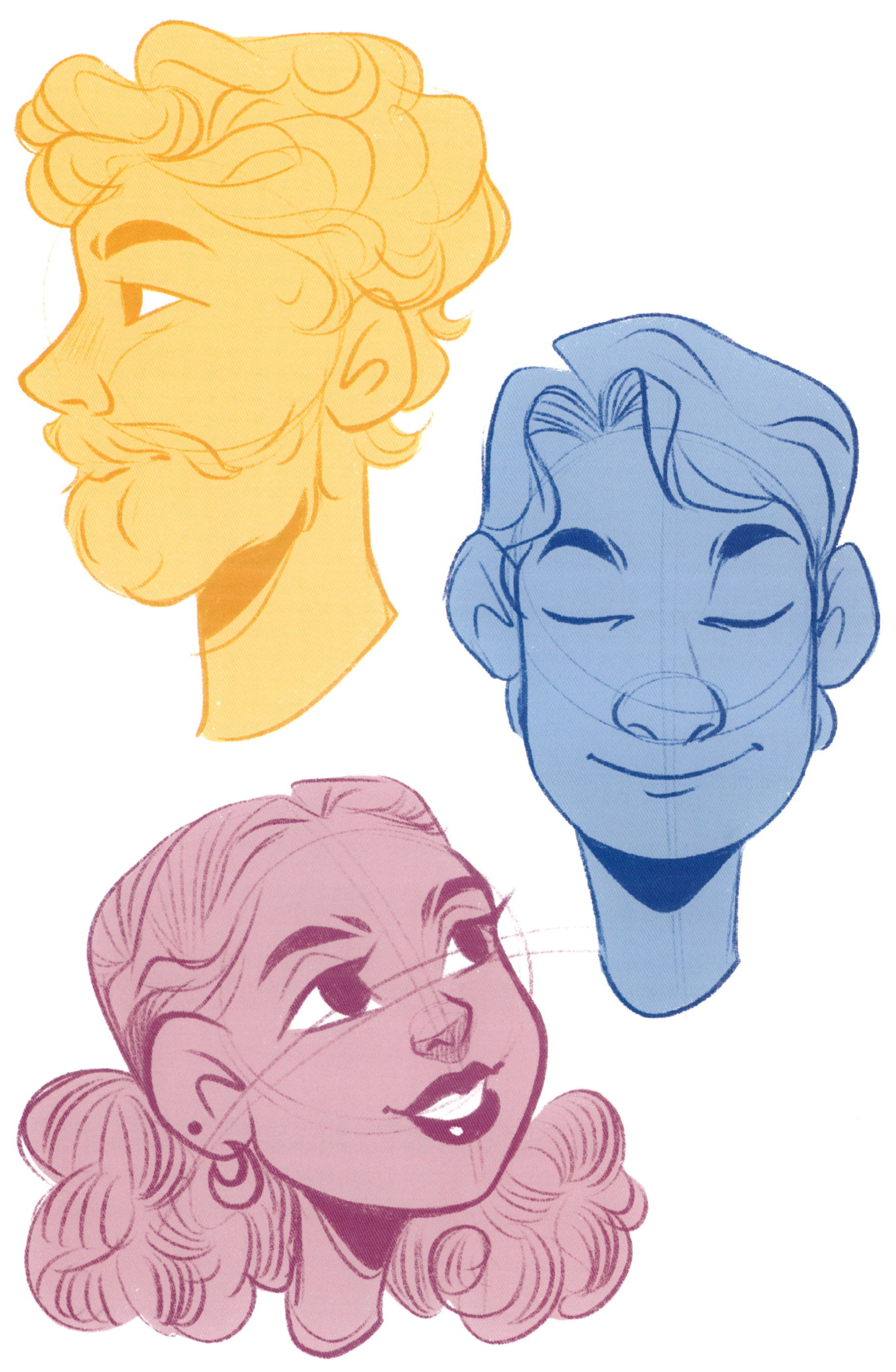

Monochromatic Art

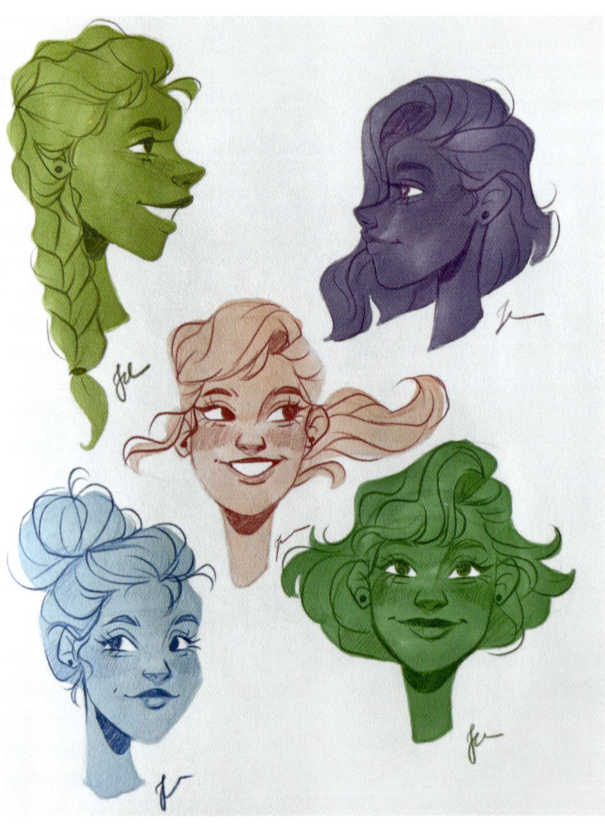

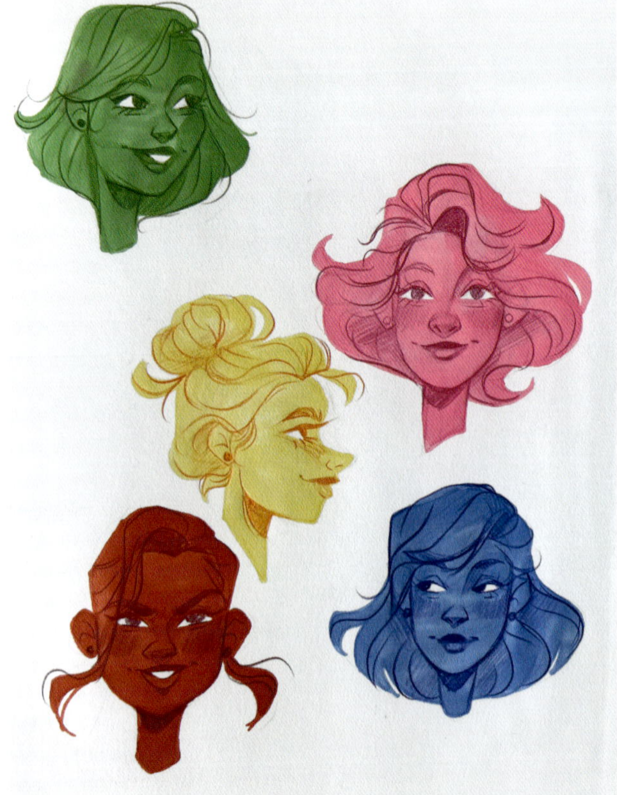

One specific style I love to draw is monochromatic characters. They are really fun and easy to do, and you can make them by combining a marker and a pencil. In this section, I'm going to share a step-by-step tutorial on how to draw these captivating and colorful monochromatic characters.

The idea behind these characters is to challenge yourself to draw using just a marker and a pencil in the same color tone. You can use any color you want, but make sure that the pencil is a little bit darker than the marker. This way there will be a contrast between the basic shape of your character that you make using the marker and the pencil scribbles that will be used for facial features and details. The process is divided into three parts: sketch, base shape, and final details.

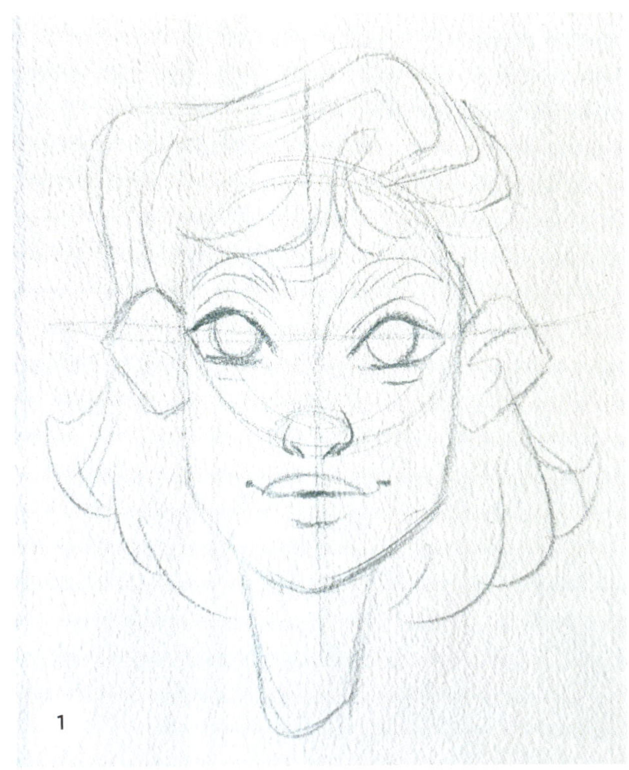

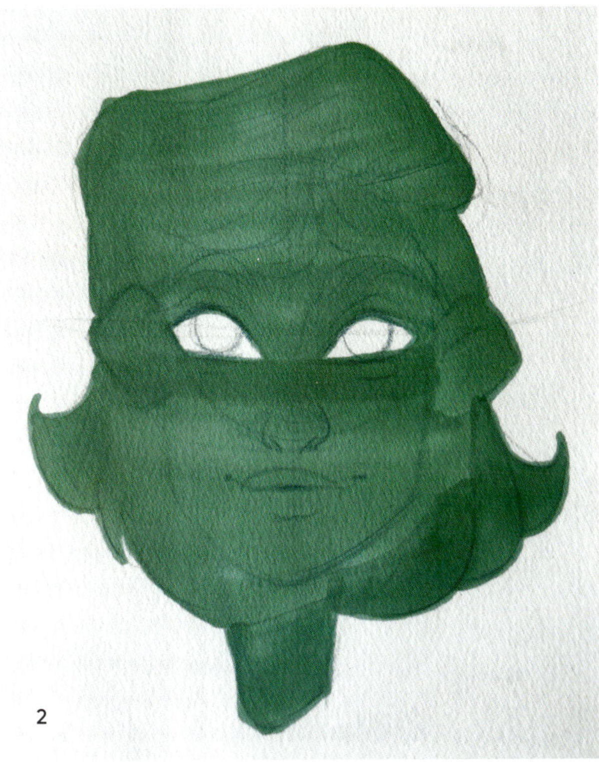

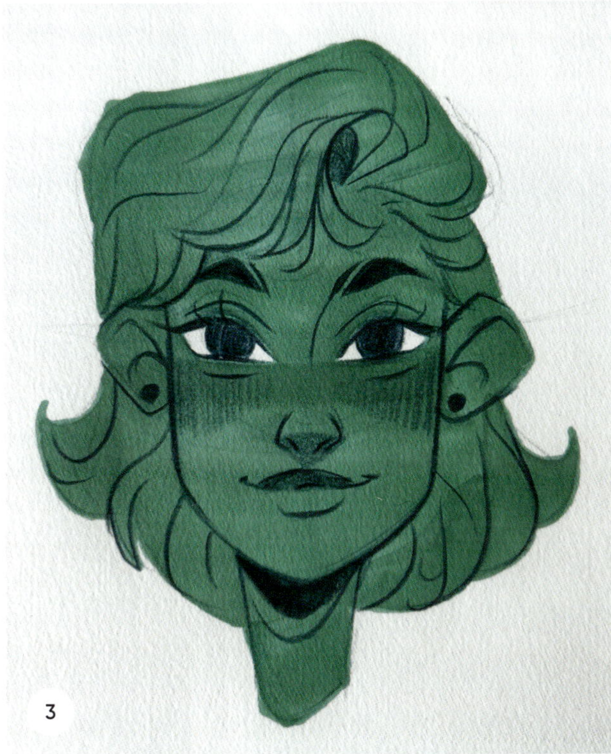

I. SKETCH

The first thing you are going to do is sketch your character so you can have an idea of where you are going to draw the shape of your character with the marker. Remember to leave the eyes and the mouth (if your character is smiling) blank.

2. BASE SHAPE

Now that you have the reference sketch, you are going to draw the base shape using your marker. Here I like to use an alcohol-based marker because the water-based ones smear more than the alcohol-based. But if you don't have an alcohol-based marker, it's okay to use a water-based one.

3. FINAL DETAILS

Now that you have the base shape placed, you are going to define the facial features and details of your character using your colorful pencil.

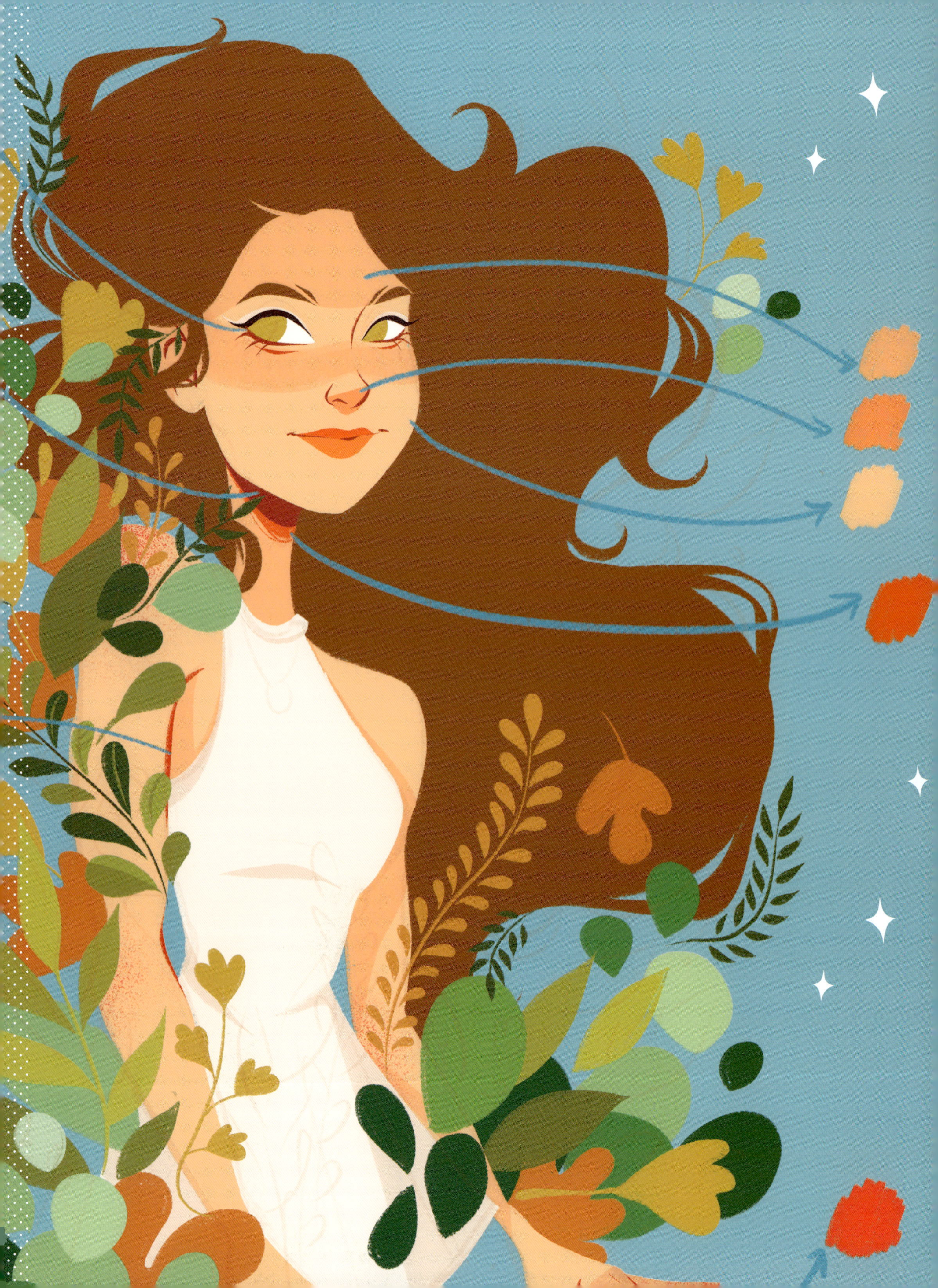

Drawing Digitally

With modern devices and easy-to-use software, more and more people are using these technologies to produce art. Remember that you can also apply many of these digital techniques and concepts to traditional art.

Remember that this is not the only correct way to produce digital drawings; there are numerous other styles and techniques that you can use. This is just a simple way that I found helps me when creating digital art.

In this chapter, we are going to cover every detail of the digital drawing process, from the rough sketch to the final art piece, so you can achieve great results with your digital creations!

Creating a Digital Drawing

In this section, we are going to cover each step in the digital drawing process, from the first brushstroke to the finished product. Essentially I make three sketches in the process of creating an illustration: the rough sketch, the "define lines" sketch, and the finalized sketch.

I like to emphasize that the way I draw digitally is a personal preference. It doesn't mean that it's the only way that's correct, but I like to share this to give you an idea of where to start when you want to draw digitally.

I currently use the Procreate app on a tablet with a digital pencil, but you can apply these principles and techniques to any app or software and digital media hardware, like a drawing tablet, for example.

ROUGH SKETCH

The rough sketch is when you start to let your imagination run free. Don't be afraid of making mistakes, and just start drawing some ideas you have. Normally, I do about three or four rough sketches, and I focus more on the proportions and movement and less on the details.

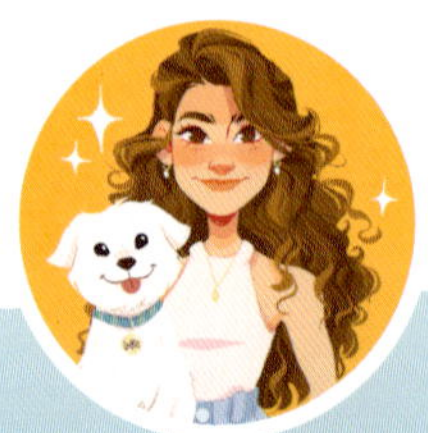

Nanda's Tips

- You can use any software or hardware to do your digital drawing. I suggest you study and know your equipment and its capabilities and resources. Be sure to know how to use your software (or app) and the names of the actions and tools it has so you can properly apply the knowledge gained in this book and other digital art courses.

- Try to draw faster and loosely! Don't lose yourself in the details. Let your creativity guide you here. One of the nice things about digital art is that going forward or backward and erasing some previous traces is very easy to do.

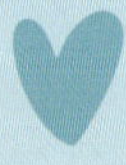

For this piece, I did four rough sketches. As you can see, these drawings are very different from each other. Here is just another example to help you get an idea of where you're going to start building your drawing, a base on which to construct your art.

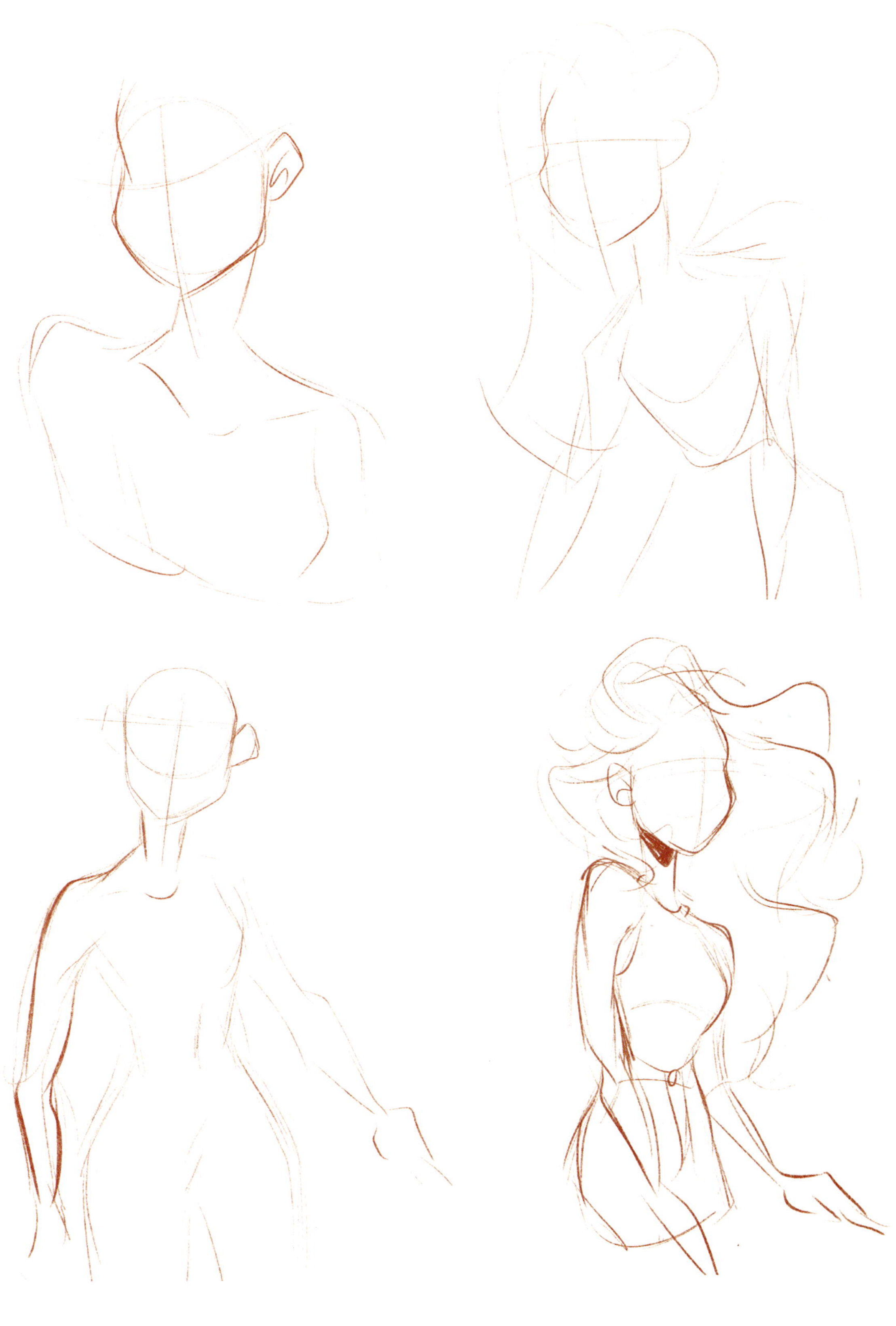

DEFINE LINES

After choosing which rough sketch is your favorite, start building your drawing on the top of that. I usually turn the opacity of the rough sketch to about 50 percent, and then create a new layer on the top of it to start my sketch, defining the lines.

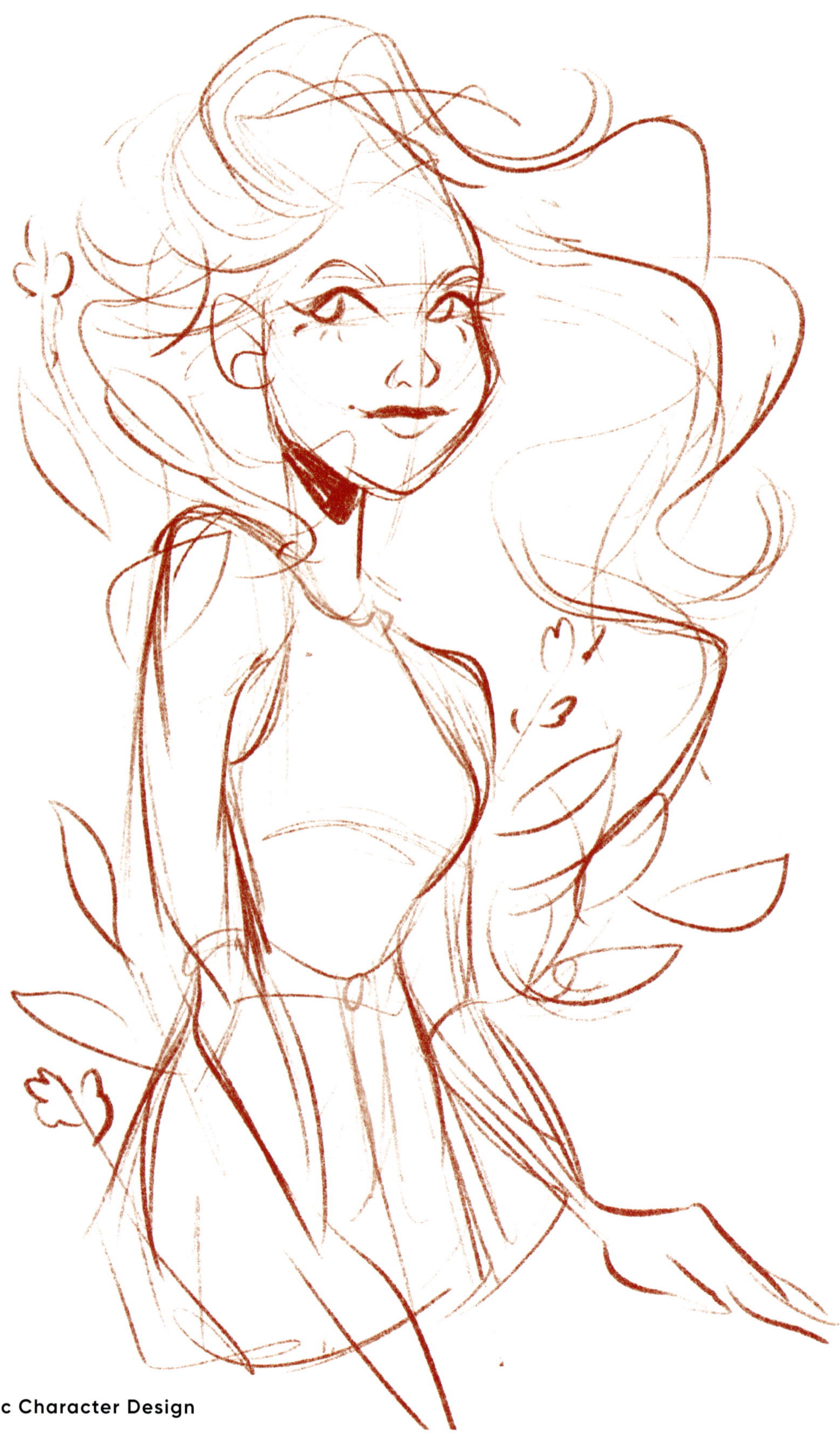

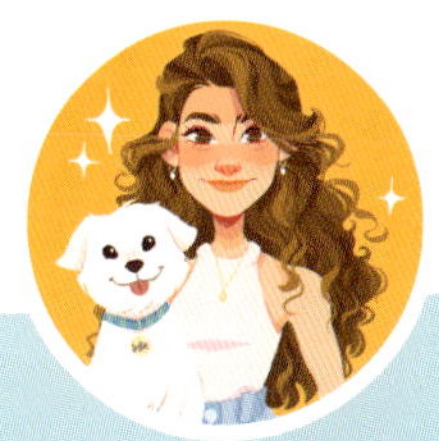

Nanda´s Tips

- Using layers is a nice resource that you should use in your digital art. They can be used to add depth to your drawing and include backgrounds or even sketches that can be hidden at the end of your process.

- Always remember that there's no problem in changing your mind during the drawing process. The most important thing is to let your creativity flow. Don't be afraid of adding, taking off, or changing something in your drawing. Being able to easily change your drawing is a big advantage of digital art.

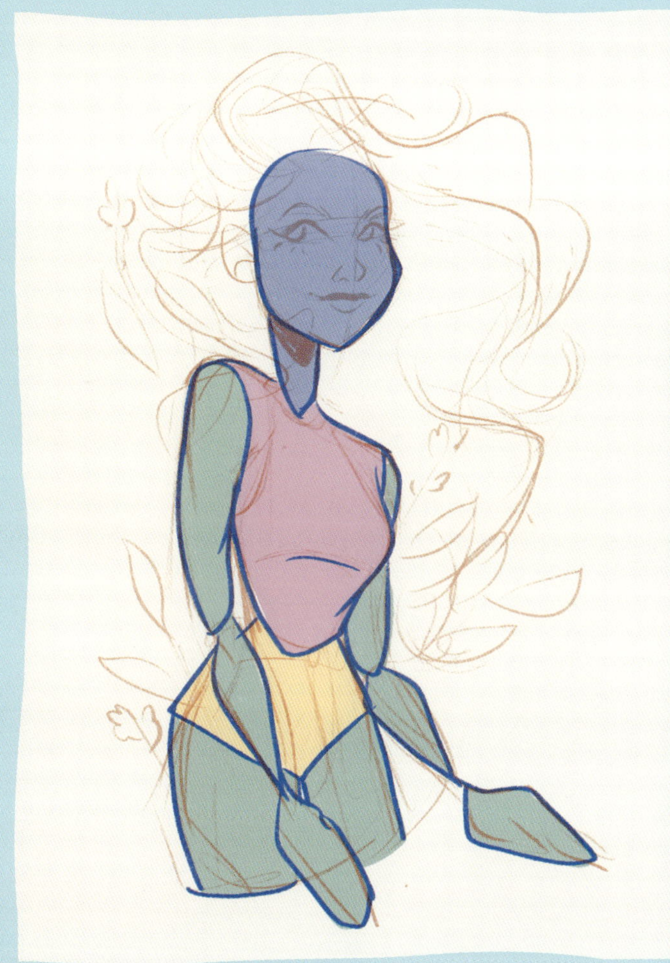

- Using a colorful pencil to sketch is just a personal preference, and you can use any color you want. I just lean toward colorful pencils for sketching because I believe it gives a more beautiful look to the drawing. Here, focus on the anatomy and proportions of your character. It is very important to give a lot of attention to the proportions in this step so you don't build your drawing wrong from the start.

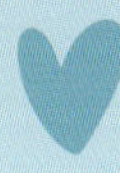

FINALIZING A SKETCH

After you have a good base for your drawing, you're going to finalize your sketch. Here, I usually hide the rough sketch layer and turn the opacity of the defined lines sketch layer to about 25 percent, and then I create another layer on top of it to redraw the sketch but in a more clean and finalized way.

Here you can start to add more details to the eyes, mouth, nose, eyebrows, hands, and hair. (You can also add more details during the process, considering that you can have additional creative ideas or even change your mind about how certain facial features should be drawn.)

After that, hide the rough sketch and the defined lines sketch, and let only the finalized sketch display.

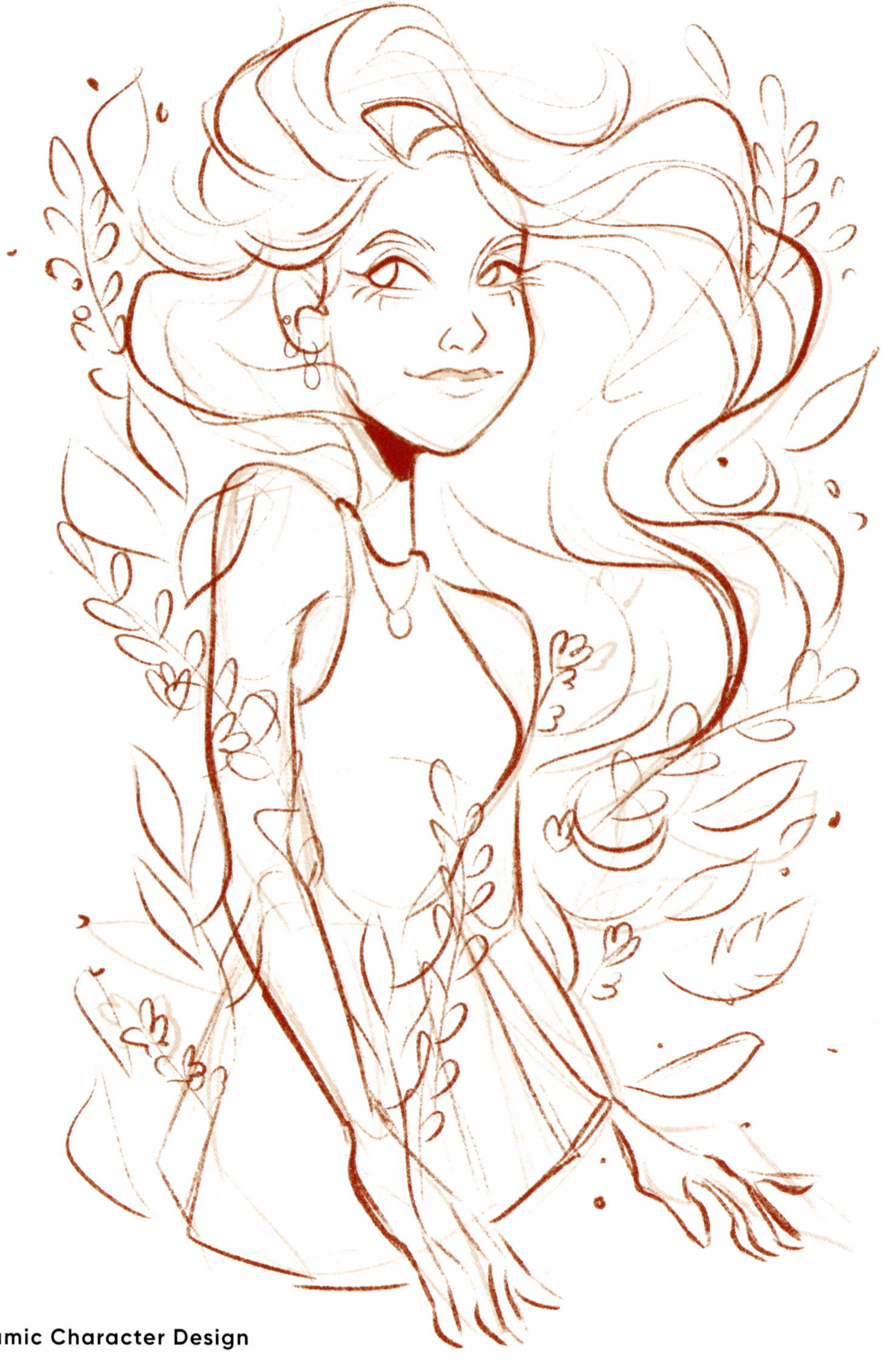

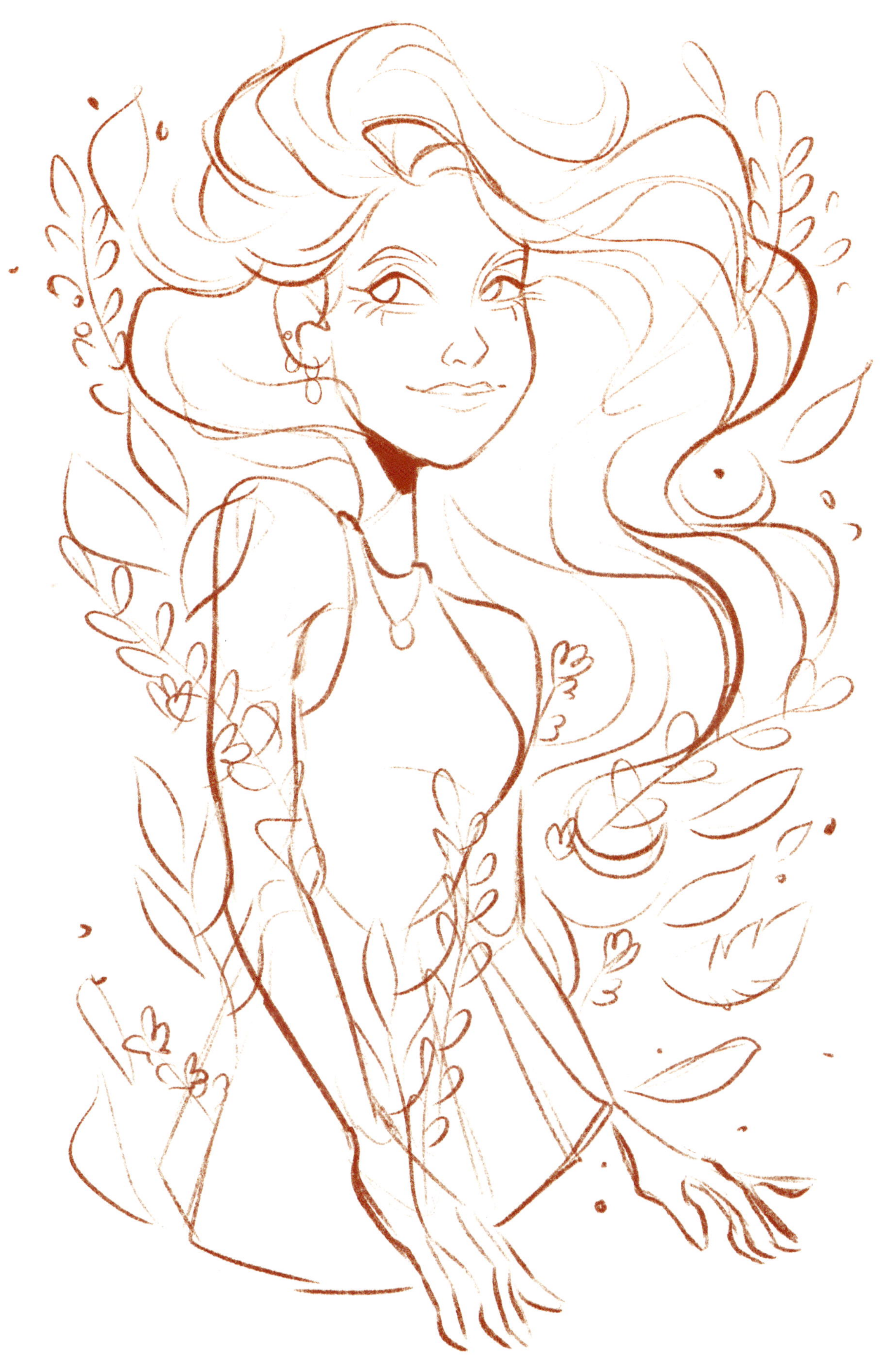

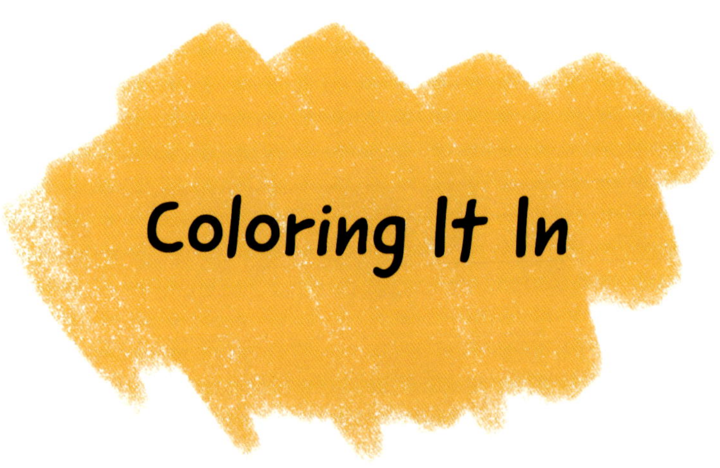

Now, let's add some color!

I use a brush with a little bit of texture to color and define shapes. In Procreate, I use the chalk brushes. You can also use the dry ink brush, shale brush, and studio pen.

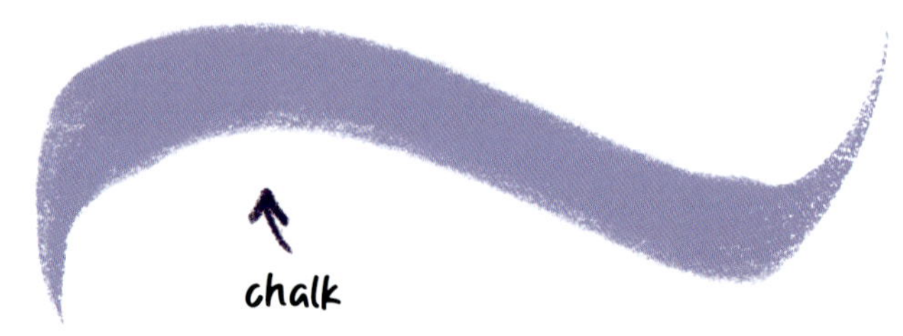

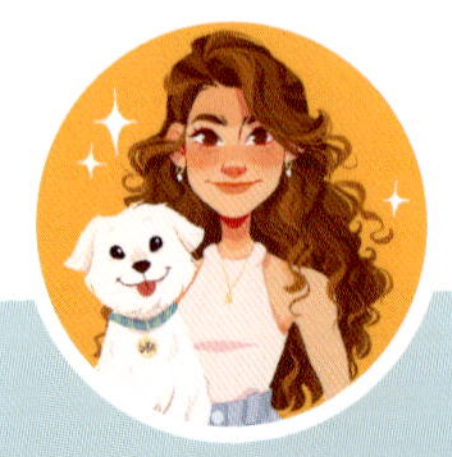

Nanda's Tip

Experiment with lots of brushes. Trying different styles and textures will give you the instruments to easily create your digital art and add some personality to your drawing.

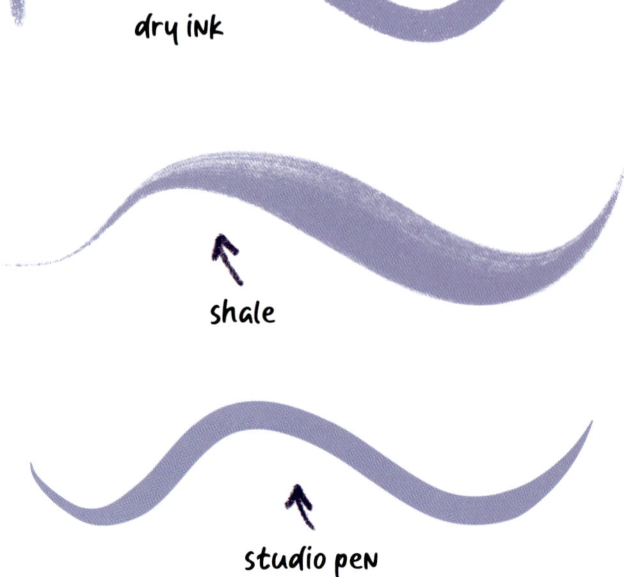

At this point, I start by turning the opacity of the finalized sketch layer to about 10 percent, and I put it on the top of every layer. As you can see, the finalized sketch is my reference for position and proportion of the next layers.

Then, under the finalized sketch layer is where I start to build the drawing.

Don't forget to leave your finalized layer on the top of all the other layers you're going to create from now on so you can have a guide for the rest of your drawing.

For this step, I like to think about each element of the body and each component as shapes, as you can see in this following example.

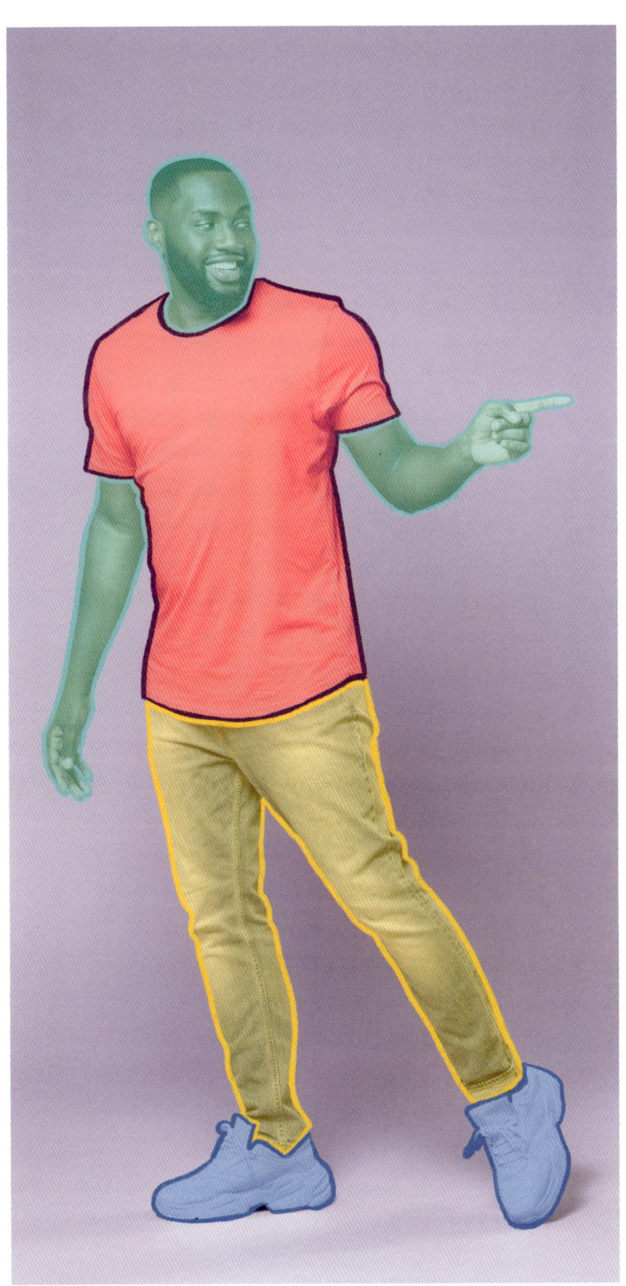

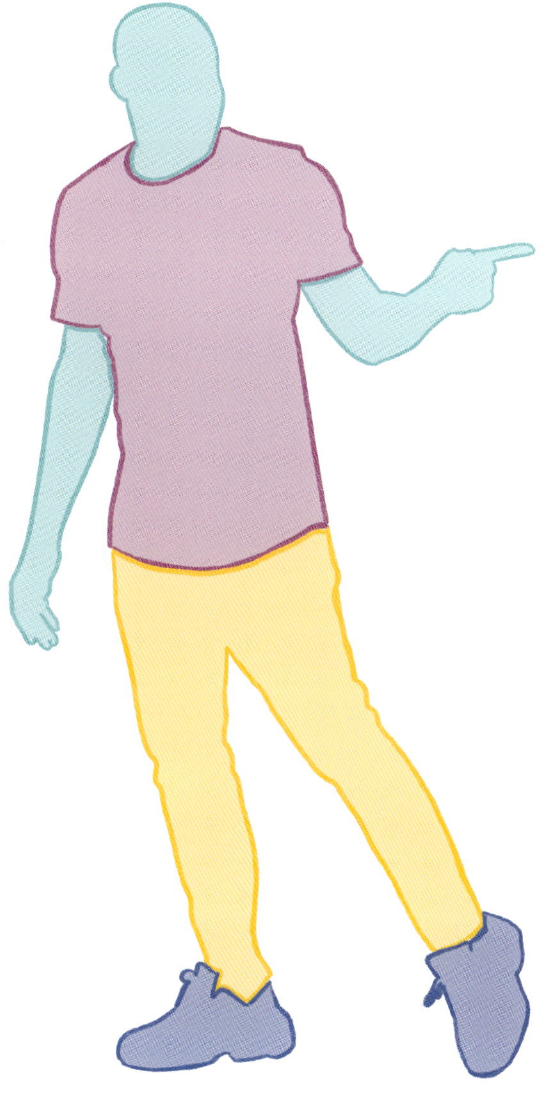

Since my drawing style is lineless, I can't simply paint inside the lines I've made because I am going to take out the finalized sketch layer in the end.

What do I mean by lineless? So you can have an idea of what I'm talking about, here is the same drawing, one with lines (top) and the other one lineless (bottom).

Identifying each component as a shape helps you construct your character without necessarily needing to keep visible lines.

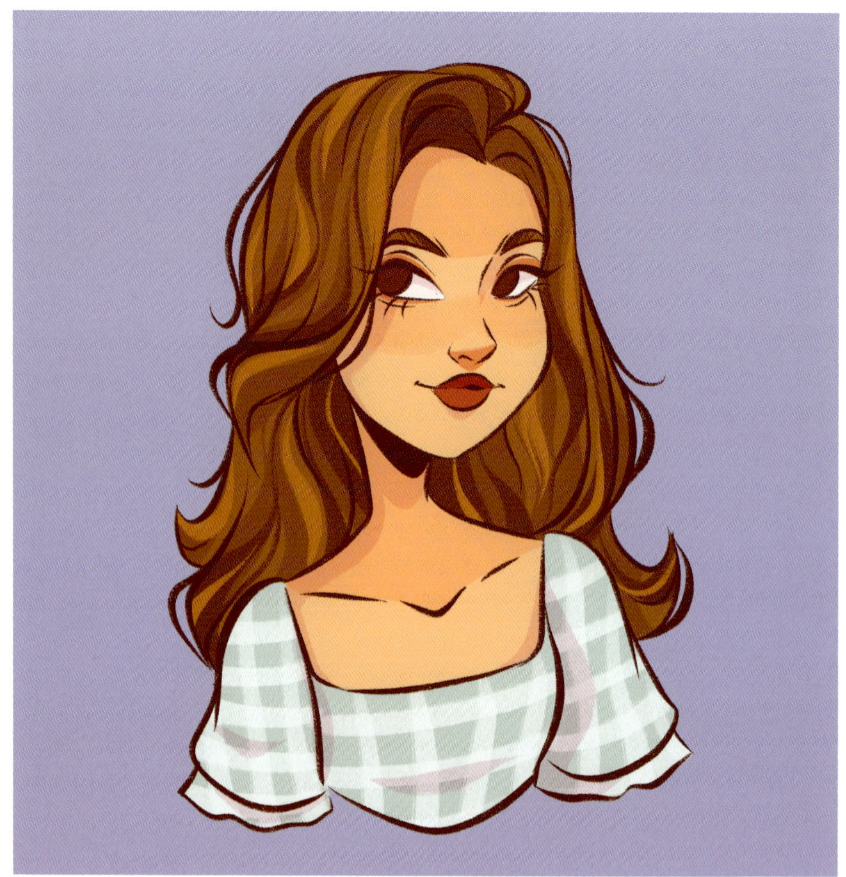

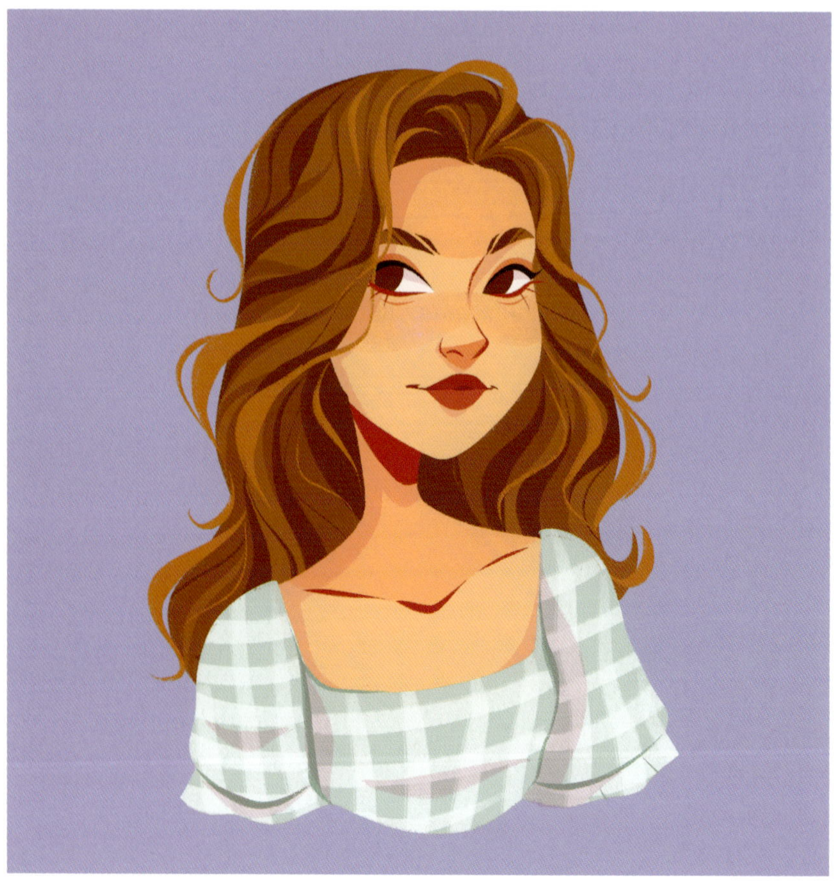

SKIN

I like to start by coloring the skin. Don't forget to create a layer only for the skin, so if you need to make any changes later on, you can make them on that specific layer. (PS: We are going to make a new layer for each part of the drawing.)

I always start with the skin because it's the base layer, so it helps you construct the rest of the drawing.

I begin by establishing the shape of the skin and then fill it in with color.

It doesn't need to be perfect since you're going to draw more layers on top of it and correct mistakes as you go.

Some artists try out colors before starting to construct the drawing, but personally I choose them throughout the development of the drawing. Choosing is part of my creative process, and selecting the colors before can restrict my creative flow. But, if you find that doing it helps you, go for it!

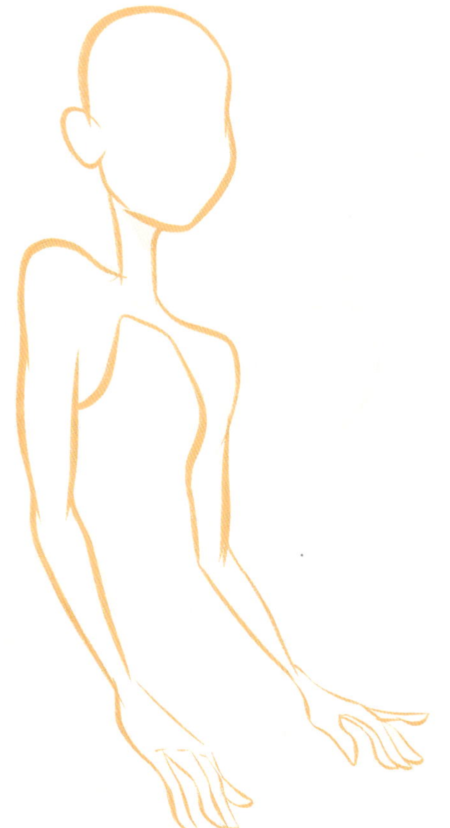

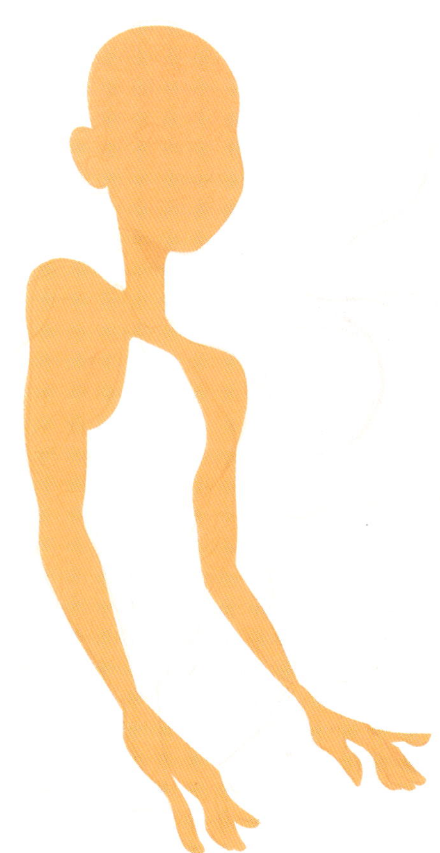

HAIR

After coloring the skin, I like to move on to the hair. This is a step when you may change the shape from your initial sketch. Your creativity flow is more important than sticking to the initial sketch because the main goal of the sketch is to help you build your drawing, not limit you to what was planned at the beginning of the process.

In this step, you start by determining the area of your hair. Draw a line to construct the shape the hair is going to have and then fill in that shape.

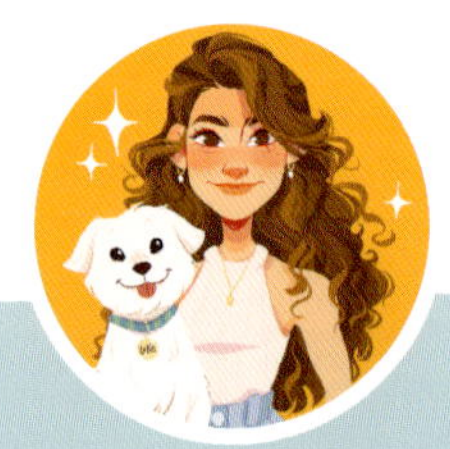

Nanda's Tip

During the process of constructing each layer, I correct some mistakes that I've made on the other layers. Adjustments are part of the process.

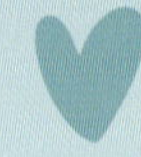

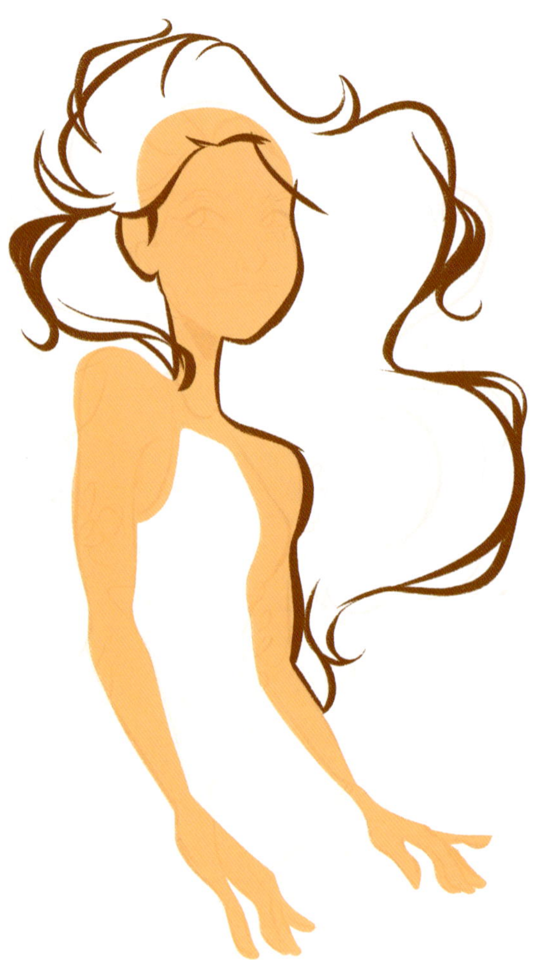

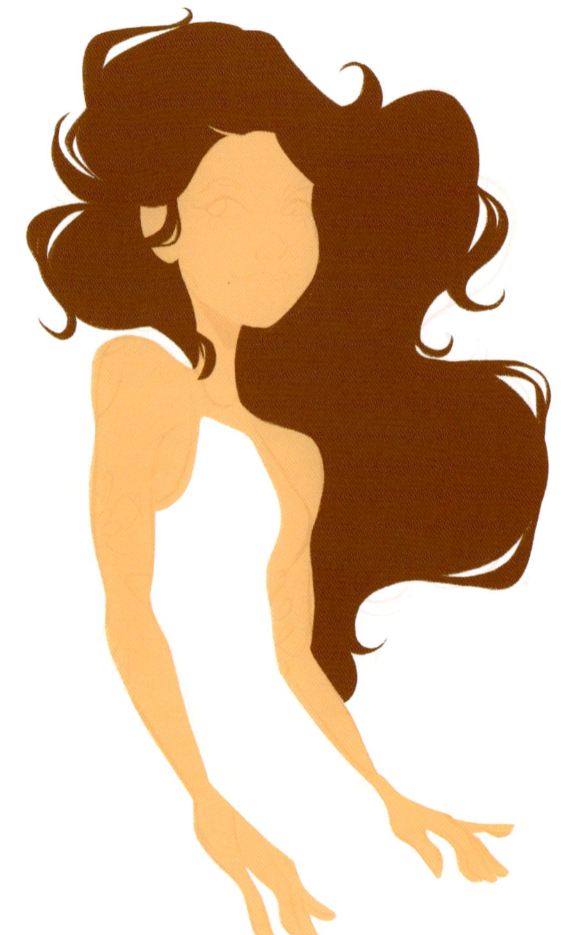

CLOTHES

The third thing I usually draw is the clothes. Just like the hair, you don't have to draw the exact outfit you did in your sketch. This is where I personally make the most changes in the process.

For this drawing, I chose a simple white dress because I want the focus to be on her hair and on the leaves, not on her clothes.

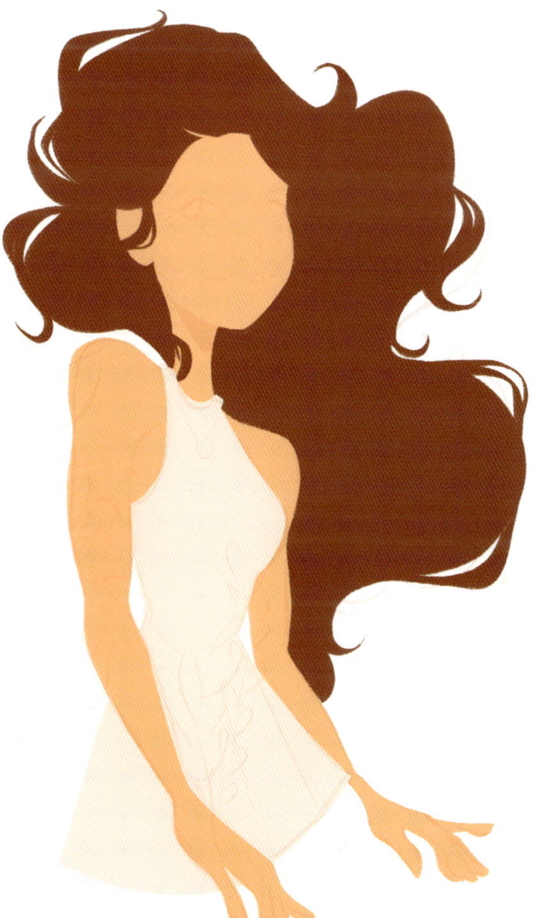

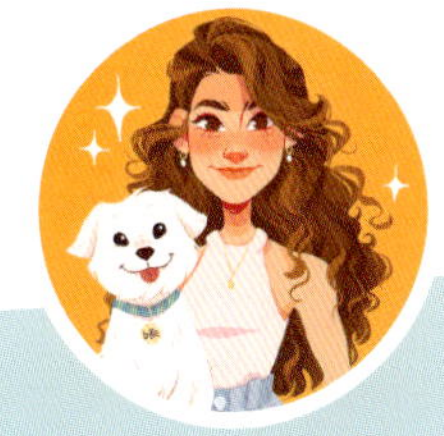

Nanda's Tips

- Clothes can bring some additional attention to your character. Sometimes it's good to have more detailed clothes full of color and with specific styles. Other times, if you want to emphasize the facial features and other characteristics, like the beauty of the hair, for example, you could draw more natural and simple clothes. It should always be in balance with the rest of your drawing.

- It can be difficult to see mistakes when I'm drawing with a lighter color on a white background, so I like to first draw in a darker color, or I change the background color to a darker one. The contrast makes it easier to see areas where I need to adjust or fill in.

- Always follow the shape of the body when you're drawing the clothes.

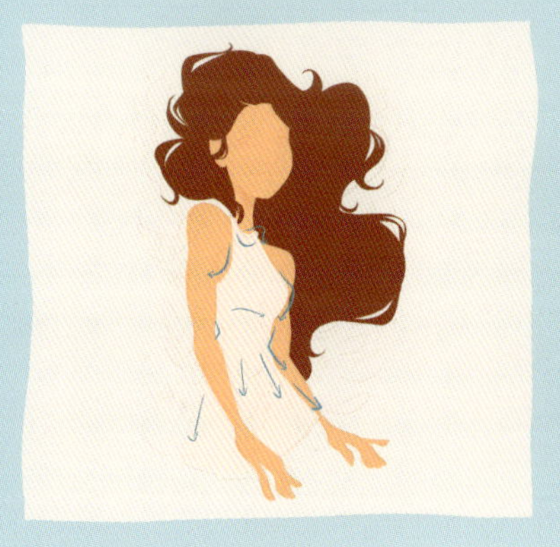

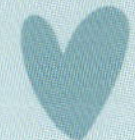

Facial Features

Now that you have the base colors and shapes on digital paper, you're going to add the facial features.

I usually create a layer for each facial feature (eyes, mouth, nose, eyelashes, and eyebrows), but remember to put them on top of all the other layers. How you're going to arrange the layers is another personal choice, but in my opinion, this is the best way to organize it.

When drawing the eyes, create a new layer for the iris that is going to be inside the layer that you did for the eye. In Procreate, for example, you can choose the option "Clipping Mask" and put it on top of the eye layer.

Remember that the same process applies to any art drawing software, which may have different names for these actions.

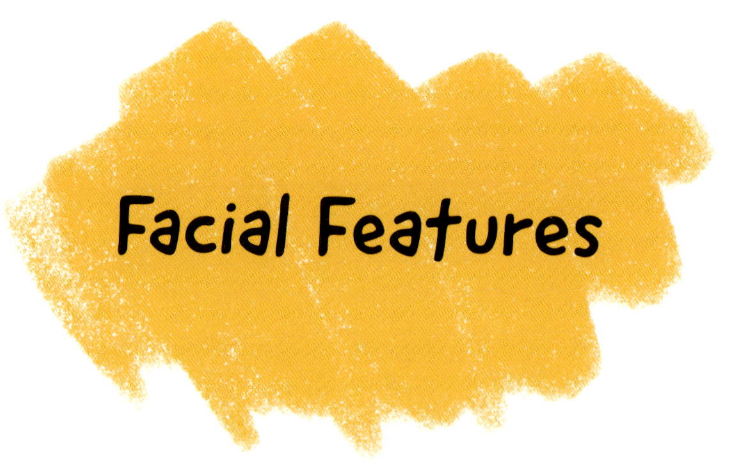

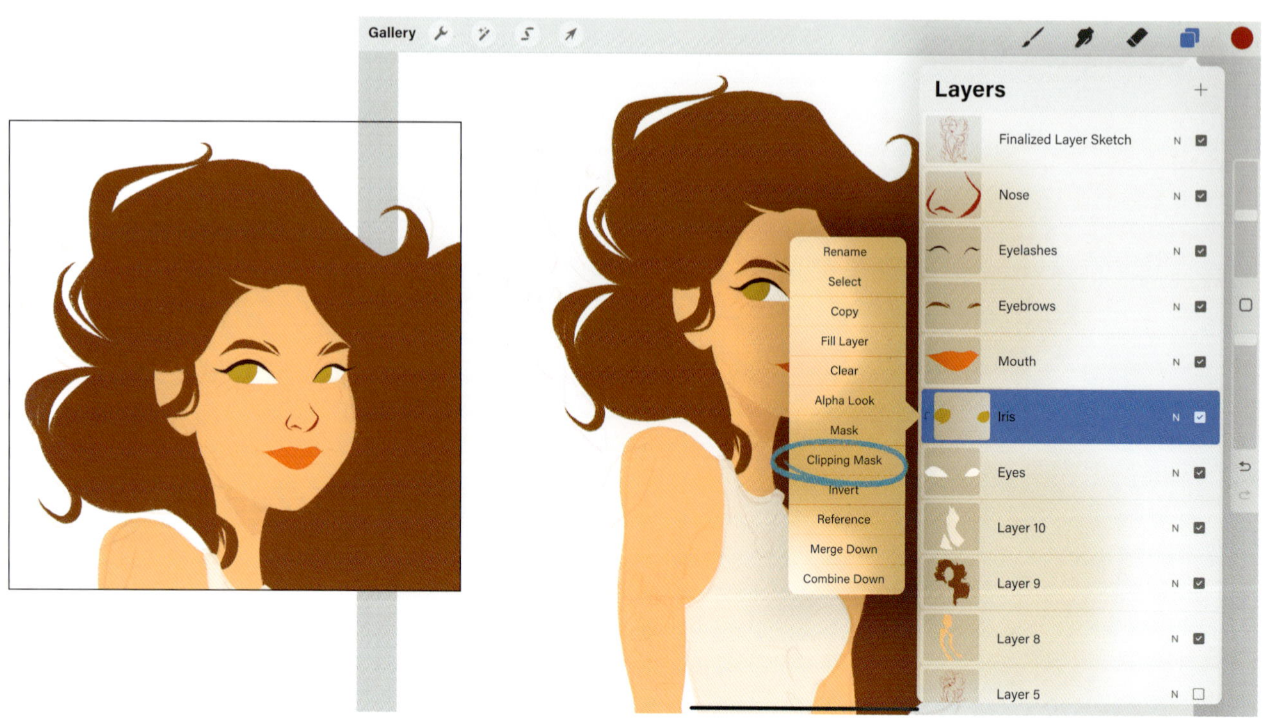

Adding Elements

In this case, the additional elements are the leaves and flowers, but they can change depending on the drawing. I like to add these extra elements after constructing the character because I have the reference for where to add them and freedom to change these elements if I want to.

Here I like to incorporate the elements into my character like they are in sync with each other—like they are one.

It isn't a problem to add some details in this step, so feel free to add whatever you want and perfect any small details you left behind in the previous steps.

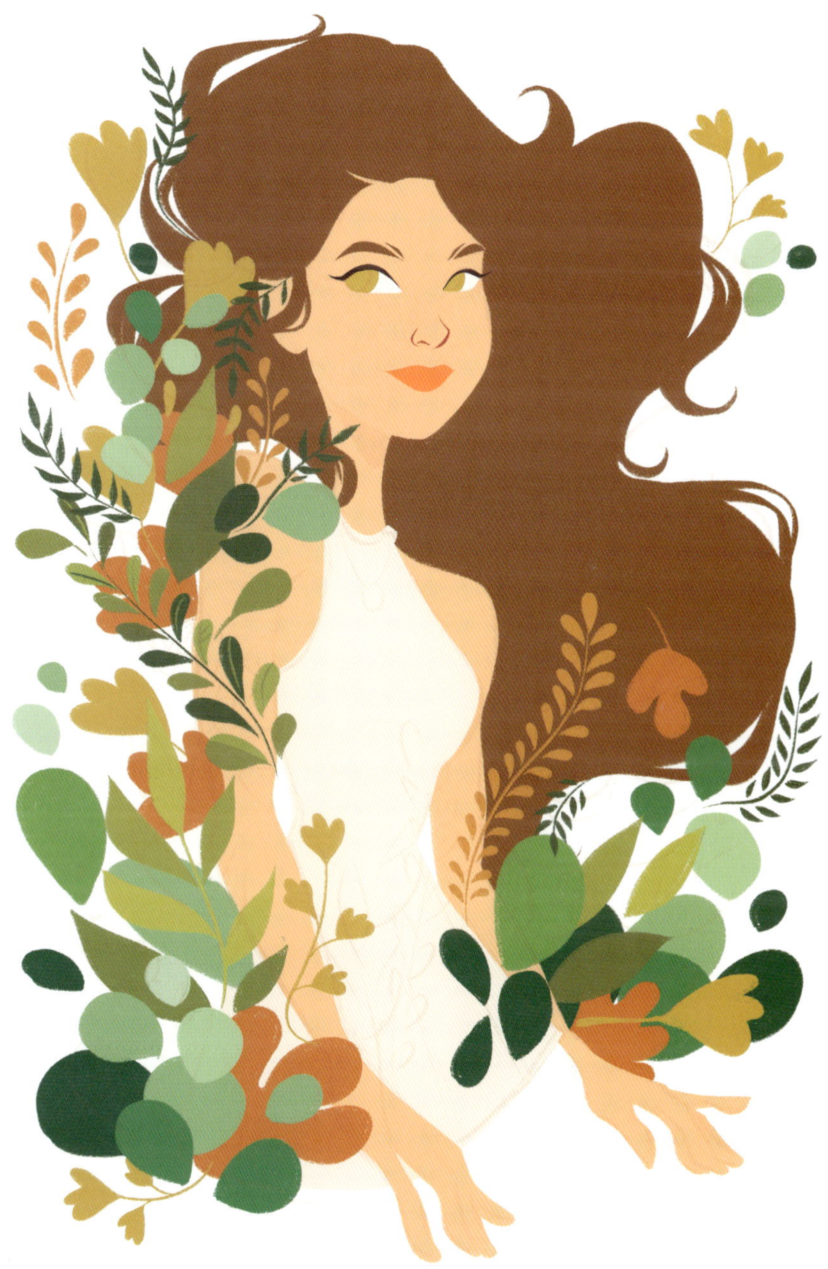

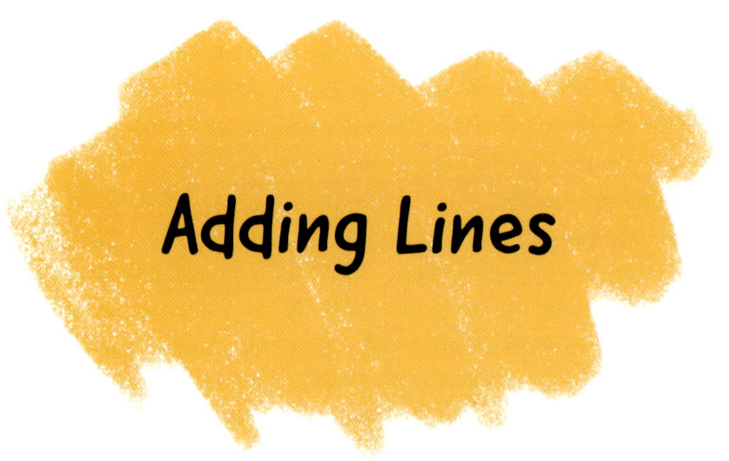

Adding Lines

Although my style is lineless, adding some lines to define shapes and the edges of your character is inevitable. It really depends on where they need to be added. Normally you will need to add lines where more finalization is required or to define a shape, like the fingers, or the division between the head and neck.

I also like to choose a really saturated and vibrant color for the lines that isn't black because other colors are visually more appealing and give some personality and style to your drawing.

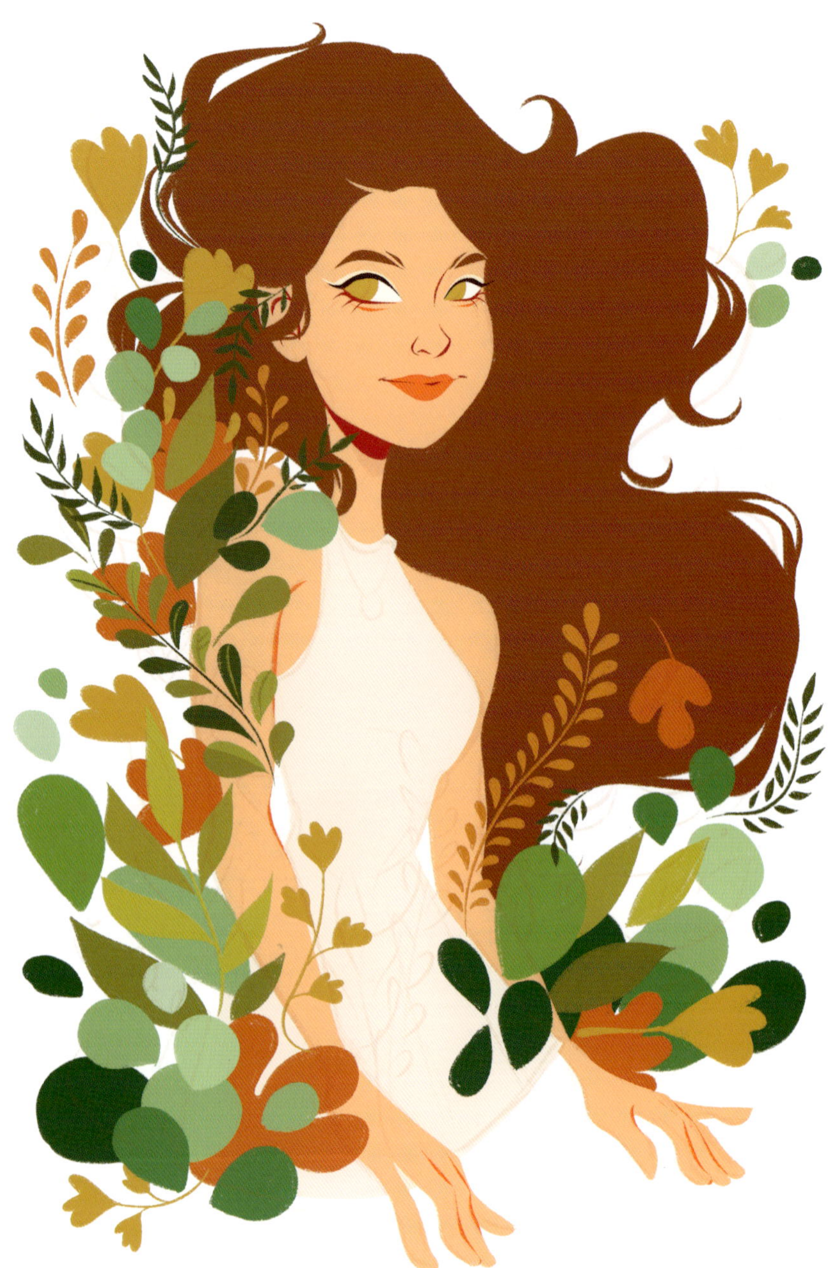

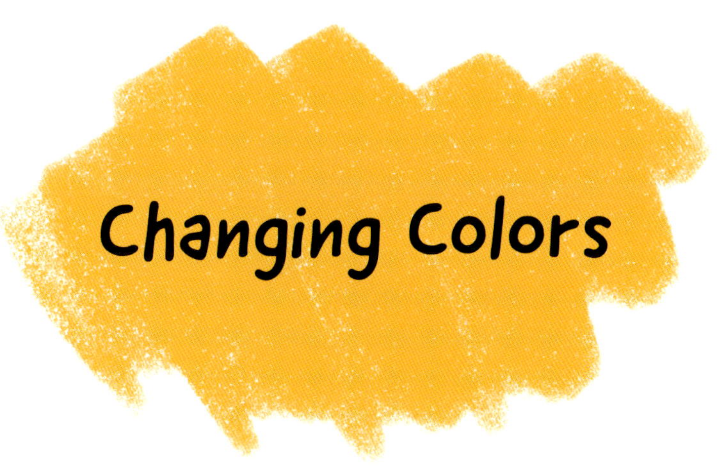

PHASE 1

I like to make the color a little bit more saturated and darker in some areas of the drawing, like the hands and elbows, to make it more realistic. In the image below, in relation to skin tones and considering the light and shadows, the hands and elbows are pinker (more saturated) than the arms. Another example is the cheeks, which would be more pink than the rest of the face.

This step is when I add the details to spice it up a bit.

As you've seen in previous sections, adding the lines helps you add the shadows and delimit where they are going to be. Here, you're going to go through each element and add the shadows and light. Choose the layer you are going to work on and lock it so you paint only inside that layer. In Procreate, I select the option "Alpha Lock" to lock the layer.

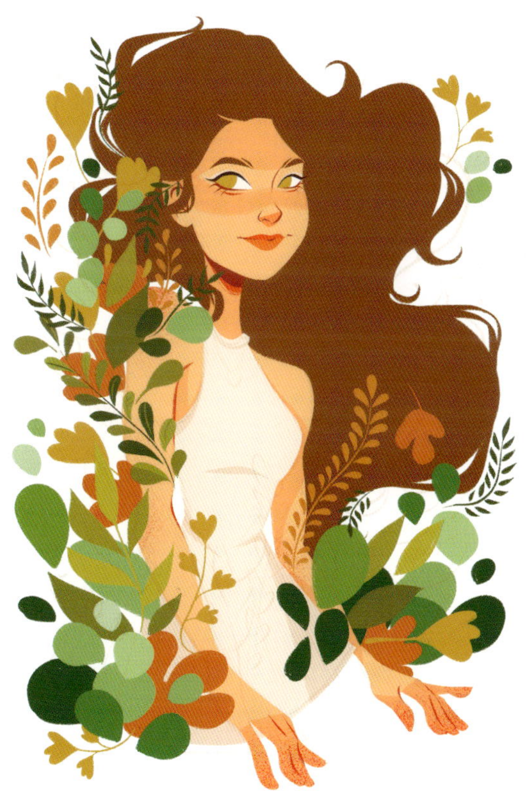

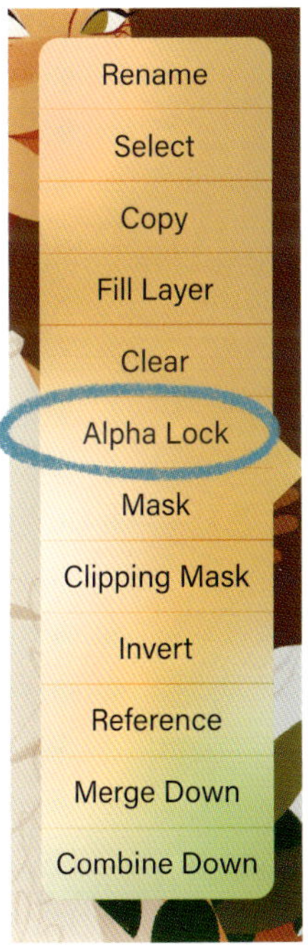

I normally use five to seven variations of the base color to create the shadows and lighting depending on where I want it to be darker or lighter. Give some space to your imagination here. Shadowing and lighting don't need to exactly match reality.

You can also use more than one brush to add some texture to your drawing.

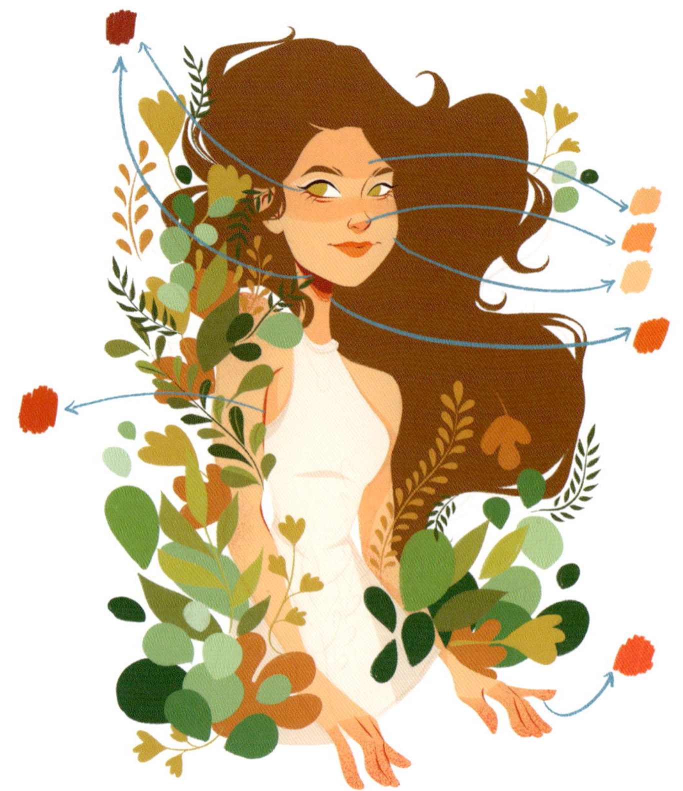

+ dark, saturated, and reddish/pink

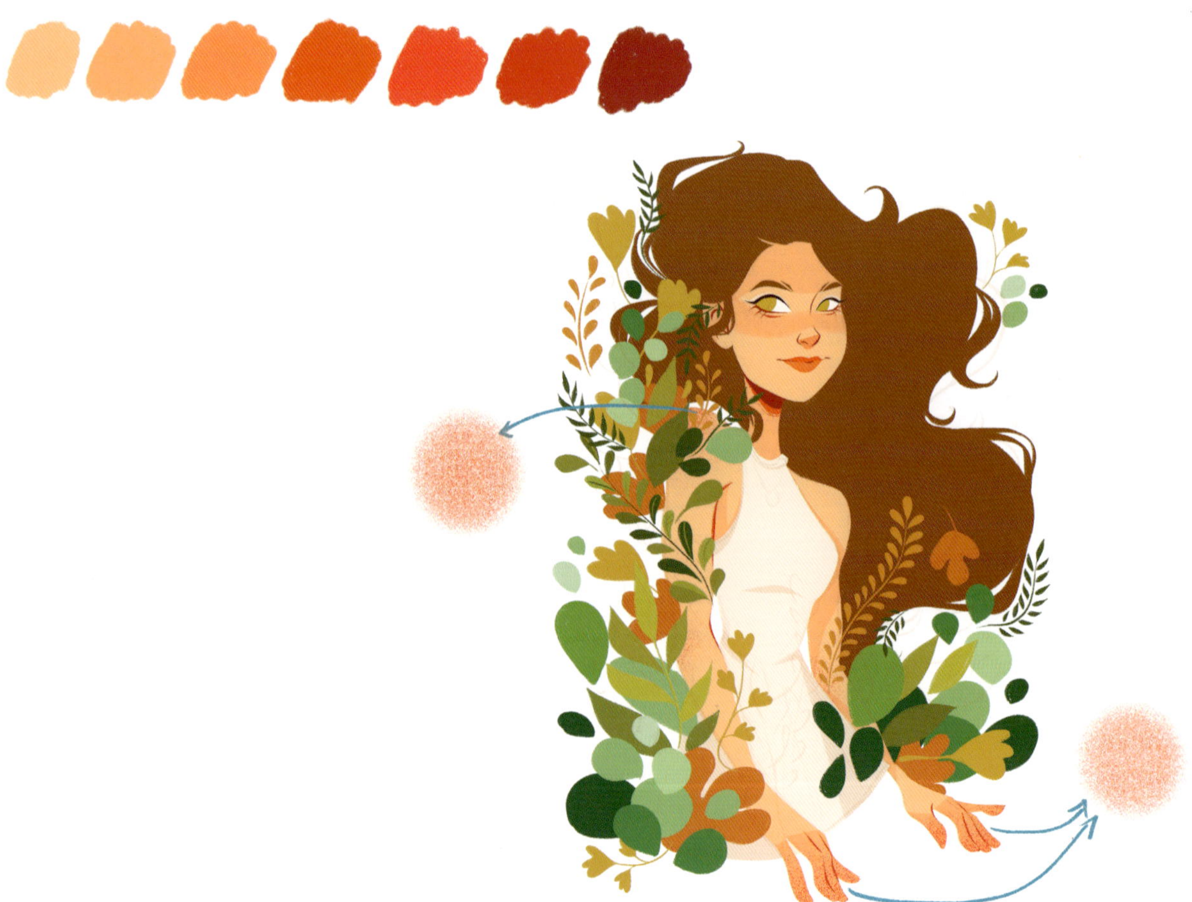

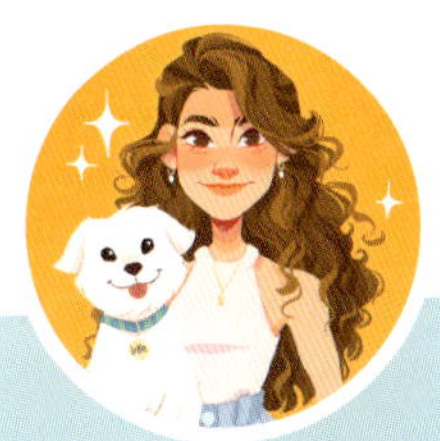

Nanda's Tip

When adding shadows, pick up the base color, and make it a little darker and more saturated. Don't make it more gray because this will make your drawing less vivid and colorful.

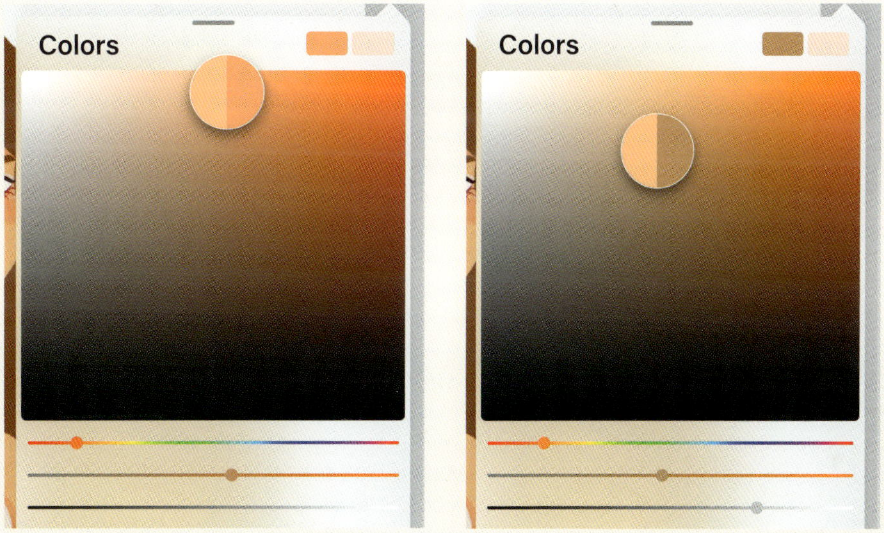

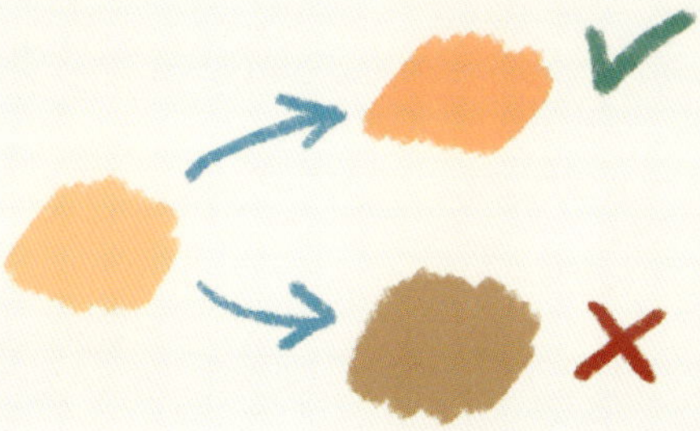

ADDING SHADOWS AND LIGHT

To understand where it makes sense to place the shadow, try to imagine that there's a spotlight pointing at your drawing, and visualize where the shadows would be formed. If you need to use a reference photo, or even take a picture of yourself with a spotlight pointing from a certain direction, do it. Use every resource that you have available.

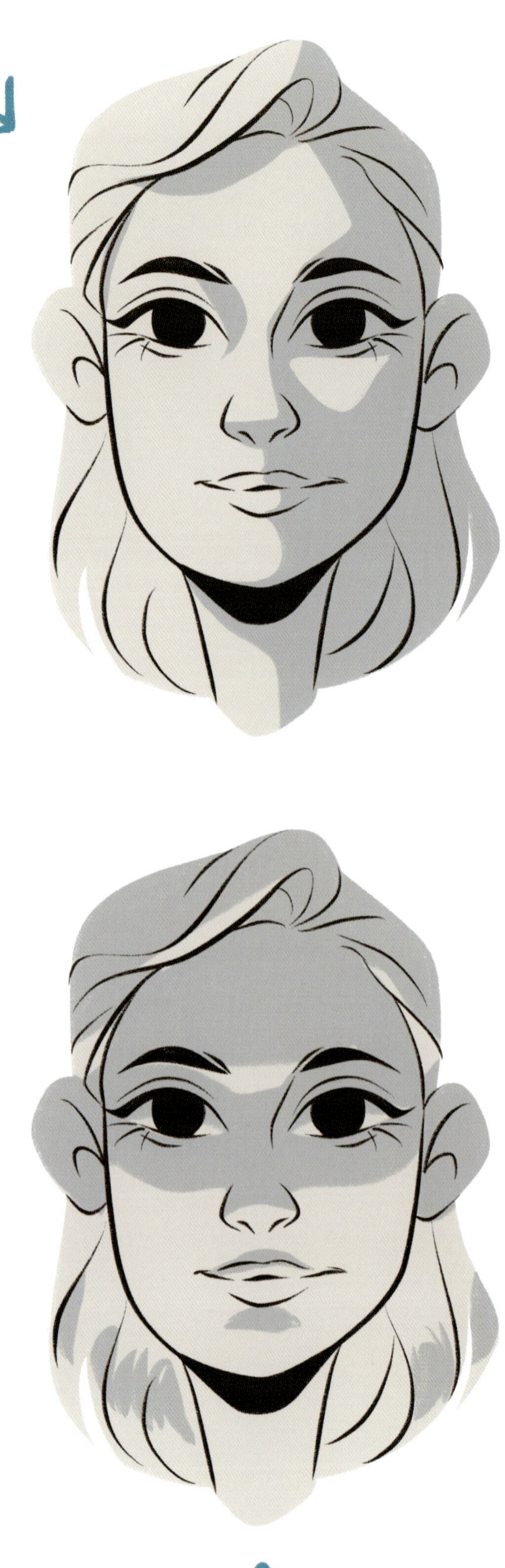

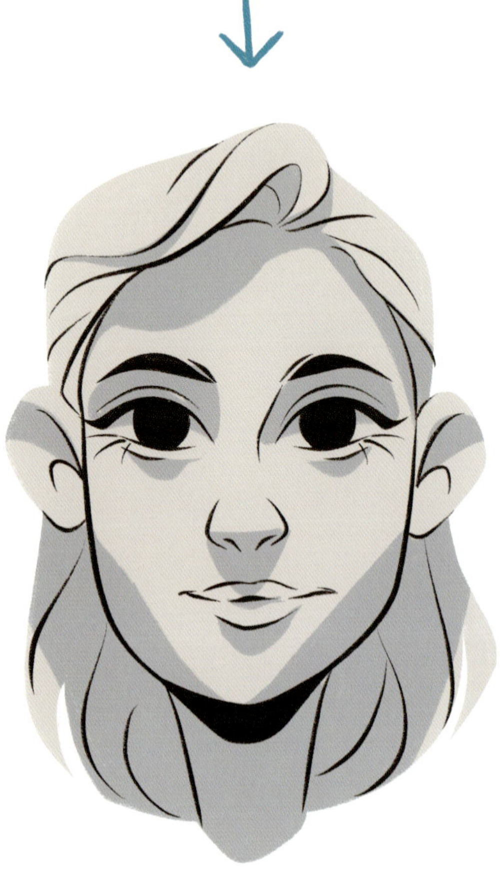

PHASE 2

I like to add an extra phase to the shadowing part: I add a new layer on top of where I want to have a shadow, choose the option "Multiply" in Procreate (which makes all the colors below that layer darker and with a background of the color you chose for your Multiply layer), and add some extra shading in places where I believe it's needed. This gives the drawing more depth and value.

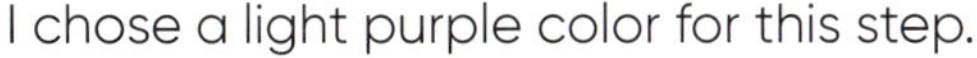

I chose a light purple color for this step.

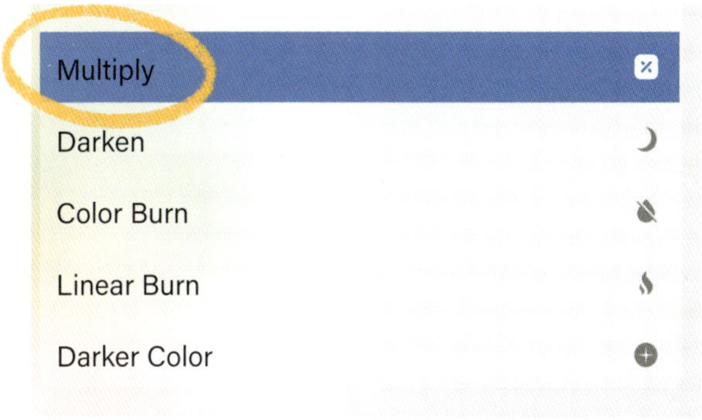

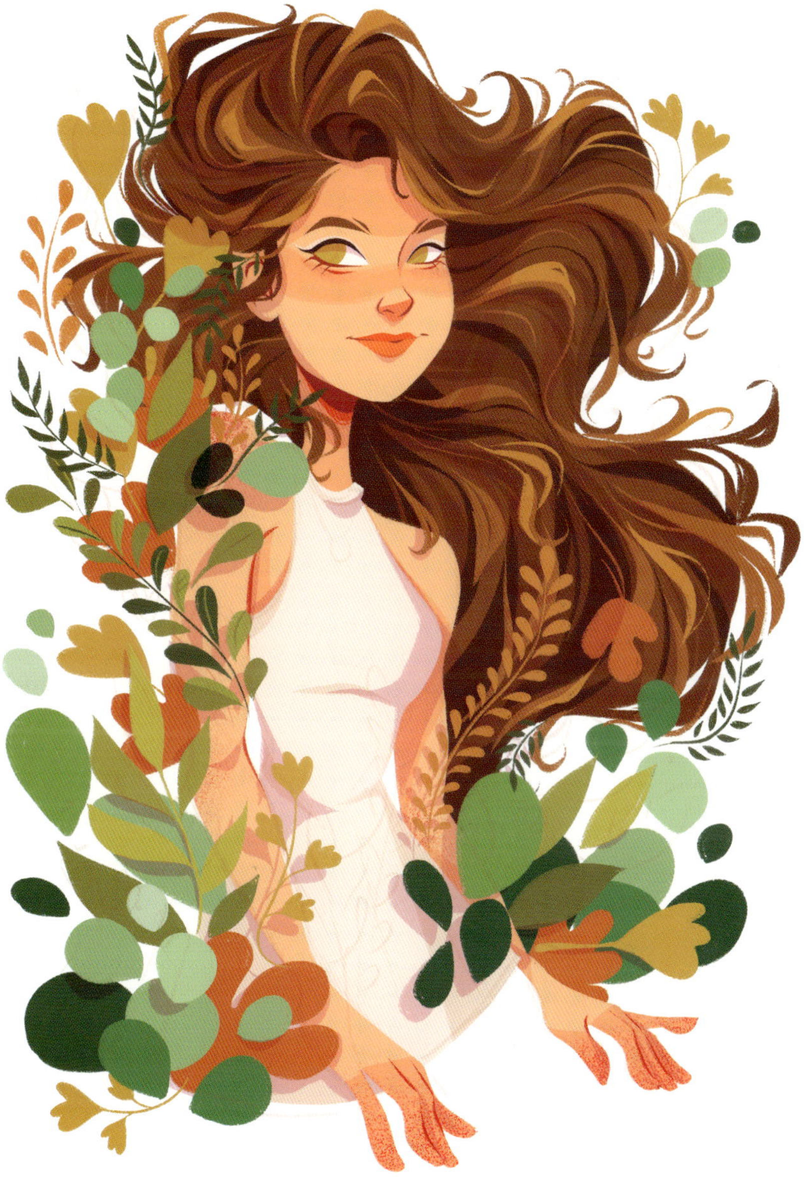

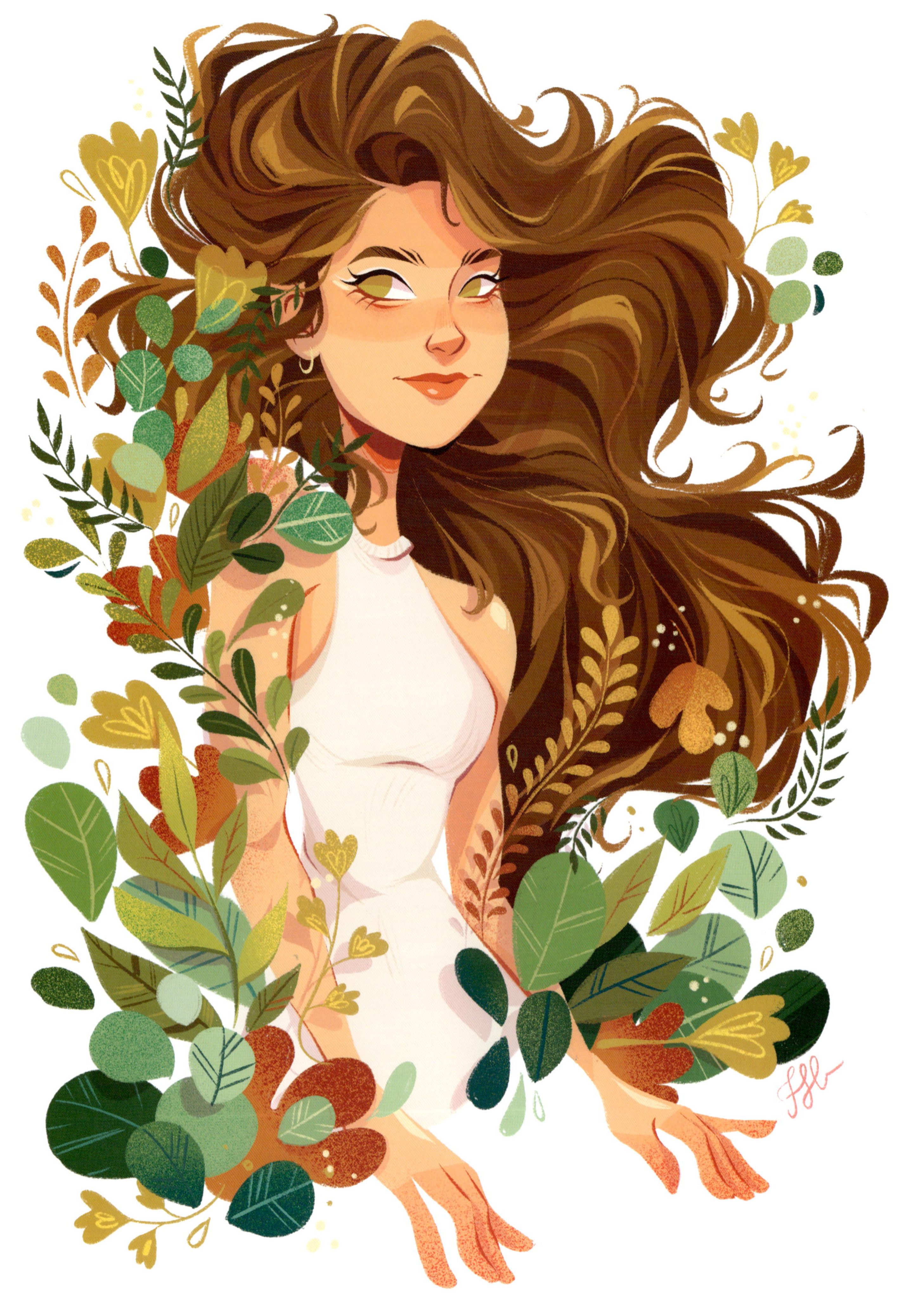

DETAILS AND FINAL TOUCHES

Now that your drawing has almost everything done, you're going to add the last details and changes to take your artwork to the next level.

First, hide the defined lines layer. After this point, you won't have any more of the sketch layers left, which will help you better see where you need to correct and add more details.

Use different brushes, correct the colors, and let your creativity run free at this point.

I like to say that this step is what differentiates the good-quality art from regular art. Sometimes artists skip this step, or they finalize their art in a kind of lazy way. So don't be lazy here. Correct any last mistakes that you need to correct, and add the details that you need to add.

If you need to take a break and finish it later, do it. Don't try to rush this stage and end up not doing your best. Take your time and give the needed attention to this step.

On the other hand, try not to lose yourself in the details. Too many details can mean a drawing has too much information, and the viewer doesn't know where to look. If your drawing doesn't seem to have much to add to it at this step, don't feel obligated to add more stuff just because. Balance is the secret of this part. It's important to know where to stop.

BACKGROUND COLOR

I like to choose the background color of my illustration when I have my character completed because I want the viewer's attention to go to my character, not to the background (if this is a plain background kind of drawing). So I want to choose a color that will enhance the drawing and make it stand out. I want the color to help the character stay the center of attention.

In this case, I ended up leaving the background white.

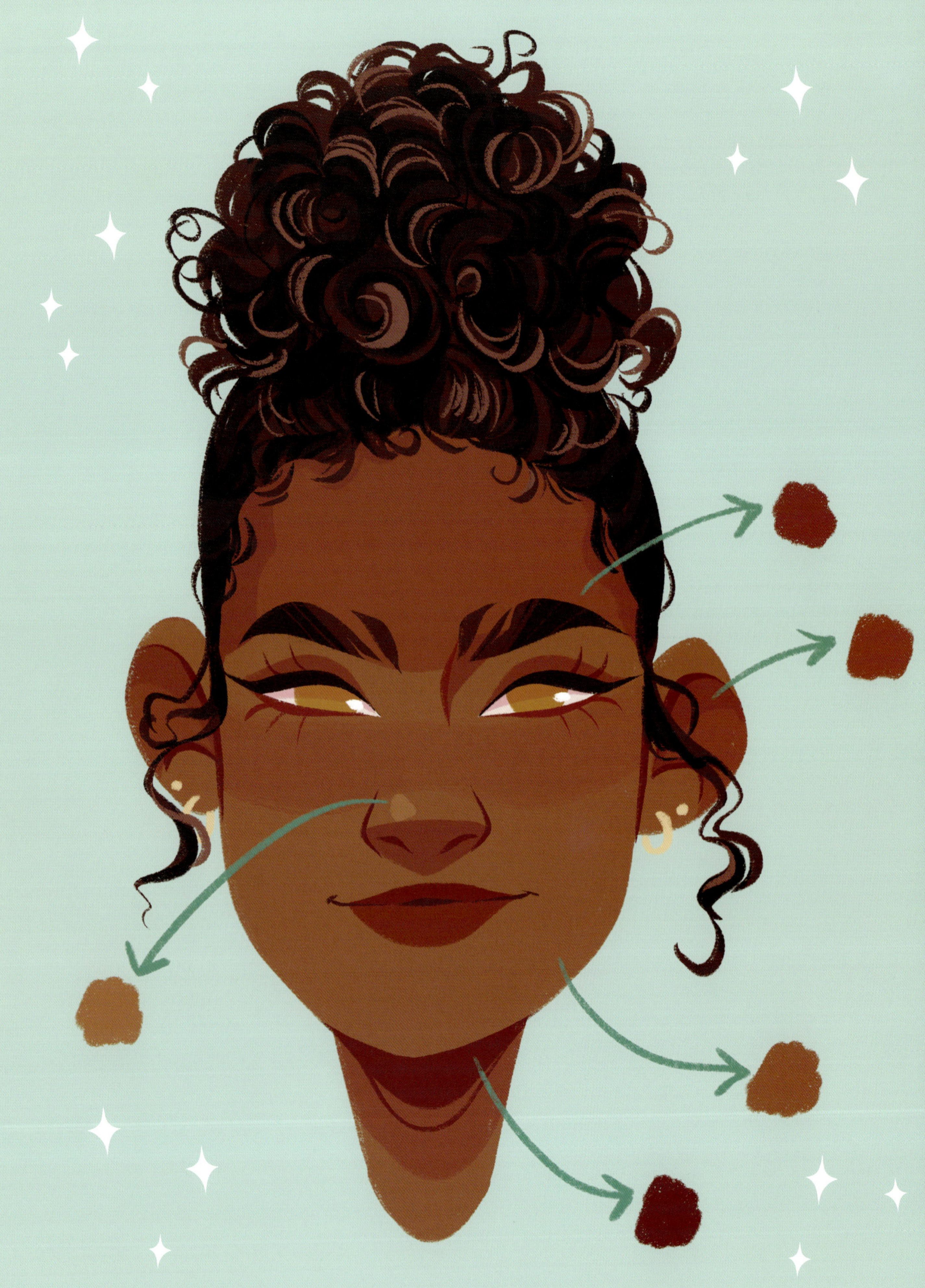

CHAPTER 5

Final Tips

In this last chapter, I have gathered some final tips about various topics that every artist should know to improve their art.

You will take a look at concepts such as complementary colors, hue, saturation and brightness, the color wheel, color selection, and many other useful techniques.

Finally, I'll cover the importance and relevance of practicing for each and every artist, as well as some tips on where to add details in your drawings.

Stay safe and keep art alive!

Color

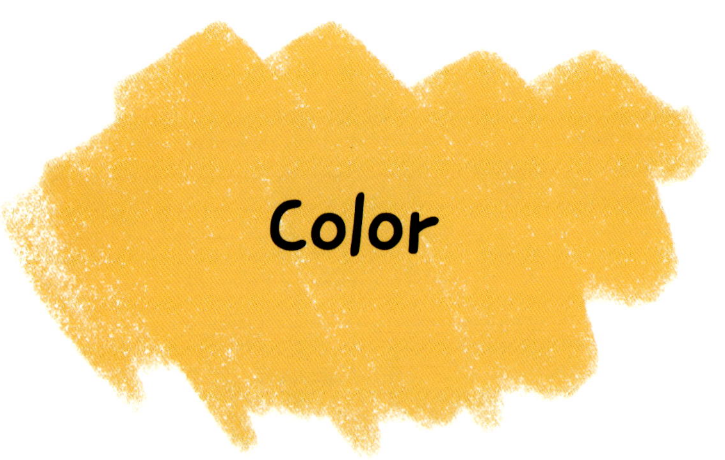

There is no doubt that color is an important element in every drawing. You can change the mood and personality of your drawing just by changing the color of the features and details of your character, the background, and so on. Knowing which color you are going to use is a really important step that will heavily influence the result of your drawing. In this section, I'm going to share some quick tips that will help you choose the colors of your drawing to create a character with harmony and color balance.

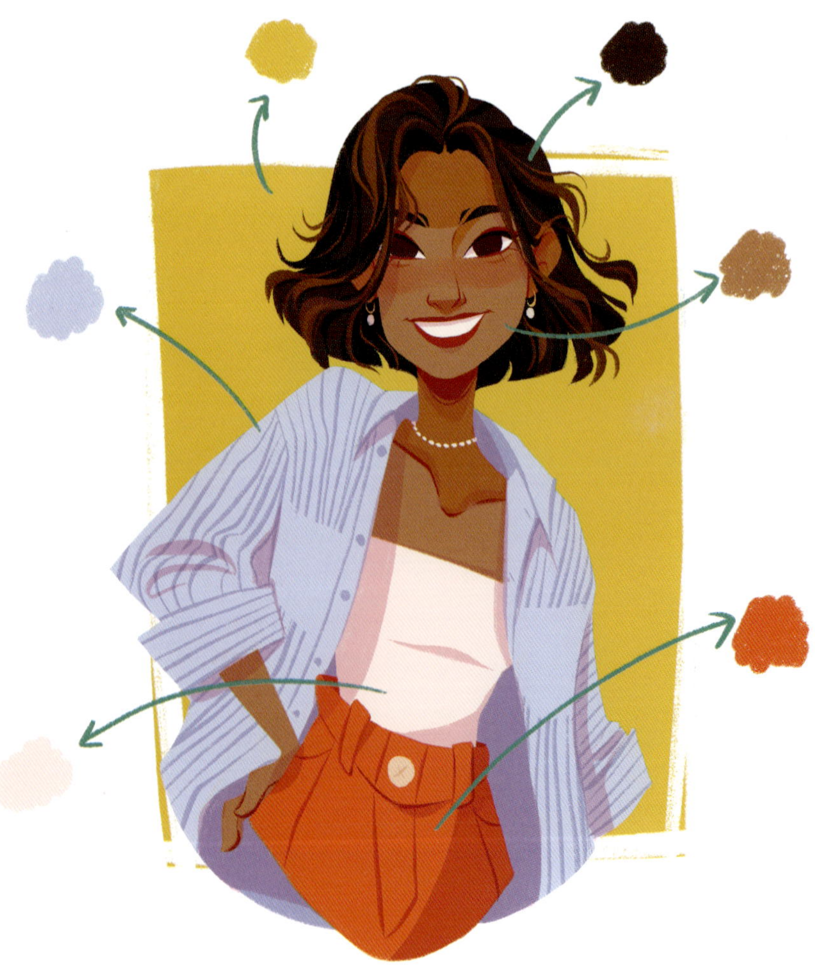

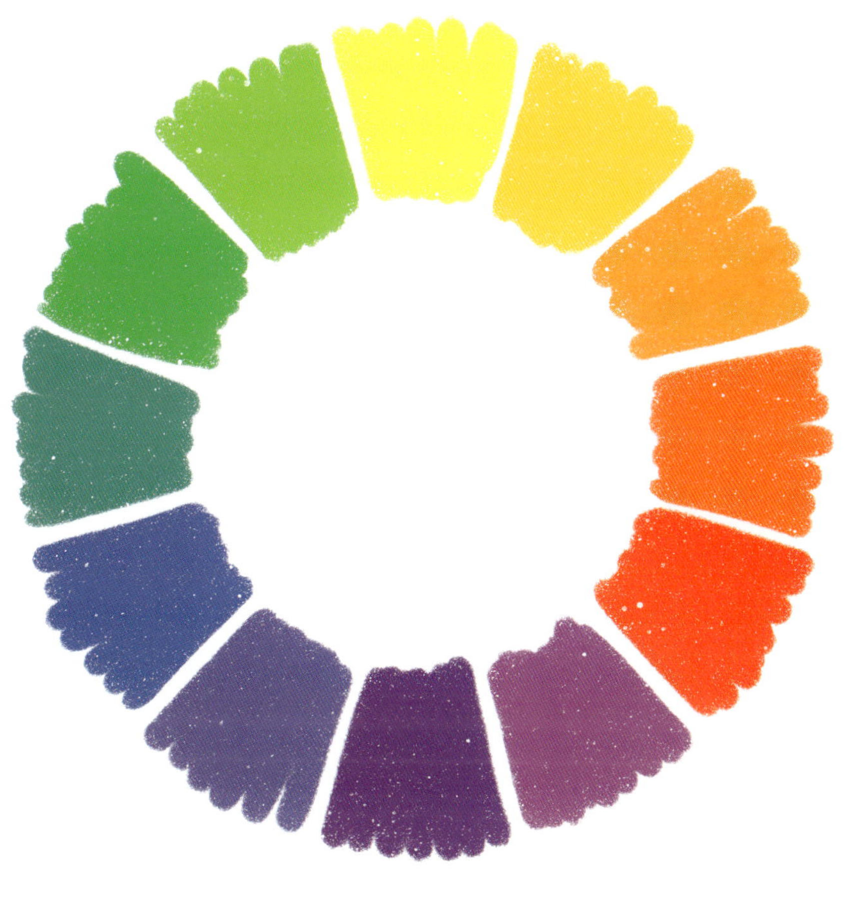

COLOR WHEEL

Before discussing my tips about choosing the colors for your drawing, I'm going to briefly talk about the color wheel, which is a tool that every artist should have an idea of how to use. It is very useful when picking colors.

The color wheel shows how colors work together and can help you identify combinations of colors and visualize how they look. Color theory is an extensive topic, but the focus of this book is on creating characters in a dynamic way. So, what I want to focus on is how you can use the color wheel as a tool, to create visually appealing and harmonic characters, with colors that work well together.

HUE, SATURATION, AND BRIGHTNESS

Before we go any further, it is important to know the difference between hue, saturation, and brightness. Hue is the color itself, saturation is the purity and intensity of the hue, and brightness is the intensity of black or white that is mixed with the hue.

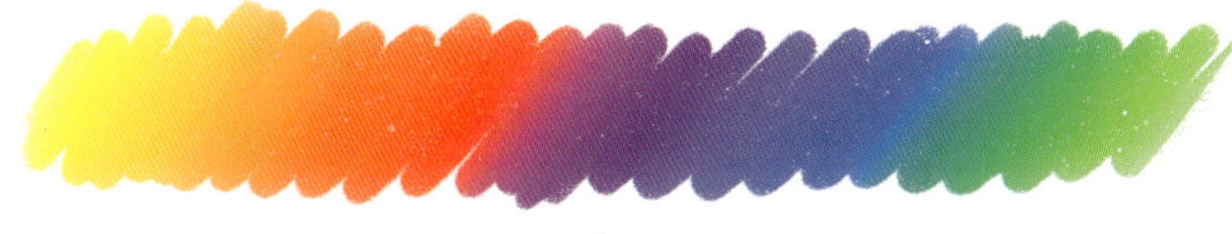

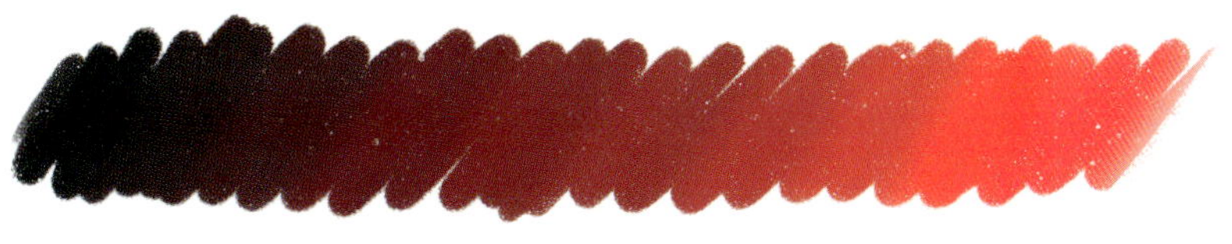

COLOR COMBINATIONS

There are unending color combinations that you can do using the color wheel. I'm going to show my three favorite ways to combine color that I use when choosing the background, the skin tone, and so on.

1. Complementary Colors

A complementary color is one that is exactly on the opposite side of the wheel from another. For example, when I want my character to stand out from the background but still need both the character and background to be colorful, I choose the complementary color from the color that appears most in my character for the background. Here is an example (below).

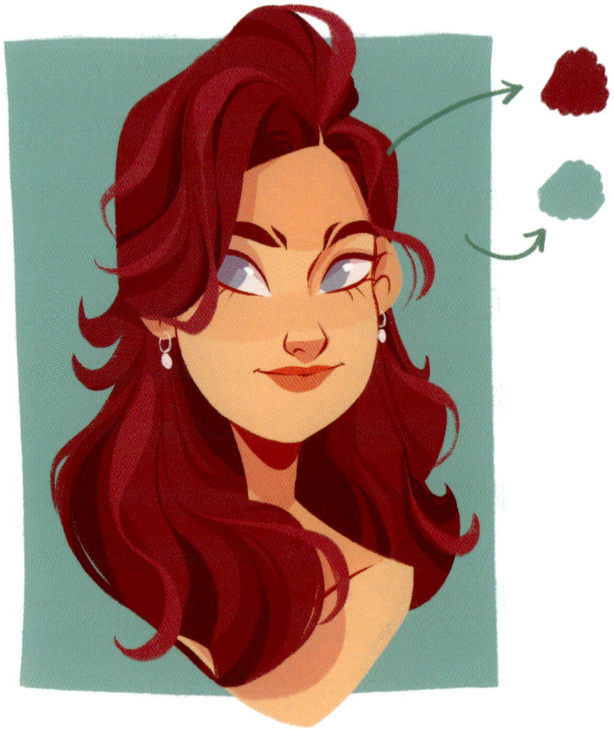

For the complementary color on the background in this one, I only changed the brightness and saturation a bit:

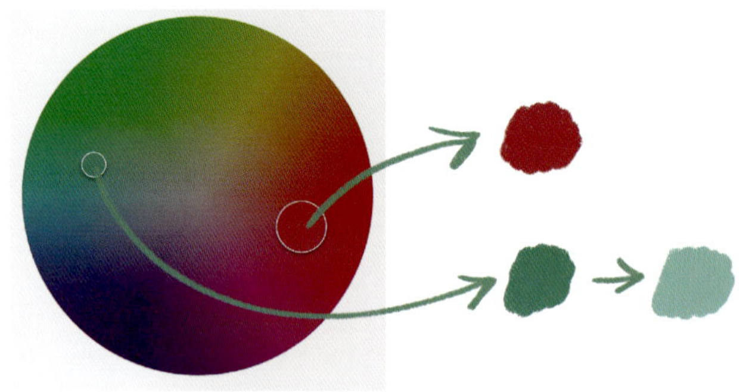

Here are some ideas of other complementary color combinations.

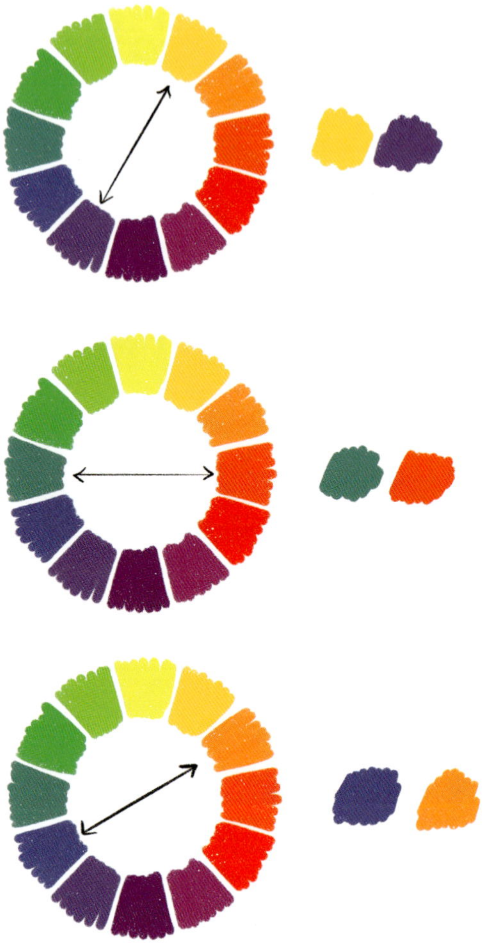

2. Analogous Colors

Analogous colors are groups of colors that are next to each other, side by side on the color wheel. They are a very helpful tool for creating a harmonic character. There are a lot of different combinations you can make using analogous colors.

You may also change the brightness and saturation of each color if you want to!

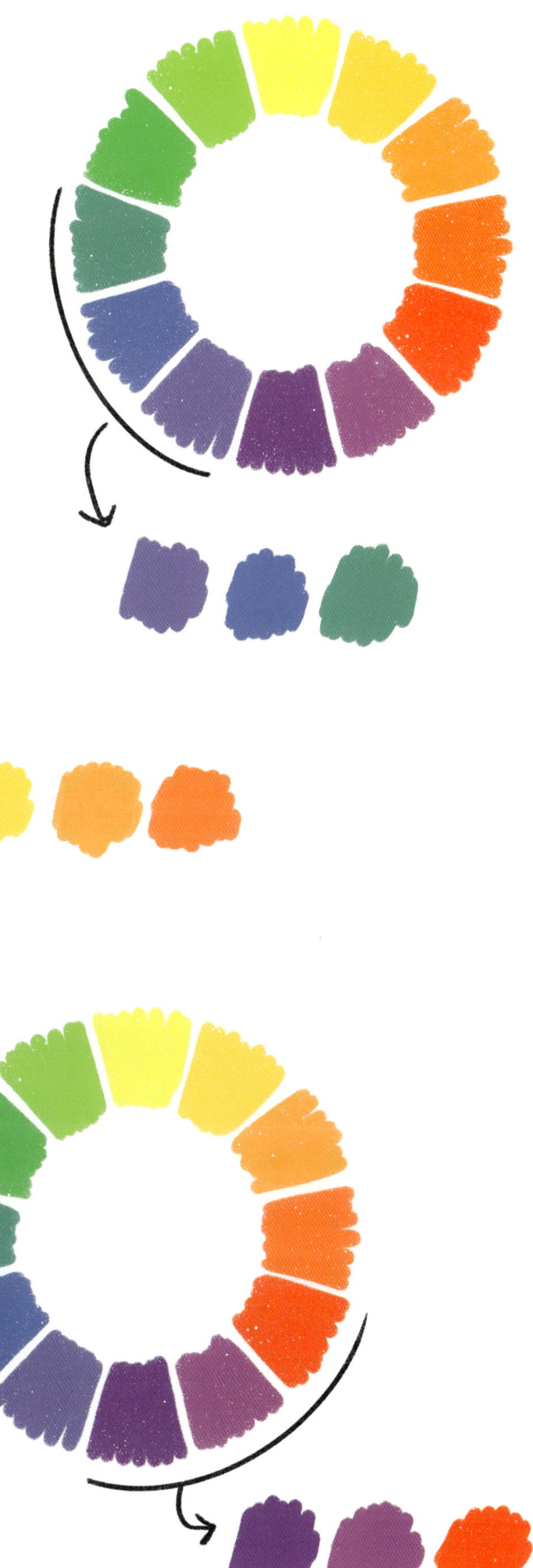

3. Monochromatic Colors

In a monochromatic color combination, you keep the hue the same but make variations of that same color, changing the brightness and saturation.

   In this image to the right, I made all these colors using the same hue and only changed the saturation and brightness. All these color tones are from the same hue, so there's a variety of combinations you can make with the same hue.

   Color combinations are a very extensive topic. I only briefly went through it, but remember that there are unlimited color combinations. Experiment with the color wheel, and don't be afraid to make mistakes and try different styles. Use a color wheel as a tool, but always let your creativity flow.

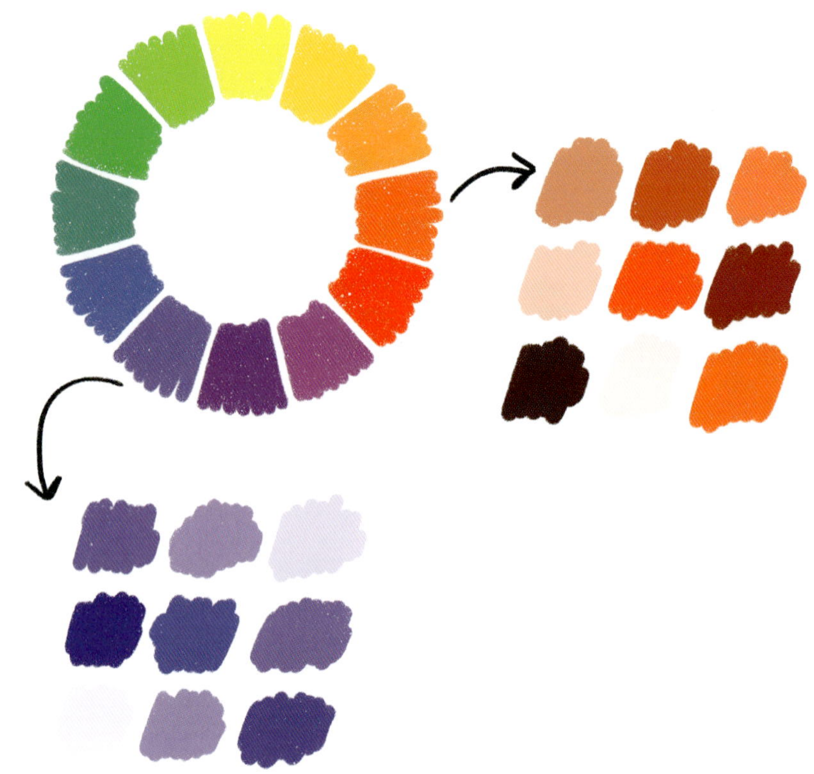

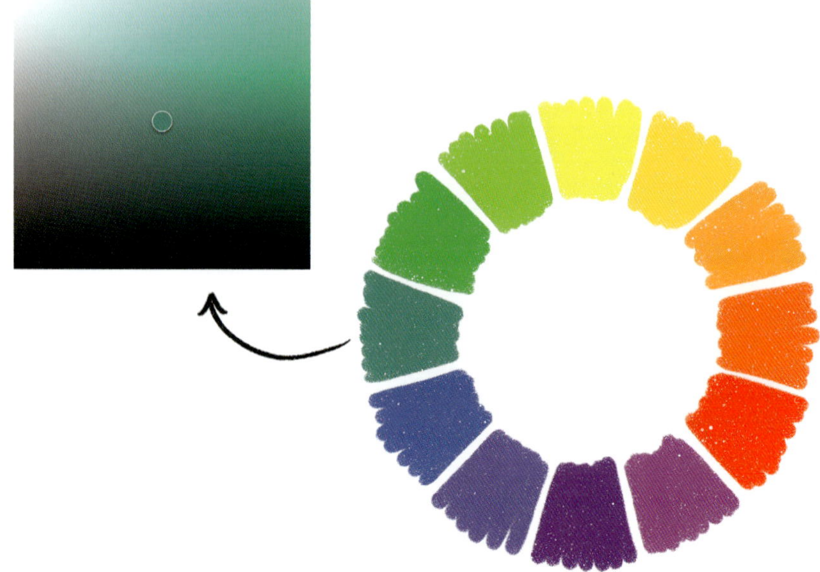

SKIN TONE

When choosing the skin tone of my character, as well as shadows and highlights, an important tip is to not only change the brightness and darkness of the midtone but also change a little bit of the hue and its saturation. This gives personality and life to the drawing and helps create a more vivid character.

As you can see from the colors on the right side, the hues are different from each other, and I just changed the saturation and brightness of each one. Doing this will give you different "background colors" in your drawing.

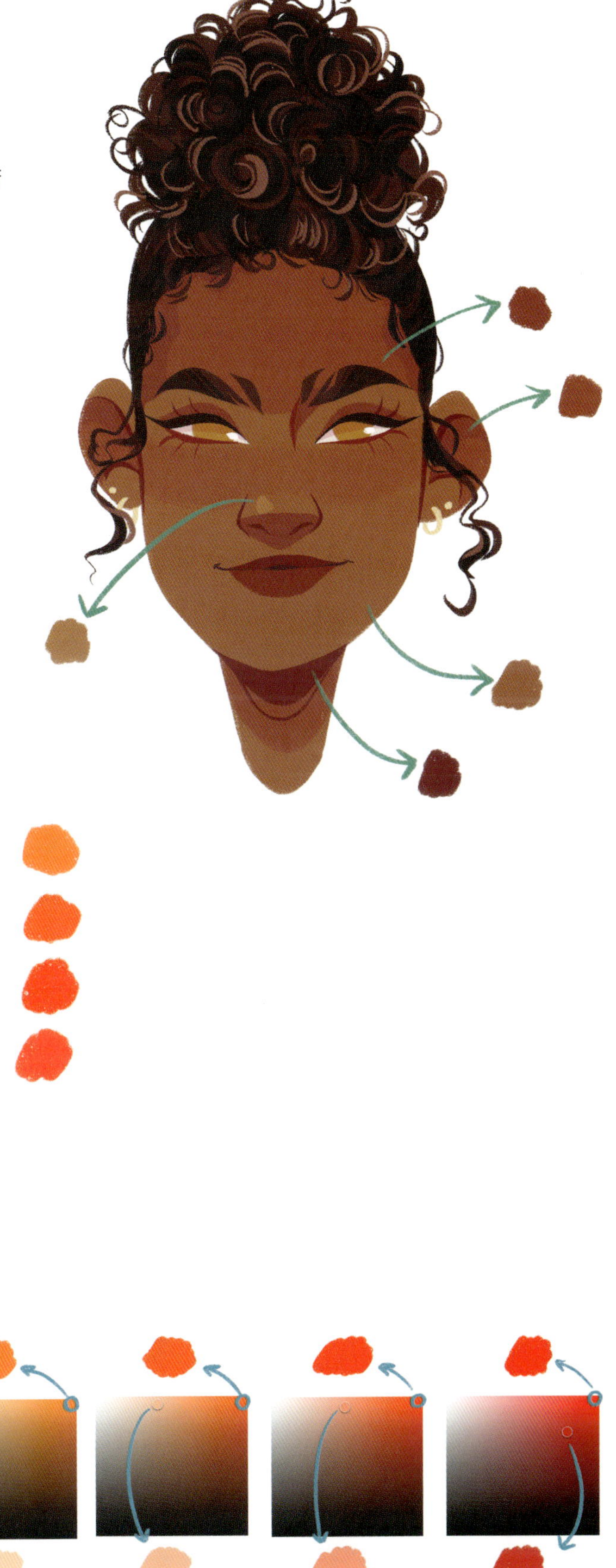

EXPERIMENT WITH COLOR

If you are indecisive about what color to choose when drawing a character, you can always make color thumbnails to help you choose the color and visualize what colors are going to work well with each other.

Also, be creative, and add colors that you don't visually see in the reference photo—it will add an artistic touch to your drawing. Always be creative during the process of your drawing. You don't need to always stick to the rules. Be original, and let your imagination flow!

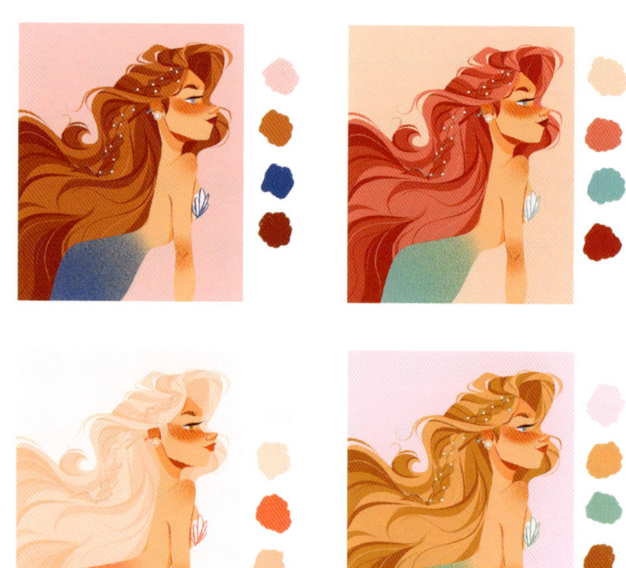

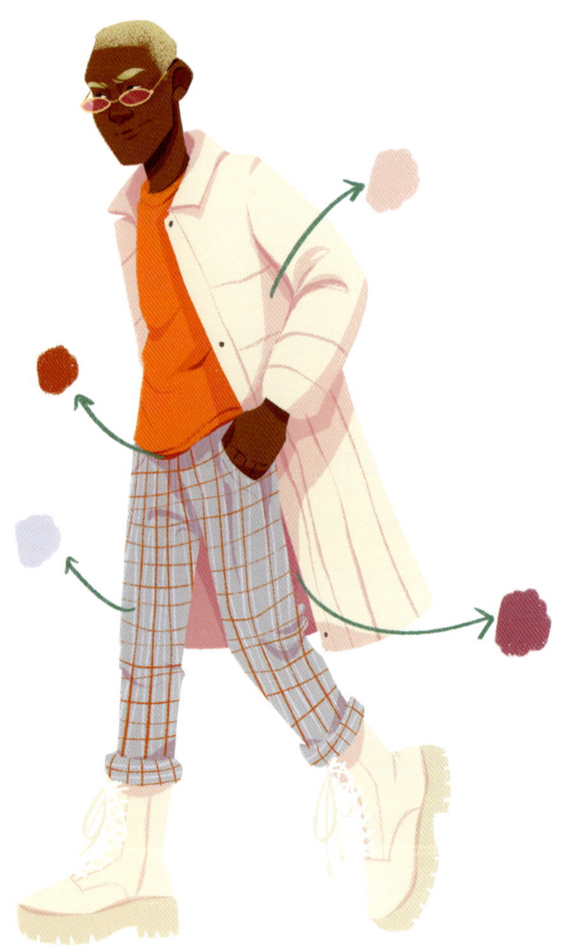

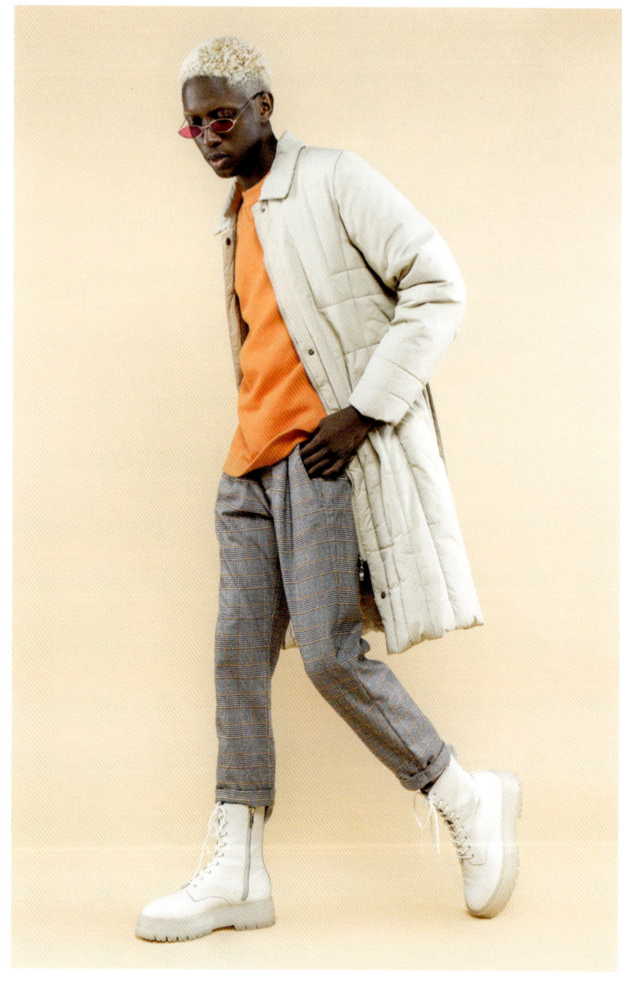

The Importance of Practicing

Practicing is something that every artist should do. I know that sometimes you just want to achieve that result quickly. Or you want to learn how to draw using different materials or in a different style, but thinking that you must practice and practice and practice sometimes demotivates you from that goal. I can guarantee you that no artist has ever achieved their level of knowledge and skill without practice.

So since you can't run from having to practice, you can find a way to make it fun and pleasurable. Practicing is not something you should be afraid of. It is something you should be happy about because it is what is going to get you to that level of art you want to achieve. I would never be where I am now with my art if I hadn't practiced a lot. And I still do. Practicing is important to improving your skills and is a place where you can trial and error as much as you want. Sketching, for example, is a form of practice you can use to help improve your artistic skills. Like I said in the sketching section, sketching gives you the opportunity to try new things without having the pressure of making them perfect.

Enjoy the process of trying, practicing, and perfecting your skills. Don't be afraid of trying new things, and let your creativity flow!

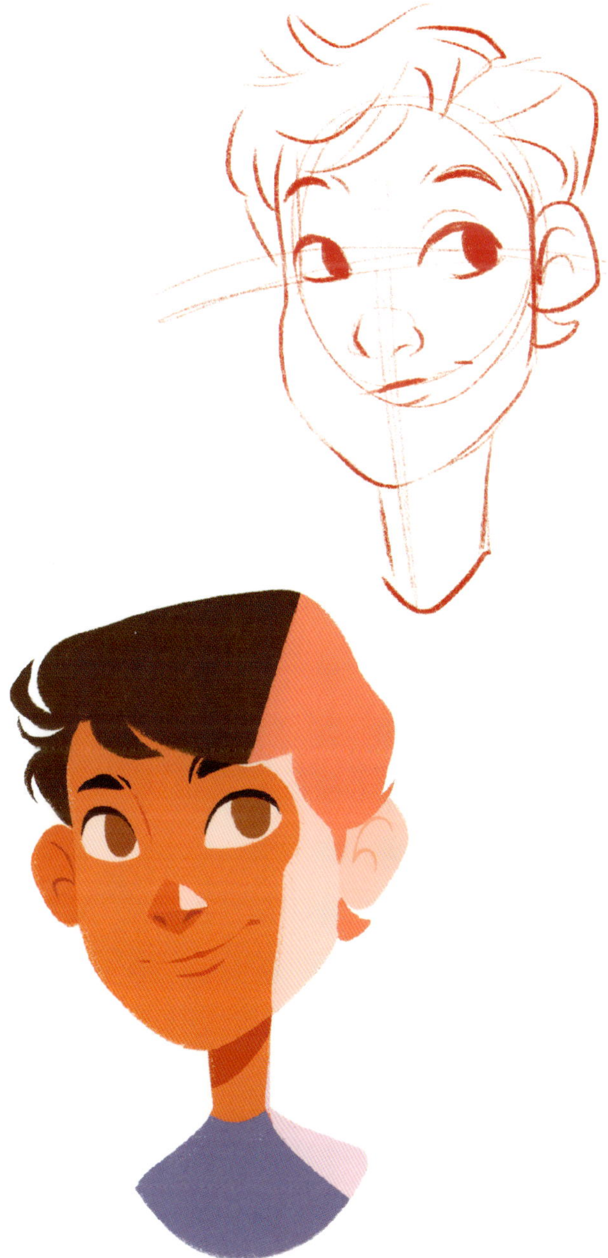

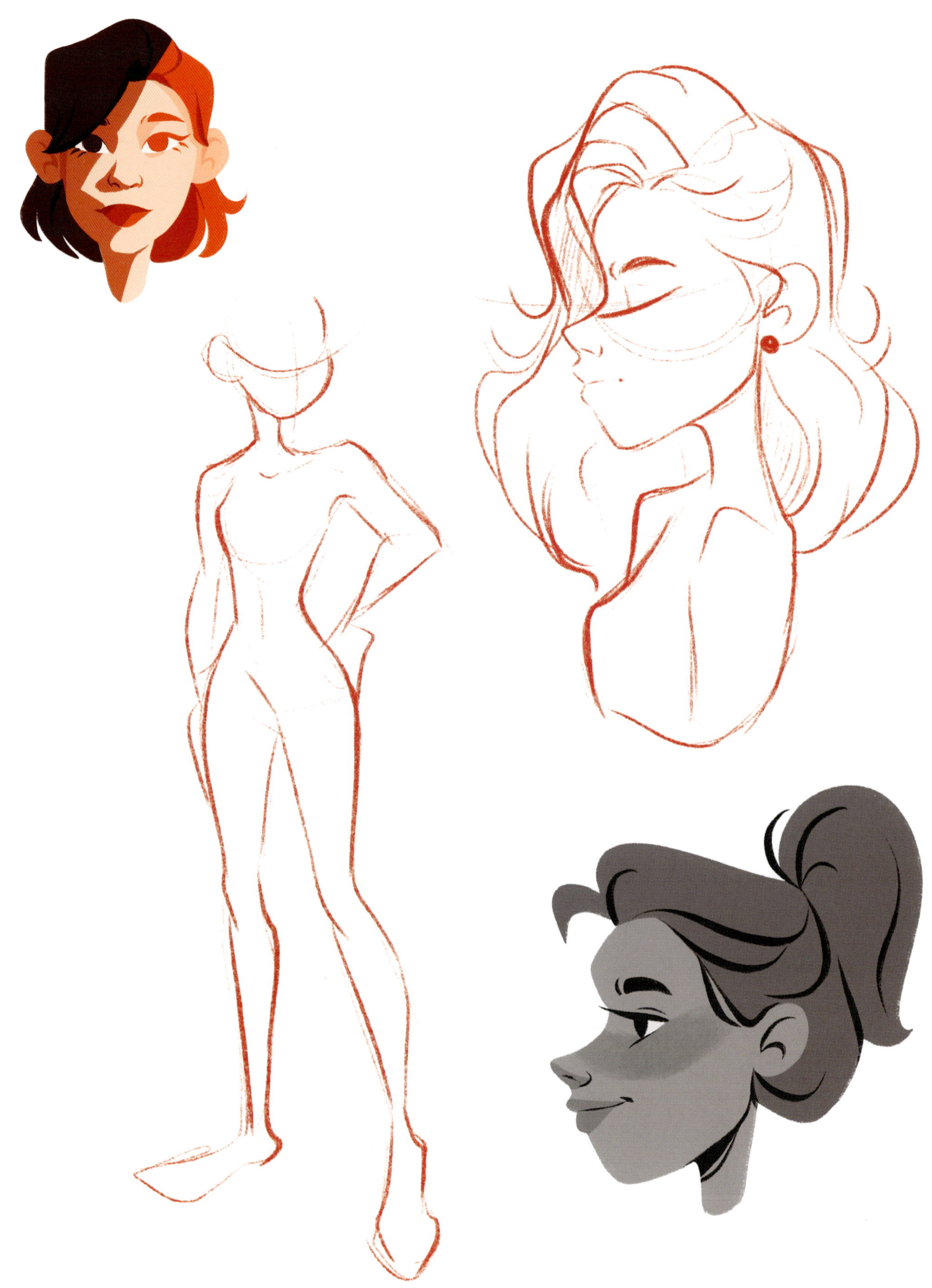

Where to Add Details

A lot of artists tend to add more details than they should, making the drawing busy, with a lot of information to process. Knowing where to add details is an important skill to develop so viewers focus their attention on the things you want and don't look at unnecessary details.

To emphasize some areas and features of your character, you can use a few techniques.

First of all, you can make the areas you want to draw more attention to a more saturated color.

As you can see, I've added more emphasis to the eyelashes, just by changing their color, making them more saturated and colorful.

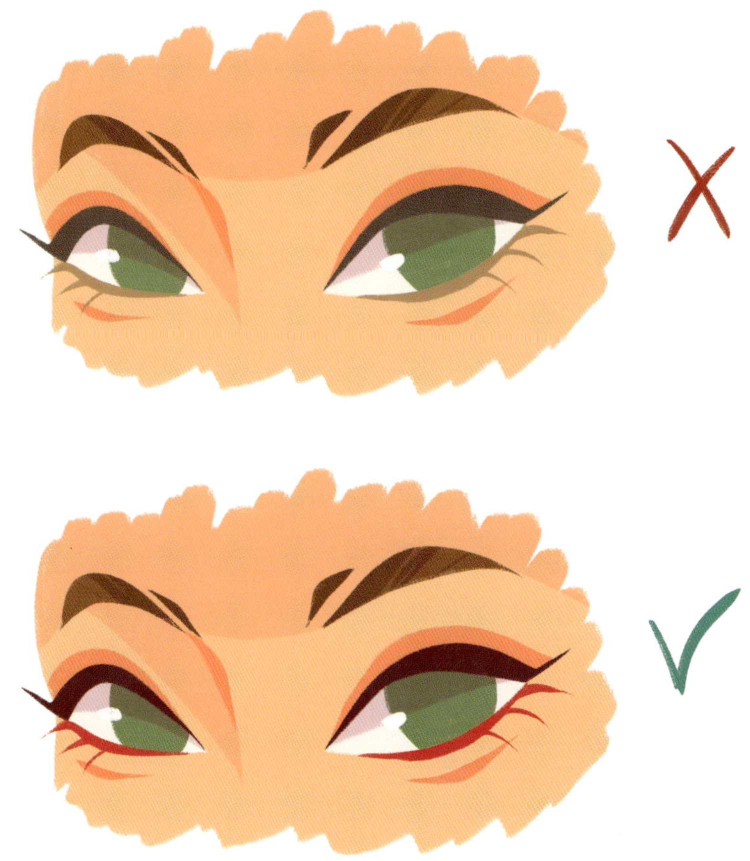

Another way to make some areas of your drawing more detailed is to thicken a few edges and parts of the line strokes you make while drawing. Do this by applying more pressure sometimes in just a few areas while making the brushstroke. This will make your drawing more organic and dynamic, and you can control where to add more details.

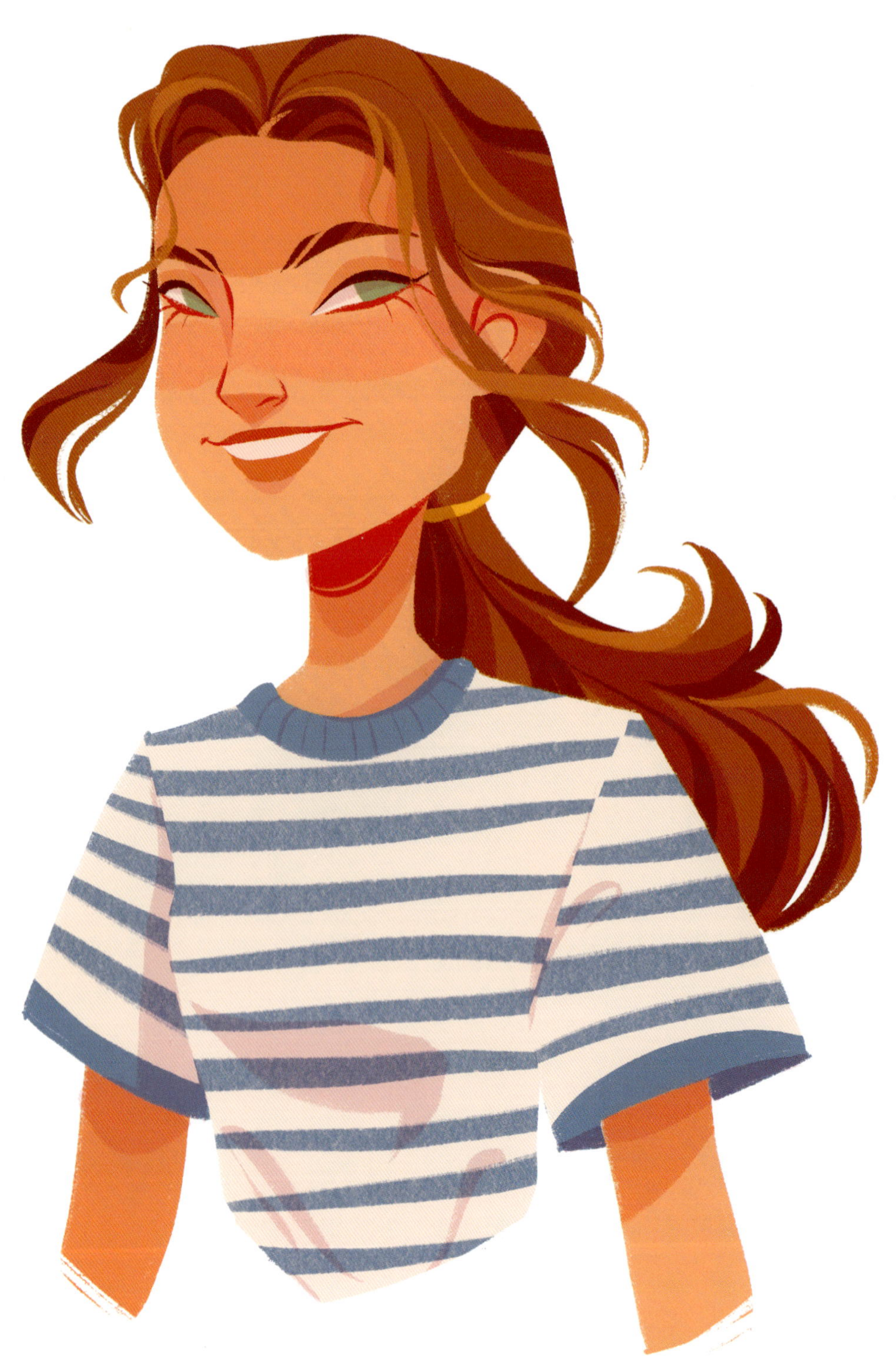

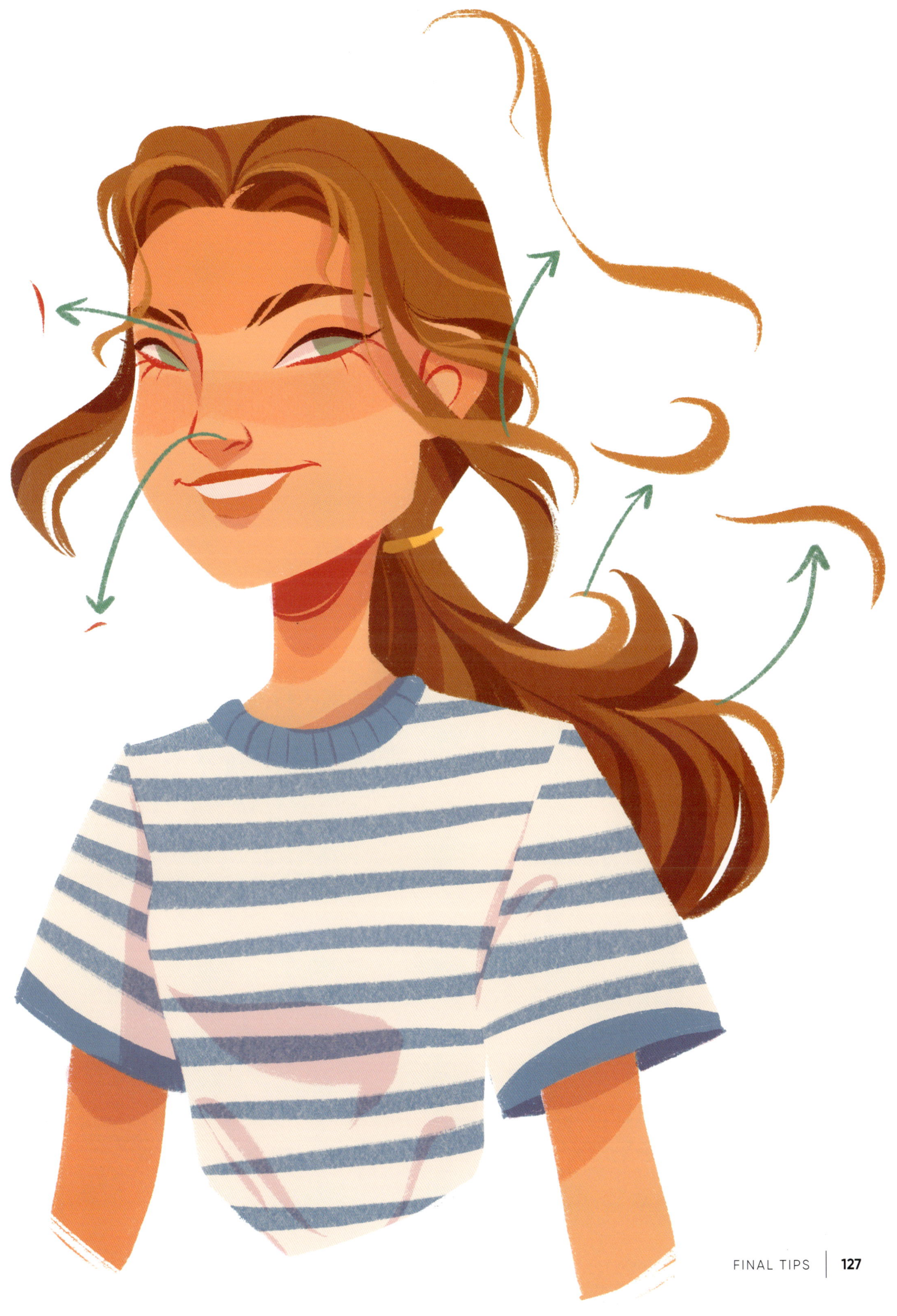

Acknowledgments

Special thanks to God, the creator of all art; my family, for all the love and support and even for modeling for some illustrations; my friends and social media followers—you are the reason I've embraced this project; and my uncle, my personal photographer.

A special thanks to my dad and also to my boyfriend, for revising and making suggestions related to the book text.

About the Artist

Fernanda is a twenty-year-old Brazilian artist who discovered her passion for art at a very young age. She has always been fascinated by creating characters and developing a unique style that has a lot of personality and color. She first started her artistic career doing commissions, book covers, and illustrations for Brazilians and other people around the world, and she still does that today. Fernanda is currently in law school, but her academic life never stopped her from investing in her art vocation. Her love for art and a lot of hard work allowed her to get here, and she believes that anyone can be an artist, as long as you never give up and always believe in yourself.

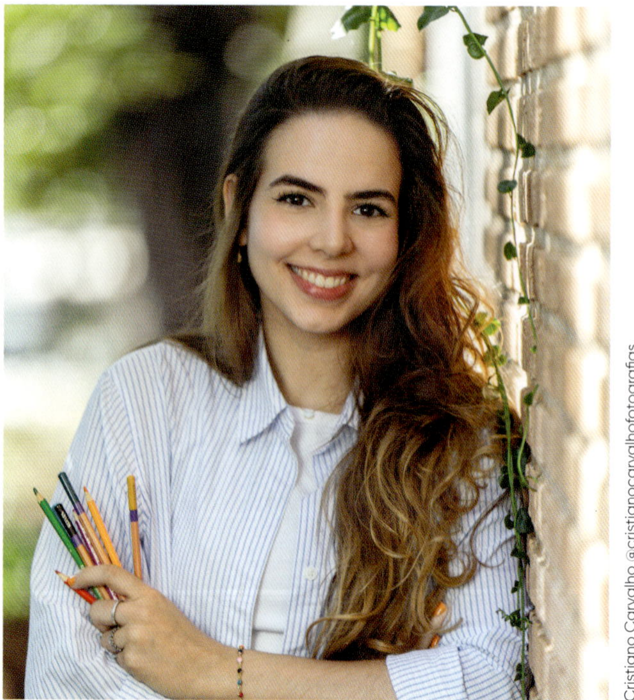

Cristiano Carvalho @cristianocarvalhofotografias